Second Edition

Cultural Diversity in Health and Illness

Second Edition

Cultural Diversity in Health and Illness

Rachel E. Spector, Ph.D., R.N.
Associate Professor
Boston College School of Nursing
Chestnut Hill, Massachusetts

APPLETON-CENTURY-CROFTS/Norwalk, Connecticut

0-8385-1395-6

85   86   87   88   89   90   /   10   9   8   7   6   5   4   3   2   1

Prentice-Hall of Australia, Pty. Ltd., Sydney
Prentice-Hall Canada, Inc.
Prentice-Hall Hispanoamericana, S.A., Mexico
Prentice-Hall of India Private Limited, New Delhi
Prentice-Hall International (UK) Limited, London
Prentice-Hall of Japan, Inc., Tokyo
Prentice-Hall of Southeast Asia (Pte.) Ltd., Singapore
Whitehall Books Ltd., Wellington, New Zealand
Editora Prentice-Hall do Brasil Ltda., Rio de Janeiro

Library of Congress Cataloging-in-Publication Data

Spector, Rachel E., 1940–
   Cultural diversity in health and illness.

   Bibliography: p.
   Includes index.
   1. Social medicine.   2. Medical anthropology.
3. Health attitudes.   4. Medical personnel and patient.
5. Medical care—United States.   6. Minorities—
Health and hygiene—United States.   I. Title. [DNLM:
1. Attitude of Health Personnel.   2. Attitude to
Health.   3. Cross-Cultural Comparison.   4. Delivery of
Health Care—United States.   5. Ethnic Groups.
6. Socioeconomic Factors.   WA 30 S741c]
RA418.S75   1985   362.1'0425   85-13387
ISBN 0-8385-1395-6

Design: Lynn M. Luchetti

PRINTED IN THE UNITED STATES OF AMERICA

To Manny, Sam, Becky, and my mother, Freda Needleman.
And to the memory of my father, Joseph J. Needleman.

Contents

Preface

In 1977 I wrote a book—the purpose of that book was to increase the reader's awareness of the dimensions and complexities involved in caring for people from diverse cultural backgrounds. I wished to share my personal experiences and thoughts concerning the introduction of cultural concepts into the education of health-care professionals. The book represented my answers to the questions: "How does one effectively expose a student to cultural diversity?" and "How does one examine health-care issues and perceptions from a broad social viewpoint?" As I had done in the classroom, I attempted to bring the reader into direct contact with the interaction between providers of care within the American health-care system and the consumer of health care.

At the time that I prepared that manuscript, I had become acquainted with the issues of health-care delivery as they primarily affected consumers of health care who were people of color—Asians, blacks, Hispanics, and Native Americans. Since that time, I have had the opportunity not only to continue to be concerned with the initial issues, but also to delve into the religious and ethnic differences that impinge upon whites who are consumers of health care. In this text's second edition, I have taken the opportunity to begin to pry open the door and to examine the differences that lie within white America with respect to beliefs and practices affecting health and illness. My work has become increasingly exciting, for the more I explore and question, the more I know that one can spend an entire lifetime researching these questions, and the answers will never be the same.

Today's health-care provider is believed to be, for the most part, a white person of middle-class background. That is truly an assumption, for if one looks at the large numbers of people who provide health-care services, one finds diverse people from all walks of life. How well do we know one another? What are considered the beliefs of consumers certainly may also apply to providers in terms of their personal health and illness beliefs and practices. Quite often we not only do not understand the world view of the consumer, we also do not understand the world views of the providers with whom we practice.

I am neither a sociologist nor an anthropologist. I am a *nurse* and a *nursing educator,* and I am committed to finding a way to alert nurses and other health-care providers to the beliefs about health and illness of a given health-care consumer. This book is an attempt to open the door to the immense diversity that exists within our American society; to demonstrate various methods one can use to open one's mind to the beliefs of others; to describe some of these beliefs; and to refer to some of the countless available resources. To this end, an annotated bibliography has been provided at the conclusion of each chapter to encourage further exploration into the appropriate literature; illustrations have been added; and activities that are fun and creative to help this material come alive for the reader have been suggested.

Those who provide health care in the 1980s and 1990s are faced with a changing system of health-care delivery. Not only has health care become far more technical and far less personal, it has become increasingly difficult for people with marginal incomes and no insurance to acquire. The mechanisms for funding health care have changed drastically in the past few years and numerous services have been curtailed. More services are being delivered in peoples' homes, and in delivering home care it is even more important to understand the cultural background of the client and family. To ensure safe and effective service to the consumer, it has become necessary to provide the student and the health-care professional with both the technical knowledge and the cultural understanding to meet the consumer's needs. Just as the society is changing, the milieu in which one practices health care is also changing. No longer is the consumer willing to "receive" care; rather, the client desires the opportunity to participate in care-related decisions. No longer can the provider dictate a regimen; efforts must be made to collaborate with the consumer in determining a treatment plan. Unless the provider has a sound understanding of the consumer's values and perceptions regarding health and illness, the consumer's needs cannot be met satisfactorily.

The essential argument of this book is that the provider of health care (nurse, physician, social worker, etc.) has been socialized into a distinct provider-culture. This provider-culture instills in its members its own norms regarding health and illness. When a member of this culture interacts with a person from a culture with differing norms, there is often a conflict in their beliefs. For this reason, I will explore issues of health and illness in three areas:

1. Provider self-awareness
2. Consumer-oriented issues surrounding delivery and acceptance of health care

3. Examples of traditional health beliefs and practices among selected populations

There is much to be learned. Books and articles have begun to
appear that address these problems and issues. It is not easy to alter
attitudes and beliefs or stereotypes and prejudices. Some social psy-
chologists state that it is almost impossible to lose all of one's prejudices. Yet alterations can be made. I believe the health-care provider
must develop a sensitivity to personal fundamental values regarding
health and illness. With acceptance of one's own values comes the
framework and courage to accept the existence of differing values. This
process of realization and acceptance can enable the health-care provider to be instrumental in meeting the needs of the consumer in a
collaborative, safe, and professional manner.

The first edition of this book was the outcome of a *promesa*, a
promise, I once made. The promise was made to a group of black and
Hispanic students I taught in a medical sociology course in 1973.
In this course, the students wound up being the "teachers," and
they taught me to see the world of health-care delivery through the
eyes of the health-care consumer, rather than through my own well-
intentioned eyes. What I came to see, I did not always like. I did not
realize how much I did not know; I believed I knew a lot. I have held
on to the promise, and my experiences over the years have been incredible. I have met people and traveled. At all times I have held on
to the idea and goal of attempting to help nurses and other providers
be aware of and sensitive to the beliefs and needs of their patients. I
know that looking inside closed doors carries with it a risk. I *know*
that people prefer to think that our society is a melting pot and that
old beliefs and practices have vanished with an expected assimilation
into mainstream American life. But many people have continued to
carry on their traditional customs and culture from their native lands,
and health and illness beliefs are deeply entwined within the cultural
and social beliefs that people have. In order to understand health and
illness beliefs and practices, it is necessary to see the person in his
unique socio-cultural world.

This book is written primarily for the student in basic nursing
education. I believe it will also be helpful for nurses in all areas of
practice, especially community health, long-term oncology and chronic
care settings, and hospice centers. I am attempting to write in a direct
manner and to use language that is understandable by all. The material is sensitive, yet I believe that it is presented in a sensitive manner. At no point is my intent to create a vehicle for stereotyping. I
know that one person will read this book and nod "Yes, this is how I
see it," and someone else of the same background will say "No, this
is not correct." This is the way it is meant to be. It is incomplete by
intent. It is written in the spirit of open inquiry, so that an issue may

be raised and so that clarification of any given point will be sought from the patient as health care is provided. The deeper I travel into this world of cultural diversity, the more I wonder at the variety. It is wonderfully exciting. By gaining insight into the traditional attitudes that people have toward health and health care, I find my own nursing practice is enhanced, and I am better able to understand the needs of patients and their families. We live in a most wonderful country. It is thrilling to be able to meet, to know, and to provide care to people from all over the world. It is the excitement of America and the excitement of nursing.

You don't need a masterpiece to get the idea.
—**Pablo Picasso**

Acknowledgments

I wish to thank the following people for their guidance and professional support: Elsie Basque, Julian Castillo, Leonel J. Castillo, Joe Colorado, Mary Crockett, Mary A. Dineen, Noreen Dresser, Celeste Dye, Terry Fermino, Laverne Gallman, Orlando Isaza, Hawk Littlejohn, Patricia McArdle, Father Richard E. McCabe, S. Dale McLemore, David Warner, and Irving Zola.

I also wish to thank my friends who have tolerated my absence at numerous social functions and the many people who have provided the numerous support services necessary for the completion of a project such as this. They include Marie Armando, Nancy O'Connell, and Karen Furlong.

Armando Aguilar, Jacqueline Clark, Mary Colman, Juan Kouri, Rosemary Lamacchia, Donna McHugh, Lori Nelson-Brackett, and Jerilyn Sasek, Boston College undergraduate and nursing students, have been helpful in reviewing the content.

Credit for the photographs in Chapter 6 goes to Robert W. Schadt, Production Coordinator, Educational Media Center, Tufts New England Medical Center, Boston, Massachusetts.

Most of all, I want to acknowledge the support and love of my husband and family. Thank you.

Introduction

The historic events of the 1960s have made our society aware of gaps that divide the multitudes of people comprising the American population. In the afermath of the events that shook the country—political assassinations, student uprisings, the civil rights movement, and riots in Watts, Detroit, and Washington, D.C.—the focus on inequality has also entered the arena of health and health-care delivery. Just as other people now state their needs, health-care consumers demand participation in and understanding of their care.

We have had to find a way of caring for the client that matches the client's perception of the health problem and its treatment. In many situations, this is not difficult; in other situations, it seems impossible. With the passage of time, a pattern emerges: for the health-care provider, the client-needs most difficult to meet are those of people who are the most "different." These people tend to be ethnic people of color—blacks, Asians, Hispanics, and Native Americans.

When there is conflict between the provider's and the client's belief systems, the provider is typically unable to understand the conflict and, hence, usually finds ways of minimizing it. Ordinarily, the provider knows too little about a client's self-perception or beliefs regarding health and illness. For the provider, all that is important is knowing the "hows" and scientific "whys." In the past, little was known of the impact this attitude had on the recipient of health care. Today we realize it was negative; thus, the issue is crucial.

The providers are usually aware of—but generally have difficulty relating to—the personal and social problems of these people, such as unemployment, underemployment, welfare, the presence of illegitimate children, and drug and alcohol abuse. Even though problems of this sort may well account in part for a client's inability to cope with or to follow any kind of medical regimen, little or nothing has been taught professionals about them and how they affected the patient or how the patient related to them.

This book will help the reader to take a good look at some major issues of health and health-care delivery. One must ask: How does the client view life? What are his beliefs, values, and norms? What is his cultural background and how does it influence his behavior? How do such factors affect the *meanings* of "health" and "illness"? What does it mean in terms of survival? (How does one person's socialization differ from that of another?)

When one completes an educational program and dons the attire of the profession—for example, the traditional white dress and cap of the nurse—little thought is given to one's fallibility. One is now sanctioned by society to enter the professional world and deliver the practiced and learned skills. One does not choose to answer to the client who fails to follow the treatment regimen of a physician or nurse, or who does not keep appointments, or who does not seek early health care. Once licensed, the provider feels secure in the scientific knowledge that took so long to master: Does he or she not "know it all"? The person who fails to comply with treatment, does not attend a clinic appointment, or delays in seeking health care is of little concern. Surely it is not the provider's fault that these situations continue to occur. Surely the fault must lie with the consumer. We continue to rationalize, to look for scapegoats, and we most often wind up by labeling the client "lazy" or "stupid." In the narrowly defined world of the health-care provider, there is only room for blaming the client—who, in this instance, is the *victim*.

According to health-care providers, there are no alternative forms of healing; there are no other healers. The American health-care provider has been socialized to believe that modern medicine as taught and practiced in Western civilization is the answer to *all* of humankind's needs. Has not modern medicine transcended all other forms of healing in technological skills and scientific understanding? With these extraordinary skills and this scientific sophistication, to cite an example, the dead can be brought back to life. When a heart or kidney fails, it can be replaced—either by a machine or by a transplanted organ. In the eyes of some consumers, however, Western medicine does not reign omnipotent, and the provider—with social, political, and humanistic concern—may be puzzled. For there are people who do not follow prescribed regimens; who fail to maintain attendance at a clinic, that is, who "elope" (the term used when a person fails to return to a clinic where he is undergoing treatment); or who spurn medical services or seek them as a last resort, and then leave the health system as quickly as possible. WHY?

The answers are deep and complex. Sometimes people fail to seek care or to take medication because they cannot afford to. The question one might then ask is: Why don't health-care seekers accept the care or medicine when it is given to them? I suggest that perhaps the consumer believes the care and medicine that are offered cannot help him.

Perhaps the consumer believes that the offered care will make him sicker or a given regimen is incompatible with his illness. Until recently a student in the health-care professions was not taught that a client may believe that the regimen or the medication that health care provides is incompatible with his illness. Much of this "incompatibility" is rooted in the opposite views the client and provider may have of a health problem. If a problem is not perceived in an agreed-upon way, the prescribed treatments may well not be complied with. One source of such perceptual incompatibility lies within one's culturally and ethnically determined perceptions of the health condition.

Those who deliver health care may ask the following questions: "Why, with today's knowledge and communication, doesn't everybody know about and believe in germs and viruses?" "Doesn't everybody know about epidemiology?" "Who has never heard of depression and schizophrenia?" "Is there anyone who doesn't believe in penicillin and thorazine?" "Shouldn't everybody believe in and practice prevention and public health?" "What is there to believe in if not the medical model of disease?"

I believe there is a fundamental difference between the health beliefs of health-care providers and the consumers. Many (if not all) of these beliefs are set in motion and determined by our socio-cultural-ethnic backgrounds. In the following pages I intend to develop these arguments:

1. That each person enters the health professions with culture-bound definitions of health and illness.
2. That health professionals bring with them distinct practices for the prevention and treatment of illness.
3. That professionals' ideas change as they are socialized into the "health-care provider culture."
4. That a schism develops between the provider of health services and the recipient.
5. That if the provider becomes more sensitive to the issues surrounding health care and the traditional health beliefs of the consumer, more comprehensive health care can be provided.

I am able to validate this theory with analyses of the works of Rosenstock[1] and Becker.[2,3] The health belief model (Fig. I-1) illustrates the consumer's perceptions of health and illness. This model can be modified to reflect the viewpoint of health-care providers. When this is implemented with the provider's viewpoint (Fig. I-2), the material provides a means of reinspecting the differences between professional and lay expectations. One may forge a link between the two and better understand how people perceive themselves in relation to illness and what motivates them to seek medical help and then follow that advice.

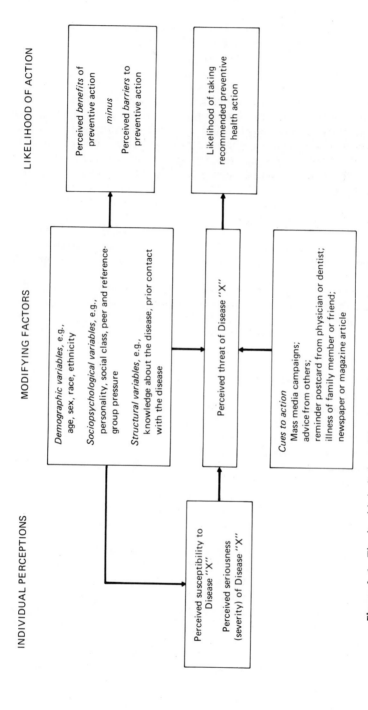

Figure I-1. The health belief model as a predictor of preventive health behavior. (Reprinted with permission from M. H. Becker et al., "A New Approach to Explaining Sick Role Behavior in Low-income Populations," *American Journal of Public Health* 64 (1974): 206.)

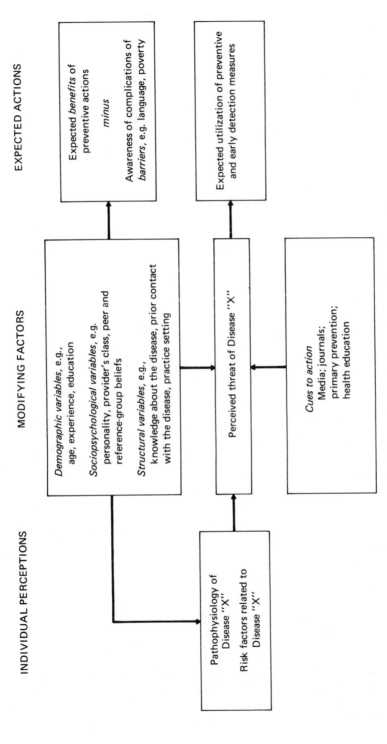

Figure I-2. The health belief model from the provider's point of view.

PERCEIVED SUSCEPTIBILITY

How susceptible to a certain condition does a person consider himself to be? For example, a woman whose family does not have a history of breast cancer is unlikely to consider herself susceptible to that disease. However, a woman whose mother and maternal aunt both died of breast cancer may well consider herself highly susceptible. In this case, the provider may concur with this perception of susceptibility on the basis of known risk factors.

PERCEIVED SERIOUSNESS

The degree of a problem's seriousness varies from one person to another. It is in some measure related to the amount of difficulty the client believes it will cause him. From his background in pathophysiology, the provider knows—within a certain range—how serious a problem is and may withhold information from the client. The provider may resort to euphemisms in explaining a problem. The patient may experience fear and dread by just hearing the name of a problem, such as in the case of cancer.

PERCEIVED BENEFITS: TAKING ACTION

What kind of action does a person take when he feels that he is susceptible, and what are the barriers that prevent him from taking action? If a person decides that the condition is serious, he may seek help from a doctor or some other significant person, or he may vacillate and delay seeking and using help. Many factors enter into the decision-making process. Several that may act as *barriers* to care are cost, availability, and the time that will be missed from work.

From the provider's viewpoint, there is a set definition of *who* should be consulted when a problem occurs; *when,* during that problem's course, help should be sought; and *what* therapy should be prescribed.

MODIFYING FACTORS

The *modifying factors* shown in Figure I-1 and I-2 indicate the areas of conflict between consumer and provider.

Demographic Variables: Race and Ethnicity
The variables of race and ethnicity are most often cited as problem areas when the provider is white and middle class and the consumer is an ethnic person of color. Chapters 1 and 2 will demonstrate the difficulty providers have in defining health and illness, and later

chapters will explore the meaning of health and illness as perceived both by the nonwhite and white person. Such perceptions vary not only among groups but also among individuals.

Sociopsychological Variables
The factors of social class, peer-, and reference-group pressures also vary between the provider and consumer and among different ethnic groups. For example, if the consumer's belief system as to the causes of illness is "traditional" and the provider's is "modern," there is inevitable conflict between the two viewpoints. This is even more evident when the provider is unaware of the consumer's traditional beliefs. Quite often, there are class differences between the consumer and provider: the reference group of the provider is that of the "technological health system" whereas the reference group of the consumer may well be that of the "traditional system" of health care and health-care deliverers.

Structural Variables
The structural variables also differ when the provider sees the problem from one angle, and the consumer sees it from a different angle. Often, each is seeing the same thing but is using different terms (or jargon) to explain it; consequently neither is understood. Reference-group problems are also manifested in this area, and the media are an important structural variable.

Unit I focuses on the provider's self-knowledge in terms of perceptions and understanding of health and illness (Chapters 1 and 2). The readers are then asked to do a family history to determine what methods were practiced in their own families to prevent and treat illness. The results of what students have learned by doing this history and what it means to them are described and discussed in Chapter 3.

Unit II focuses on the broad issues of health-care delivery, culture, and healing.

Much of the idealism that has been associated with the delivery of health care is not justified. Providers are naive in their knowledge and awareness of the harsh realities of health care. In Chapter 4, the reader is exposed to the multifaceted problems of health-care delivery and some of the more negative aspects of the system, as well as the important issue of human rights.

The concept of culture and the role it plays in one's perception of health and illness are explored. This is first done in broad and general terms: What is culture? How is it transmitted? What is ethnicity? How does it affect a person? These and other issues are analyzed in Chapter 5. The concept of culture is then taken from its broad anthropologic and sociologic definitions and brought into concrete and specific terms.

The concept of faith is also explored. It is an increasingly important issue, which is evolving to a point where the professional must have some understanding of this phenomenon. Faith plays a major role in treatment—in outcome and in success of cure. People of diverse backgrounds today acknowledge using faith healers and other types of healers. In Chapter 6 the philosophy of the holistic approach to health care is examined. A discussion of healing and alternative healers is presented.

Once the study of each of these components has been completed, the text moves on to explore various ethnic groups in more detail. Chapter 12 is a presentation of a case study that describes a situation in the Mexican border areas of Texas where both traditional and modern health care is practiced. It describes the ongoing use of the *partera*, a lay midwife within the Mexican culture. The practice of the *partera* and the issues surrounding this practice are discussed.

These pages cannot do full justice to the richness of any one health-belief system. By presenting some of the beliefs and practices and suggesting background reading, however, the book can begin to sensitize the reader to the needs of a given group of people.

The Epilogue is devoted to an overall analysis of the book's contents and how best to apply this knowledge in health planning, health education, and health-care delivery for both the consumer and the health-care professional.

REFERENCES

1. Irwin M. Rosenstock, "Why People Use Health Services," *Millbank Memorial Fund Quarterly* 44, no. 3 (July 1966): 94–127.
2. Marshall H. Becker et al., "A New Approach to Explaining Sick Role Behavior in Low-Income Populations," *American Journal of Public Health* 64 (1974): 205–216.
3. Marshall H. Becker, *The Health Belief Model and Personal Health Behavior*. Thorofare, N.J.: B. Slack, 1974.

BIBLIOGRAPHY

Allport, Gordon W. *The Nature of Prejudice* (abridged). Garden City, N.Y.: Doubleday, 1958.
    This book is a classic study of prejudice—the how, what, who, when, and why. Excellent background reading for study of race relations and for understanding the issues that underlie prejudice.
Jung, Carl G., editor. *Man and His Symbols*. Garden City, N.Y.: Doubleday, 1964.
    Jung and others illustrate the various ways man explains his relationship to self, others, world, and nature by the use of art.

FUTHER SUGGESTED READING

Spector, Rachel E. "Health and Illness among Ethnic People of Color," *Nurse Educator* 2, no. 3 (May–June 1977): 10–16.

Second Edition

Cultural Diversity in Health and Illness

UNIT I

Provider Self-awareness

Unit I enables the reader to become aware of beliefs about health and illness. The reader is helped to:

1. Reexamine and redefine the concepts of health and illness
2. Understand the multiple relationships between health and illness
3. Associate the concepts of good and evil and light and dark with health and illness
4. Trace your family's practices in:
   a. The protection and maintenance of health
   b. The prevention of illness
   c. The diagnosis and treatment of illness
5. Understand the behavioral variations in health and illness
6. Understand the variety of influences that your culture and ethnicity have on the interpretations of the concepts of health and illness

Before you read Chapter 1, please answer the following questions:

1. How do you define health?
2. How do you keep yourself healthy?

Before you read Chapter 2, please answer the following questions:

1. How do you define illness?
2. What would you define as a minor or "not serious" medical problem? Give examples.
3. How do you know when a given health problem does not need medical attention?
4. Do you "self-diagnose" when a health problem presents itself? Give examples.
5. Do you use over-the-counter medications? Which ones and when?

CHAPTER 1

Health

Life is an adventure in a world where nothing is static; where unpredictable and ill-understood events constitute dangers that must be overcome, often blindly and at great cost; where man himself, like the sorcerer's apprentice, has set in motion forces that are potentially destructive and may someday escape his control. The very process of living is a continual interplay between the individual and his environment, often taking the form of a struggle resulting in injury or disease. Complete and lasting freedom from disease is but a dream remembered from imaginings of a Garden of Eden designed for the welfare of man.

—René Dubos, Mirage of Health

To begin our quest for a deeper understanding of the problems surrounding the delivery of adequate health care, let us ask: "What is health?" One response may be a flawless recitation of the standard definition of the World Health Organization (WHO), given with great assurance—a challenge is neither expected nor welcomed but may evoke an intense dispute in which the assumed right answer is completely torn apart. Answers such as "homeostasis," "kinetic energy in balance," "optimal functioning," and "freedom from pain" are opened to discussion. Experienced health-care providers may be unable to give a comprehensive, acceptable answer to such a seemingly simple question. It is difficult to give a definition that makes sense without the use of some form of medical jargon. It is also challenging to define "health" in terms that a lay person could understand. (We lack skill in understanding "health" from the layman's perspective.)

One example of the many definitions of health is in the *American Heritage Dictionary:*

n. 1. The state of an organism with respect to functioning, disease, and abnormality at any given time. 2. The state of an organism functioning normally without disease or abnormality. 3. Optimal functioning with freedom from disease and abnormality. 4. Broadly, any state of optimal functioning, well being, or progress. 5. A wish for someone's good health, expressed as a toast.[1]

Murray and Zentner define health as "a purposeful, adaptive response, physically, mentally, emotionally and socially, to internal and external stimuli in order to maintain stability and comfort."[2] The WHO defines health as a "state of complete physical, mental, and social well being and not merely the absence of disease."

These definitions—varying in scope and context—are essentially those that the student, practitioner, and educator within the health professions agree convey the meaning of "health." The most widely used and recognized definition is that of WHO. Within the socialization process of the health-care deliverer the denotation of the word is that contained in the WHO definition; for other students the meaning of the word "health" becomes clear through the educational experience.

In analyzing these definitions, one is able to discern subtle variations in denotation. If this occurs in the denotation of the word, what of the connotation? That is, are health-care providers as familiar with implicit meanings as with those that are more explicit? If the following comment (made in a discussion of an article by Irwin M. Rosenstock) is accurate, then the educational process is indeed deficient:

> Whereas health itself is in reality an elusive concept, in much of research, the stages involved in seeking medical care are conceived as completely distinct. The health professions are becoming increasingly aware of the lack of clarity in the definition of health.[3]

The framework of both education and research in the health professions continues to rely on the more abstract definitions of the word "health." When the broader connotations are considered, one can conceive that health is regarded not only as the absence of disease but also as a reward for "good behavior." In fact, a state of health is regarded by many people as the reward one receives for "good" behavior and illness as punishment for "bad" behavior. Frequently people state, "She is so good; no wonder she is so healthy." The mother admonishes the child, "If you don't do such and such, you'll get sick." Situations and experiences may be avoided for the purpose of protecting and maintaining one's health. On the other hand, some people seek out challenging, albeit dangerous, situations with the hope that they will experience the thrill of a challenge and still emerge in an intact state of health. One example of this is driving at high speeds.

There is also the viewpoint that health is the freedom from and the absence of evil. In this context, health is analogous to day, which equals good, which equals light. Conversely, illness is analogous to night, which equals evil, which equals dark. Illness, to some, is seen as a punishment for being bad or doing evil deeds; it is the work of vindictive evil spirits. In the "modern" education of health-care providers, these concepts of health and illness are rarely, if ever, discussed. Yet it can be maintained that—if these concepts of health and illness are believed by people within the general population, including consumers of health-care services—understanding these varying ideas is important for the provider.

We each enter the health-care community with our own culturally based concept of health. During the educational and socialization process in our profession—nursing, medicine, or social work—we are expected to shed these beliefs and adopt the standard definitions. In addition to shedding these old beliefs, we learn, if only by unspoken example, to view as deviant those who do not accept the prevailing, institutional connotation of the word "health."

The material that follows illustrates the complex process necessary to enable providers to return to and appreciate their former interpretations of health, to understand the vast number of meanings the word "health" has, and to be aware of the difficulties that exist with definitions such as that of the World Health Organization.

HOW DO YOU DEFINE HEALTH?

You have been requested to describe the term *health* in your own words. An initial response to this request is frequently a recital of the WHO definition. What does this definition really mean? The following is a representative sample of actual responses:

1. Being able to do what I want to do.
2. Physical and psychological well-being, "physical" meaning that there are no abnormal functions with the body, all systems are without those abnormal functions that would cause a problem physically, and "psychological" meaning that one's mind is capable of a clear and logical thinking process and association.
3. Being able to use all of your body parts in the way that you want to—to have energy and enthusiasm.
4. Being able to perform your normal activities, such as working, without discomfort and at an optimal level.
5. The state of wellness with no physical or mental illness.
6. I would define health as an undefined term. It depends on the situations, individuals, and other things.

In the initial step of the "unlocking" process,* it begins to become clear that there is not a set rule that states what health really is. We can all agree on the WHO definition, but when asked "What does that mean?" we are unable to clarify or to simplify that definition. As we

---

*The "unlocking" process includes those steps taken to help break down and understand the definitions of both terms, *health* and *illness*, in a "living" context. It consists of persistent questioning: "What is Health?" No matter what the response, the question "What does that mean?" is asked. Initially, this causes much confusion, but in classroom practice—as each term is written on the blackboard and analyzed—the air clears and the process begins to make sense.

begin to perceive a change in the connotation of the word, we may experience dismay, as that emotional response accompanies the breaking down of ideas. When this occurs, we begin to realize that as we were socialized into the provider-culture by the educational process, our understanding of *health* changed and we moved a great distance from our older understanding of the term. The following list includes the definitions of health given by students at various levels of education and experience. The students ranged in age from 19-year-old college juniors to adult nursing trainees and graduate students in both nursing and social work.

- *Junior students*
  A system involving all subsystems of one's body that constantly work on keeping one in physical and mental condition.
- *Senior students*
  Ability to function in activities of daily living to optimal capacity without requiring medical attention.
  Mental and physical wellness.
  The state of physical, mental, and emotional well-being.
- *RN students*
  Ability to cope with stressors. Absence of pain—mental and physical.
  State of optimal well-being, both physically and emotionally.
- *Graduate students*
  State of well-being that is free from physical and mental distress. I can also include in this social well-being, even though this may be idealistic.
  Not only the absence of disease, but a state of balance or equilibrium of physical, emotional, and spiritual states of well-being.

It appears that the definition becomes more abstract and technical as the student advances in the educational program. The terms explaining "health" take on a more abstract and scientific character with each year of removal from the lay way of thinking.

Can these layers of jargon be removed and can we help ourselves once again to view health in a more tangible manner?

In probing this question let us think back to the way we perceived health before our entrance into the educational program. I believe that the farther back one can go in one's memory of earlier concepts of health the better. Again, the question "What is health?" is asked over and over. Initially, the responses continue to include such terms and phrases as "homeostasis," "freedom from disease," or "frame of mind." Slowly, and with considerable prodding, we are able to recall earlier perceptions of health: once again, health becomes a *personal, experiential* concept, and the relation of *health* to *being* returns. The fragility and instability of this concept are also recognized as the term gradually acquires meaning in relation to the term *being*.

This process of unlocking a perception of a concept takes a considerable amount of time and patience. It also engenders dismay that briefly turns to anger and resentment. One may question why the definitions acquired and mastered in the learning process are now being challenged and torn apart. The feeling may be that of taking a giant step backward in a quest for new terminology and new knowledge.

Yet with this unlocking process, one is able to perceive the concept of health *in the way that a vast number of health-care consumers may perceive it.* The following illustrates the transition that the concept passed through in an unlocking process from the WHO definition to the realm of the health-care consumer:

- *Initial responses*
  Feeling of well-being, no illness.
  Homeostasis.
  Complete physical, mental, and social well-being.
- *Secondary responses*
  Frame of mind.
  Subjective state of psychosocial well-being.
  Activities of daily living can be performed.
- *Experiential responses*
  (Health becomes tangible; the description is illustrated by using qualities that can be seen, felt, or touched.)
  Shiny hair.
  Warm, smooth, glossy skin.
  Clear eyes.
  Shiny teeth.
  Being alert.
  Being happy.
  Freedom from pain.
  Harmony between body and mind.

Even this itemized description does not completely answer the question, "What is health?" The words are once again subjected to the question, "What does that mean?" and once again the terms are stripped down and a paradox begins to emerge. For example, "shiny hair" may in fact be present in an ill person or in a person whose hair has not been washed for a long time. In the healthy person, clean, well-groomed hair with luster may not always be present.

It becomes clear that no matter how much one goes around in a circle in an attempt to define "health," the terms and meanings attributed to the state can be challenged. As a result of this prolonged discussion, one never really comes to an acceptable definition of health. Yet, by going through the intense "unlocking" process, one is able finally to understand the ambiguity that surrounds the word. We are, accordingly, less likely to view as deviant those people who have other beliefs and practices in relation to their own health and health care.

HOW DO YOU KEEP YOURSELF HEALTHY?

Preventive Care and Health Maintenance

There are multiple ways of viewing health and there are many areas
of disagreement with respect to how this word can be defined. "Health
is not merely an end in itself, but rather a means of attaining human
well-being within the natural constraints in which man finds himself."[4] To state it another way:

> ... any aspect of health for an individual, or the determiners of what he
> does or does not do in relation to some aspect of health, is some combi-
> nation of the effects of his physical body: what he knows about it, what
> he feels about it, and how significant others react to it.[5]

The preparation of health-care workers tends to organize education from a perspective of illness; rarely (or superficially) does it include a study of the concept of *health*. Today, however, the emphasis
is shifting from acute care to preventive care. The need for the provider of health services to comprehend this concept is, therefore, crucial. If this movement for preventive health care is to take hold, become
firmly entrenched, and thrive, multiple issues must be resolved in answering the question, "What is health?" Unless the provider is able
to understand health from the viewpoint of the consumer, a barrier of
misunderstanding is perpetuated. It is difficult to reexamine complex
definitions dutifully memorized at an earlier time. Yet an understanding of health from a client's viewpoint is essential to the establishment
of preventive health-care services because the perception of health is
a complex psychological process. It is selective in that "man sees what
he wants to see or expects to see."[6] There tends to be no established
pattern in what individuals and families see as their health needs and
how they go about practicing their own health care.[7] Yet their perception of health is sanctioned and given meaning when it is brought
to a level of awareness where it can be interpreted and used in planning.[8]

Health maintenance and the prevention of illness are by no means
new concepts. As long as human beings have existed, they have used
a multitude of methods—ranging from magic and witchcraft to
present-day immunization—in an ongoing effort to maintain good
health and prevent debilitating illness. Raquel Cohen sees prevention
as "a plea for early intervention to help people deal more successfully
with the difficulties arising from man's struggles to adapt to society."[9] Another current viewpoint regarding prevention is advanced by
Richard Stark: "Health maintenance has become our national obses-
sion. Logic suggests that in order to maintain health we must prevent
disease, and that is best accomplished by eating balanced meals, ex-
ercising regularly, and seeing the doctor once a year for a checkup."[10]
The annual ritual of visiting a physician has been extensively pro-
moted by the medical establishment and is viewed as effective by nu-

---

HEALTHFUL HINTS FROM LONG AGO

A sassafras root carried in the pocket guards against illness. (Superstition of Old Saint Simons)

Asafetida worn on a string around the neck protects a child from many diseases; and, a buckeye carried in the pocket protects against rheumatism. (Blue Ridge and Great Smoky Mountains)

A single, pierced nutmeg, worn around the neck on a string, will protect you from boils, croup, body lice, and various lung diseases. (New England)

A well-ventilated bedroom will prevent morning headaches and lassitude. (1914 Almanac)

---

merous lay people. A doctor's statement is often required by a person seeking employment or life insurance.[11] Furthermore, the annual physical examination has been advertised as the key to good health. A "clean bill of health" is considered essential for social, emotional, and even economic success. This clean bill of health is bestowed only by the members of the medical profession. The general public has been conditioned to believe that health is guaranteed if a disease that may be developing is discovered early and treated with the ever-increasing varieties of modern medical technology.[12] Yet for all those who believe in and practice the annual physical and screening for early detection of a disease, there are those—both within and outside the health-care professions—who do not subscribe to it.[13] Preventive medicine grew out of clinical practice associated either with welfare medicine or with industrial or occupational medical practice. The approach of preventive medicine and health maintenance is now developing as a new focus for health-care practice in the United States.[14]

Health Diaries
Keeping a 30-day health diary is recommended to increase awareness of one's own health status and health practices. If an illness occurs, record what is done for it, why it is done, and what type of health-care services were used.

Comments will be most revealing! We recognize that, in spite of the fact that we are learning "proper" methods of health maintenance, we have poor nutritional and sleeping habits and rarely, if ever, seek medical help for what some of us consider "serious" bodily complaints. At best, seeking care is delayed until we give up the idea that our symptoms will disappear. This diary has a very sobering effect. It is also used as an additional "humanizing" tool. The term *humanizing* is used here because just as we treat ourselves or delay in seeking help, we also ought not to judge people who, for various reasons, treat themselves or delay in seeking health care.

The following exercise is designed to help the reader tune in to his own daily health status.

Keep a daily record of your health status and behavior for 30 days. Include in this record medications taken (prescription and nonprescription), eating, sleeping, exercise, and recreational activities. When appropriate, note the reasons for your actions.

The daily record, or diary, enables you to see how you react to the various stresses and strains of daily life. It reveals the intricacies of your daily life-style—the things you take for granted. For example: Do you eat three balanced meals a day? Do you get enough rest? Do you exercise?

At the end of 30 days reread this diary and analyze it in relation to recommended health practices.

Typical entries for such a record follow.

- *Monday*
  overslept (went to bed 3:00 AM)
  skipped breakfast
  dozed in class
  coke and cheese crackers for lunch
  2 aspirins (headache)
  hamburger and french fries for supper
  crashed at 8:00 PM

- *Tuesday*
  up at 6:30 for clinical
  milk and toast for breakfast
  exercise—walk in hospital corridors
  supper—lasagne, wine
  headache—2 aspirins
  bed 8:00 PM (couldn't study)

- *Wednesday*
  up at 7:00 for 8:30 lecture
  walked to hospital
  no breakfast (not hungry)
  peanut butter & jelly for lunch
  PM snack—milk & candy bar
  study until 2:00 AM
  2 aspirins (headache)

- *Thursday*
  up at 6:30 for clinical
  coffee and cheese sandwich for breakfast
  walked to hospital (it rained)
  almost slept on ward
  no lunch (out of funds—no time to cash check)
  coke
  walked in hospital corridors

In summary, this chapter has attempted to deal solely with the concept of *health*. The multiple denotations and connotations of the word have been explored. A method for helping you to "tune in" to your health has been included.

REFERENCES

1. *American Heritage Dictionary of the English Language,* s.v. "health."
2. Ruth Murray and Judith Zentner, *Nursing Concepts for Health Promotion* (Englewood Cliffs, N.J.: Prentice-Hall, 1975), p. 6.
3. Discussion of article by Irwin M. Rosenstock, "Why People Use Health Services," *Millbank Memorial Fund Quarterly* 44, no. 3 (July 1966): 94–127.
4. Herman E. Hilleboe, "Preventing Future Shock: Health Developments in the 1960's and Imperative for the 1970's," *American Journal of Public Health,* February 1972, p. 139.
5. Robert D. Russell, "Teaching for Meaning in Health Education: The Concept Approach," *Journal of School Health* 71 (January 1966): 13–14.
6. Francis L. Harmon, *Principles of Psychology* (Milwaukee: Bruce Publishing Co., 1938), p. 14; William N. Dember, *The Psychology of Perception* (New York: Holt, 1960), pp. 3–4.
7. Alexander A. Schneiders, *Introductory Psychology* (New York: Rinehart, 1960), p. 185.
8. Andiel Knutson, *The Individual, Society, and Health Behavior* (New York: Russell Sage Foundation, 1965), p. 159.
9. Raquel Cohen, "Principles of Preventive Mental Health Programs for Ethnic Minority Populations," *American Journal of Psychiatry* 128, no. 12 (June 1972): 79–83.
10. Richard Stark, "The Case Against Regular Physicals," *New York Times Magazine* (25 July 1976), p. 10.
11. Stephen B. Yohalen, *New York Times Magazine* (15 August 1976), p. 58.
12. Manuel Spector and Rachel Spector, "Is Prevention Myth or Reality?" *Health Education* 8, no. 4 (July-August 1977): 23–25.
13. Ibid.
14. John G. Freymann, "Medicine's Great Schism: Prevention vs. Cure," *Medical Care* 13, no. 7 (July 1975): 533.

CHAPTER 2

Illness

The world of illness is the one that is most familiar to the nurse and other providers of health care. It is in this world that the provider feels most comfortable and useful.

There are many questions to be answered: What determines illness? How does someone know when he is ill? What provokes a person to seek help from the health-care system? At what point does self-treatment seem no longer possible? Where does a person go for help? And to whom?

We tend to regard illness as the absence of health, yet it has been demonstrated in the preceding chapter that *health* is at best an elusive term that defies a specific definition! Let us look at the present issue more closely. Is illness the opposite of health? Is it a permanent condition or a transient condition? How does one know that he is ill?

The *American Heritage Dictionary* defines "illness" as "Sickness of body or mind. b. sickness. 2. *obsolete*. Evil; wickedness."[1]

As with *health,* the word "illness" can be subjected to extensive analysis. What is illness? A generalized response, such as "abnormal functioning of a body's system or systems," evolves into more specific assessments of what we observe and believe to be wrong. Illness is a "sore throat," a "headache," or a "fever"—the latter determined not necessarily by the measurement on a thermometer, but by the flushed face; the warm-to-hot feeling of the forehead, back, and abdomen; and the overall malaise. Or, the diagnosis of "intestinal obstruction" becomes described as pain in the stomach (really the abdomen, but lay people call it stomach), a greater pain than that caused by "gas," accompanied by severely upset stomach, nausea, vomiting, and marked constipation.

Essentially, we are being pulled back in the popular direction and encouraged to reuse lay terms. We initially resist this because we want to employ professional jargon. (Why reuse lay terms when our knowledge is so much greater?) It is crucial that we be called to task for using jargon; we must learn to be constantly conscious of the way in which the laity perceives illness and health care.

Another factor emerges as the word "illness" is stripped down to its barest essentials. Many of the characteristics attributed to health occur in illness, too. A rude awakening or "reality shock" comes about when one realizes that a person perceived as healthy by clinical assessment may then—by a given set of symptoms—define himself as ill (or vice versa). For example, in summertime one may see a person with a red face and assume that he has a sunburn. The person may, in fact, have a fever. A person recently discharged from the hospital, pale and barely able to walk, may be judged ill. However, that individual may consider himself *well* because he is much better than when he entered the hospital—now he is able to walk! Thus perceptions are relative, and, in this instance, the eyes of the beholder have been befuddled by inadequate information. Unfortunately, at the provider's level of practice, we do not always ask the person: "How do you view your state of health?" Rather, we determine his state of health by objective and observational data.

As is the case with the concept of health, one learns in nursing or medical school how to determine what illness is and how people are expected to behave when they are ill. Once these terms are separated and examined, the models that health-care providers have created tend to carry little weight. There is little agreement as to what, specifically, illness is, but one nonetheless has a high level of expectation as to what behavior should be demonstrated by both the client and provider when illness occurs. One discovers that we have a vast amount of knowledge with respect to the acute illnesses and the services that must ideally be provided for the acutely ill person. However, when the contradictions surface, one finds that one has minimal knowledge of the vast "gray" area: e.g., whether someone is ill or becoming ill with what may later be an acute episode. Because of the ease with which one often identifies cardinal symptoms, one finds that he is able to react to acute illness and may have negative attitudes toward those who do not seek help when the first symptom of an acute illness appears. The questions that then arise are: What is an acute illness, and how does one differentiate between it and some everyday indisposition that most people treat by themselves? When does one draw the line and admit that the disorder is out of the realm of adequate self-treatment?

These are certainly very difficult questions to answer, especially when careful analysis shows that even the symptoms of an acute illness tend to vary from one person to another. In many acute illnesses, the symptoms are so severe that the person experiencing them has little choice but to seek immediate medical care. Such is the case with a severe myocardial infarction. But what about the person who experiences mild discomfort in the epigastric region? One might say, "I have indigestion," and self-medicate with baking soda, an antacid, milk, or Alka Seltzer. A person who experiences mild pain in the left arm may delay seeking care, believing the pain will disappear. Obviously, this person may be as ill as the person who seeks help during the onset of symptoms, but will, like most people, minimize these small aches because of not wanting to assume the sick role.

THE SICK ROLE

The work of Talcott Parsons helps explain the phenomenon of "the sick role." In our society, a person is expected to have the symptoms viewed as illness confirmed by a member of the health-care profession. In other words, the sick role must first be legitimately conferred on this person by the keepers of this privilege: one cannot legitimize one's own illness and have one's own diagnosis accepted by the society at large. "A legitimate procedure for the definition and sanctioning of the adoption of the sick role is fundamental for both the social system and the sick individual."[2]

Role is defined sociologically (1) as the set of expectations and behaviors associated with a specific position in a social system (social role) or (2) as the way a person tends to react to a social situation (individual role).[3] Illness "is not merely a 'condition' but also a social role."[4] There are four main components inherent in the sick role:

1. "The sick person is exempted from the performance of certain of his/her normal social obligations."[5] An example is a student nurse who has a severe sore throat and decides that she does not want to go to her clinical assignment. In order for her to be exempted from the day's activities, she must have this symptom validated by someone in the health services, either a physician or the nurse on duty. Her claim of illness must be legitimized or socially defined and validated by a sanctioned provider of health-care services.

2. "The sick person is also exempted from a certain type of responsibility for his/her own state."[6] For example, an ill person cannot be expected to control the situation or be spontaneously cured. The student with the sore throat is expected to seek help and then to follow the advice of the attending physician or nurse in promoting recovery. The student is not responsible for recovery except in a peripheral sense.

3. "The legitimization of the sick role is, however, only partial".[7] When one is "sick," one is in an undesirable state and *should* recover and leave this state as rapidly as possible. The student's sore throat is acceptable only for a while; beyond a reasonable amount of time—as determined by the physician, peers, and the faculty—legitimate absence from the clinical classroom setting can no longer be claimed.

4. "Being sick, except in the mildest of cases, is being in need of help."[8] The type of help, as defined by the majority sector of American society and other Western countries, is that of the

physician. In seeking the help of the physician, the person now not only bears the sick role but in addition takes on the role of patient. Patienthood carries with it a certain prescribed set of responsibilities, some of which include compliance with a medical regimen, cooperation with the health-care provider, and following orders without asking too many questions. All of this leads to the illness experience.

THE ILLNESS EXPERIENCE

The experience of an illness is determined by what illness means to the sick person. Furthermore, illness refers to a specific status and role within a given society. Not only must illness be sanctioned by a physician in order for the sick person to assume the sick role, but it must also be sanctioned by the community or social structure of which the person is a member. This experience can be divided into four stages that are sufficiently general to apply to any society or culture.

Onset
"Onset" is the time when the person experiences the first symptoms of a given problem.[9] This event can be slow and insidious or rapid and acute. When the onset is insidious, the patient may not be conscious of symptoms or may think that, by waiting, the discomfort will go away. If, on the other hand, the onset is acute, the person is positive illness has occurred and immediate help must be sought. "This stage is seen as the prelude to legitimization of illness."[10]

Diagnosis
In the diagnostic stage of the illness experience, the disease is identified or an effort is made to identify it.[11] The person's role is now sanctioned, and at this point the illness is socially recognized and identified. At this point the health-care providers make decisions pertaining to appropriate therapy. During the period of diagnosis, the person experiences another phenomenon: dealing with the unknown, which includes fearing what the diagnosis will be.

For many people, going through a medical work-up is an unfamiliar experience. This is made doubly difficult because they are asked and expected to relate to strange people who are doing unfamiliar and often painful things to their bodies and minds. To the lay person, the environment of the hospital or the physician's office is both strange and unfamiliar, and it is natural to fear these qualities. Quite often, the ailing individual is faced with an unfamiliar diagnosis. Nonetheless, the person is expected to follow closely a prescribed treatment plan that is usually detailed by the health-care providers, but which in all likelihood may not accommodate a particular life-style. The situation is that of a horizontal-vertical relationship: the patient being figuratively and literally in the former position, the professional in the latter.

Patient Status

During the period of being a patient the person adjusts to the "social aspects of being ill and gives in to the demands of his/her physical condition."[12] The sick role becomes that of patienthood, and the person is expected to shift into this role as society determines it should be enacted. The person must make any necessary life-style alterations, become dependent on others in some circumstances for the basic needs of daily life, and adapt to the demands of the physical condition as well as to treatment limitations and expectations. The environment of the patient is highly structured. The boundaries of the patient's world are determined by the providers of the health-care services, not by the patient. Therein lies the conflict.

There has been much written describing the environment of the hospital and the roles that people in such an institution play. As was stated, the hospital is typically unfamiliar to the patient, who, nevertheless, is expected to conform to a predetermined set of rules and behaviors, many of which are unwritten and undefined for the patient—let alone *by* the patient.

Recovery

The final stage—recovery—is "generally characterized by the relinquishing of patient status and the assumption of pre-patient roles and activities."[13] There is often a change in the roles a person is able to play and the activities performed once recovery takes place. Often recovery is not complete. The person may be left with an undesirable or unexpected change in body image or in the ability to perform expected or routine everyday activities. One example might be that of a woman who enters the hospital with a small lump in her breast and who, after having surgery, subsequently returns home with only one breast. Another example is that of a man who is a laborer entering the hospital with a backache and returning home after a laminectomy. When he returns to work, he cannot reassume his job as a loader. Obviously, an entire life-style must be altered to accommodate such newly imposed changes.

From the viewpoint of the provider, this person has recovered: his body no longer has the symptoms of the acute illness that made surgical treatment necessary. In the eyes of the former patient illness persists because of the inability to perform as in the past. So many changes have been wrought that it is no wonder if he seems perplexed and uncooperative. Here, too, there is certainly conflict between society's expectations and the person's expectation. Society releases the person from the sick role at a time when, subjectively, the person may not be ready to relinquish it.

Table 2-1 is a tool designed for the assessment of the patient dur-

TABLE 2-1. A TOOL FOR THE ASSESSMENT OF THE PATIENT DURING THE FOUR STAGES OF ILLNESS

Onset	Diagnosis	Patient Status	Recovery
A. The Meaning of the Illness			
1. What symptoms does this patient complain of? 2. How does he judge the extent and kind of disease? 3. How does this illness fit with his image of health? Himself? 4. How does the disease threaten him? 5. Why did he seek medical help?	1. Does he understand the diagnosis? 2. How does he interpret the illness? 3. How can he adapt to the illness? 4. How does he think others feel about it?	1. Has his perception of the illness changed? 2. What are the changes in his life as a consequence of it? 3. What is his goal in recovery—the same level of health as before the illness, attainment of a maximal level of wellness, or perfect health? 4. How does he relate to medical professionals? 5. What are his social pressures leading to recovery? 6. What is motivating him to recover?	1. What are signs of recovery? 2. Can he reassume his prepatient role and functions? 3. Has his self-image been changed? 4. How does he see his present state of health—as more vulnerable or resistant?
B. Behavior in Response to Illness			
1. How does he control anxiety? 2. How are affective responses to concerns expressed? 3. Did he seek some form of health care before he sought medical care?	1. What treatment agents were used?	1. How does he handle the patient role? 2. How does he relate to the medical personnel?	1. Are there any permanent after-effects from this illness? 2. How does he reassume his old role?

Adapted from Alksen et al.[14]

17

ing the four stages of illness. Originally designed as a sociologic measuring tool, the material has been altered here to meet the needs of the health-care provider in achieving better understanding of patient behavior and expectations. If the provider is able to obtain answers from the patient to all of the questions raised in the table, understanding of the patient's behavior and perspective and subsequent attempts to provide safe, effective care become possible.

Another method of dividing the illness experience into stages was developed by the late Dr. Edward A. Suchman. He described the five components that follow.

The Symptom Experience Stage
The person is physically and cognitively aware that something is wrong and responds emotionally.[15]

The Assumption of the Sick Role Stage
The person seeks help and shares the problem with family and friends. After moving through the lay referral system, seeking advice, reassurance, and validation, the person is temporarily excused from such responsibilities as work, school, and other activities of daily living as the condition dictates.[16]

The Medical Care Contact Stage
The person then seeks out the "scientific" rather than the "lay" diagnosis, wanting to know: "Am I really sick?" "What is wrong with me?" "What does it mean?" At this point the sick person needs some knowledge of the health-care system, what the system offers, and how it functions. This knowledge assists in selecting resources and in interpreting the information received.[17]

The Dependent-Patient Role Stage
The patient is now under the control of the physician and is expected to accept and comply with the prescribed treatments. The person may be quite ambivalent about this role, and certain factors (physical, administrative, social, or psychological) may create barriers that will eventually interfere with treatment and the willingness to comply.[18]

The Recovery or Rehabilitation Stage
The role of patient is given up at the recovery stage, and the person resumes—as much as possible—his former roles.[19]

In summary, this chapter has introduced the reader to the concept of illness, as explored from the pure act of definition and then broadened through the sociological aspects of roles and behaviors. The writings of a number of sociologists have been examined in terms of applicability to nursing practice, observation, and experience.

REFERENCES

1. *American Heritage Dictionary of the English Language*, s.v. "illness."
2. David Mechanic, *Medical Sociology* (New York: Free Press of Glencoe, 1968), p. 80.
3. David Popenoe, *Sociology* (New York: Appleton, 1974), p. 681.
4. Talcott Parsons, "Illness and the Role of the Physician: A Sociological Perspective," in *Medical Care: Readings in the Sociology of Medical Institutions*, W. Richard Scott and Edmund H. Volkart, editors (New York: Wiley, 1966), p. 275.
5. Ibid.
6. Ibid.
7. Ibid.
8. Ibid., p. 276.
9. Lois Alksne et al., *"A Conceptual Framework for the Analysis of Cultural Variations in the Behavior of the Ill"* (unpublished report, New York City Department of Health, n.d.), p. 2.
10. Ibid., p. 3.
11. Ibid.
12. Ibid.
13. Ibid.
14. Lois Alksne et al., op. cit.
15. Edward A. Suchman, "Stages of Illness and Medical Care," *Journal of Health and Human Behavior* 6, no. 3 (Fall 1965): 114.
16. Ibid., p. 115.
17. Ibid.
18. Ibid.
19. Ibid., p. 116.

BIBLIOGRAPHY

Apple, Dorian, editor. *Sociological Studies of Health and Sickness: A Source Book for the Health Professions.* New York: McGraw-Hill, 1960.

This anthology covers such areas as the recognition of the need for health care, the patient's viewpoint, psychosocial process in illness, and the organization of hospitals. The essays address such broad questions as "Should I have a check-up?" "What occurs when patient and physician misunderstand each other?" "What are the psychosocial determinants of illness?" and "What is the social organization of hospitals?"

Bakan, David. *Disease, Pain and Sacrifice: Toward a Psychology of Suffering.* Chicago: University of Chicago Press, 1968.

Bakan explores the conviction that amelioration of suffering through understanding is the superior option. He describes the aspects of suffering from biological, psychological, and existential standpoints. Very highly recommended.

Becker, Marshall, H. *The Health Belief Model and Personal Health Behavior.* Thorofare, N.J.: B. Slack, 1974.

This monograph traces the history of the health belief model and its various uses in explaining and understanding health behavior in both health and illness.

Dubos, René Jules. *Man Adapting.* New Haven, Conn.: Yale University Press, 1965.

―――. *Man, Medicine and Environment.* New York: Praeger, 1968.

―――. *Mirage of Health.* Garden City, N.Y.: Doubleday, Anchor Books, 1961.

In these three books Dubos analyzes various aspects of human beings and their relationship to the environment. He does not explore wonder drugs but rather the wonders of life.

Freeman, Howard; Levine, Sol; and Reeder, Leo G., editors. *Handbook of Medical Sociology.* 2nd ed. Englewood Cliffs, N.J.: Prentice-Hall, 1972.

This handbook helps to bridge the knowledge gap that exists between the biologic and social sciences. It explores such areas as the sociology of illness; practitioners, patients, and medical settings; the sociology of medical care; and the strategy, method, and status of medical sociology.

Herzlich, Claudine. *Health and Illness: A Social Psychological Analysis.* Translated by Douglas Graham. New York: Academic Press, 1973.

Herzlich reports findings based on a study conducted in France in the 1960s: an exploration of people's attitudes toward health and illness. It investigates topics such as the individual, the way of life, and the genesis of illness; nature, constraint, and society; mechanisms and dosage; health and illness; the dimensions and limits of illness; the sick and the healthy; and health and illness behavior.

Jackson, Robert C., and Morton, Jean. *Family Health Care: Health Promotion and Illness Care.* Based on the proceedings of the 1975 Annual Institute for Public Health Social Workers, University of California, Berkeley.

In this work, attention is given to the broad topics of perspectives of health services to the family, strategies for the promotion of health and family functioning, and family-focused care for the ill.

Jaco, E. Gartly, editor. *Patients, Physicians, and Illness: Sourcebook in Behavioral Science and Medicine.* Glencoe, Ill.: Free Press, 1958.

This anthology is a sourcebook in behavioral science and medicine. It covers a wide range of topics including social and personal components of illness and health; community and sociocultural aspects of medical care and treatment; and the patient. Authors include Lyle Saunders, Talcott Parsons, and Mark Zborowski.

Kiev, Ari, editor. *Magic, Faith and Healing: Studies in Primitive Psychiatry Today.* New York: Free Press of Glencoe, 1964.

Another anthology, Kiev's book explores the wide number of abnormal states of mood, thought, and behavior and the multitude of "folk" ways that are employed throughout the world to treat disorders.

Knutson, Andie, L. *The Individual, Society and Health Behavior.* New York: Russell Sage Foundation, 1965.

Herein human beings are dealt with as members of society; emphasis is placed on those aspects of their behavior that are of concern to public health. The study covers a broad range of topics, including the general characteristics of humankind; men and women in their social environment; values, attitudes, and beliefs; and the communication process.

Leff, S., and Leff, Vera. *From Witchcraft to World Health.* New York: Macmillan, 1957.

Leff and Leff report on a battle that is fought to save lives. The book relates the history of public health from the medicine man to WHO. It covers such topics as primitive humans and Egyptian, Greek, and Roman medicine, and follows the development of public health through the twentieth century.

Lynch, L. Reddick, editor. *The Cross-Cultural Approach to Health Behavior.* Rutherford, N.J.: Fairleigh Dickenson University Press, 1969.

This book explores the interrelationships between sociocultural background and health behavior. The articles that are included investigate the values and beliefs about health of many people through the United States and the world.

Mechanic, David. *Medical Sociology: A Selective View.* New York: Free Press of Glencoe, 1968.

Three major sections comprise this book. The first section substantively develops a view of illness as part of the larger social interest and deviant behavior. The second explores such issues as the factors that affect mortality and morbidity. The third analyzes the various organizational contexts of practitioner-patient interactions.

Opler, Marvin K., editor. *Culture and Mental Health.* New York: Macmillan, 1959.

This anthology on social psychiatry demonstrates ways in which cultural patterns affect mental health in a worldwide perspective. Opler includes papers from every continent where work has been done.

Paul, Benjamin, editor. *Health, Culture, and Community: Case Studies of Public Reactions to Health Programs.* New York: Russell Sage Foundation, 1955.

Numerous case studies of public reactions to health programs are reported in this anthology. The cases demonstrate to health workers the kind of working relationship that ought to exist between the providers of health care and social scientists.

Pearsall, Marion. *Medical Behavioral Science: A Selected Bibliography of Cultural Anthropology, Social Psychology, and Sociology in Medicine.* Louisville: University of Kentucky Press, 1963.

An outstanding bibliography of books published through 1962 that relate to health-care practices by means of cultural anthropology, social psychology, and sociology.

Popenoe, Cris. *Wellness.* Washington, D.C.: YES! Inc., 1977.

This book is an annotated bibliography that contains numerous books relevant to health. A sample of topics that are presented includes anatomy and physiology, body work, cooking, healing, and use of herbs. Good reference.

FURTHER SUGGESTED READINGS

BOOKS

Alksne, L.; Wellin, E.; Suchman, E.; and Patrick, S. *A Conceptual Framework for the Analysis of Cultural Variations in the Behavior of the Ill.* Unpublished report, New York City Department of Health, n.d.

Blum, Henrick L. *Expanding Health Care Horizons.* Oakland, Calif.: Third Party Associates, 1976.

Cannon, Walter B. *The Wisdom of the Body.* New York: Norton, 1939.

Carlson, Rick J. *The End of Medicine.* New York: Wiley, 1975.

Dember, William N. *The Psychology of Perception.* New York: Holt, 1960.

Dubos, René. *Beast or Angel? Choices that Make us Human.* New York: Scribners, 1974.

Harmon, Francis L. *Principles of Psychology.* Madison: University of Wisconsin Press, 1951.

Murray, Ruth, and Zentner, Judith. *Nursing Concepts for Health Promotion.* Englewood Cliffs, N.J.: Prentice-Hall, 1975.

Popenoe, David. *Sociology.* New York: Appleton, 1974.

Schneiders, Alexander A. *Introductory Psychology.* New York: Rinehart, 1960.

White, Kerr L., editor. *Life and Death and Medicine.* San Francisco: Freeman, 1973.

ARTICLES

Becker, M. H., et al. "A New Approach to Explaining Sick Role Behavior in Low-Income Populations." *American Journal of Public Health* 64 (1974): 205–216.

Belloc, N. B. "Relationship of Health Practices and Mortality." *Preventive Medicine* 2 (1973): 67–81.

Boyce, Tom, and Michael, Max. "Nine Assumptions of Western Medicine." *Man and Medicine* 1 (Summer 1976): 311–335.

Brody, Howard. "The Systems View of Man: Implications for Medicine, Science and Ethics." *Perspectives in Biology and Medicine* 17 (1973): 71–92.

Cohen, Raquel. "Principles of Preventive Mental Health Programs for Ethnic Minority Populations." *American Journal of Psychiatry* 128, no. 12 (June 1972): 79–83.

Dubos, René. "The Diseases of Civilization: Achievements and Illusions." In *Mainstreams of Medicine: Essays on the Social and Intellectual Context of Medical Practice,* edited by Lester King. Austin: University of Texas Press, 1971.

Engel, George L. "The Need for a New Medical Model: A Challenge for Biomedicine." *Science* 196 (8 April 1977): 129–36.

Freyman, John G. "Medicine's Great Schism: Prevention vs. Cure." *Medical Care* 12, no. 7 (July 1975): 533.

Glazier, William H. "The Task of Medicine." *Scientific American* 228 (April 1973): 13–17.

Hayes-Bautista, David, and Harveston, Dominic S. "Holistic Health Care." *Social Policy* 7 (March/April 1977): 7–13.

Hilleboe, Herman E. "Preventing Future Shock: Health Developments in the 1960's and Imperative for the 1970's." *American Journal of Public Health,* February 1972, p. 139.

Parsons, Talcott. "Illness and the Role of the Physician: A Sociological Perspective." In *Medical Care: Readings in the Sociology of Medical Institutions,* edited by W. Richard Scott and Edmund H. Volkort. New York: Wiley, 1966.

Rosenstock, Irwin M. "Why People Use Health Services." *Millbank Memorial Fund Quarterly* 44, no. 3 (July 1966): 94–127.

Russell, Robert D. "Teaching for Meaning in Health Education: The Concept Approach." *Journal of School Health* 71 (January 1966): 13–14.

Sheldon, Alan. "Toward a General Theory of Disease and Medical Care." In *Systems and Medical Care,* edited by Alan Sheldon, Frank Baker, and Curtis P. McLaughlin. Cambridge: MIT Press, 1970.

Spart, Richard. "The Case Against Regular Physicals." *New York Times Magazine*, 25 July 1976, pp. 10, 11, 38–41.

Spector, Manuel, and Spector, Rachel E. "Is Prevention Myth or Reality?" *Health Education* 8, no. 4 (July-August 1977): 23–25.

Suchman, Edward A. "Stages of Illness and Medical Care." *Journal of Health and Human Behavior* 6 (Fall 1965): 114–28.

CHAPTER 3

Familial Folk Remedies

"As modern medicine becomes more impersonal, people are recalling with some wistfulness old country cures administered by parents and grandparents over the generations."[1] If this practice occurs within the general population, does it not also occur among those who deliver health care? Given the difficulty of defining health and illness—it can be assumed that the reader may also have little or no working knowledge of personally practiced "folk medicine" within his own family. In addition to exploring the already described questions regarding the definitions of health and illness, readers should describe how they treat their minor illnesses and how they prevent illness. A common form of self-medication and treatment is the use of aspirin for headaches and colds or occasional diet supplements with vitamins. Initially, one may admit to using tea, honey, and lemon, and hot or cold compresses for headaches and minor aches and pains. For the most part, however, our answers tend to be more oriented toward the health-care system for the treatment of minor illness. In an attempt to bring to consciousness one's knowledge of familial folk remedies, the following procedure is useful.

Interviewing your maternal* grandmother or grandaunt, and your mother, obtain answers to the following questions:

1. What is the family's ethnic background?
   Country of origin?
   Religion?
2. What did *they* do to maintain health?
   What did *their mothers* do?
3. What did *they* do to prevent illness?
   What did *their mothers* do?

---

*An explanation for this choice follows in the text.

4. What home remedies did *they* use to treat illness?
   What did *their mothers* use?

There are two reasons for exploring your familial past. First, it draws your attention to your ethnic heritage and belief system. Many of your daily habits relate to early socialization practices that are passed on by parents or additional significant others. Many behaviors are both unconscious and habitual, and much of what you believe and practice is passed on in this manner. By digging into the past, remote and recent, you can recall some of the rituals you observed either your parents or grandparents perform: you are then better able to realize their origin and significance. There are many beliefs and practices that are ethnically similar. Socialization patterns also tend to be similar among ethnic groups. Religion also plays a role in the perception of, interpretation of, and behavior in health and illness.

The maternal side is selected for the interview because in today's society of interethnic and interreligious marriages, it is assumed that the ethnic beliefs and practices related to health and illness of the family will be more in tune with the mother's family than with the father's. By and large, nurturance has been the domain of women in most cultures and societies. The mother tends to be the person within a family who cares for family members when illness occurs; she also tends to be the prime mover in preventing illness and seeking health care. It is the mother who tells the child what and how much to eat and drink, when to go to bed, and how to dress in inclement weather. She shares her knowledge and experience with her offspring, but usually the daughter is singled out for such experiential sharing.

A second reason for this examination of familial health practices is to sensitize yourself to the role your ethnic heritage has played. You must reanalyze the concepts of health and illness and, once again, view your own definitions from another perspective. If the familial background is presented in a nursing class setting, the peer group can see these people in a different light: a group observes similarities and differences among its members. You discover peer beliefs and practices that you originally had no idea existed. You may then be able to identify the "why" behind many daily health habits, practices, and beliefs.

Quite often you may be amazed to discover the origins of these health practices. Reflecting on their origin may also help to explain the "mysterious" behavior of a roommate or friend. It is interesting to discover crossethnic practices within one's own group. Some people have believed that a given practice was an "original," practiced only by their family. Many religious customs, such as "the blessing of the throats," are now conceptualized in terms of health and illness behavior. Table 3-1 lists a sample of responses to the questions that students obtained from members of the maternal side of their families.

TABLE 3–1. FAMILY HEALTH HISTORIES OBTAINED FROM STUDENTS OF VARIOUS ETHNIC BACKGROUNDS AND RELIGIONS

Austrian (United States), Jewish

Health Maintenance
Eat wholesome foods, homegrown fruits and vegetables
Bake own bread
Prevention
Camphor around the neck (in the winter) in a small cloth bag to prevent measles and scarlet fever
Home Treatment
Sore throat: Go to the village store, find a salted herring, wrap it in a towel, put it around the neck, and let it stay there overnight; gargle with salt water
Boils: Fry chopped onions, make a compress and apply to the infections

Black and Native American, Baptist

Health Maintenance
Eat balanced meals three times a day
Dress right for the weather
Prevention
Keep everything clean and sterile
Stay away from people who are sick
Regular checkups
Blackstrap molasses
Home Treatment
Bloody nose: Place keys on a chain around neck to stop
Sore throat: Suck yolks out of egg shell; honey and lemon; baking soda, salt, warm water, onions around the neck; salt water to gargle

Black African (Ethiopia), Orthodox Christian

Health Maintenance
Keep the area clean
Pray every morning when getting up from bed
Prevention
Eat hot food, such as pepper, fresh garlic, lemon
Home Treatment
Eat hot and sour foods, such as lemons, fresh garlic, hot mustard, red pepper
Make a kind of medicine from leaves and roots of plants mixed together
Colds: Hot boiled milk with honey
Evil eye: They put some kind of plant root on fire and make the man who has the evil eye smile and the man talks about his illness

Canadian, Catholic

Health Maintenance
Cleanliness
Food: people should eat well (fat people used to be considered healthy)
Prayer: health was always mentioned in prayer
Prevention
Sleep
Lots of good food
Elixirs containing herbs and brewed, given as a vitamin tonic
Wear camphor around the neck to ward off any evil spirit; use Father John's medicine November to May

TABLE 3-1—Continued

Home Treatment
Kidney problems: Herbal teas
Colds: Hot lemons
Infected wounds: Raw onions placed on wounds
Cough: Shot of whiskey
Sinuses: Camphor placed in a pouch and pinned to the shirt
Fever: Lots of blankets and heat make you sweat out a fever
Headache: Lie down and rest in complete darkness
Aches and pains: Hot Epsom salt baths
Eye infections: Potatoes are rubbed on them or a gold wedding ring is placed on them and the sign of the cross is made three times

Eastern Europe (United States), Jewish

Health Maintenance
Go to doctor when sick (mother)
Health care for others, not self (mother)
Reluctantly sought medical help (grandmother)
Health for self not a priority (grandmother)
Physician twice a year (mother)
Doctor only when pregnant (grandmother)
Prevention
Observe precautions, such as dressing warmly, not going out with wet hair; getting enough rest, staying in bed if not feeling well (mother)
Not much to prevent illness—very ill today with chronic diseases (grandmother)
Vitamins and water pills
Home Treatment
Colds: Fluids, aspirin, rest
Stomach upset: Eat light and bland foods
Muscle aches: Massage with alcohol
Sore throat: Gargle with salt water; tea with lemon and honey
Insomnia: Glass of wine
Chicken soup used by mother and grandmother.

English, Baptist

Health Maintenance
Eat well; daily walks; read; keep warm
Home Treatment
Earache: Honey and tea, warm cod-liver oil in ear; stay in bed
Cold: Heat up glass and put on back

English, Catholic

Health Maintenance
Lots of exercise; proper sleep; lots of walking; no drinking or smoking; hard work
Bedroom window open at night
Take baths
Never wear dirty clothing
Good housekeeping
Immediate clean-up after meals; washs pan before meals
Rest
Prevention
Maintain a good diet; fresh vegetables; vitamins; little meat; lots of fish; no fried foods; lots of sleep

(continued)

TABLE 3-1—Continued

English, Catholic—Continued

Strict enforcement of life-style
Keep kitchen at 90°F in winter and house will be warm
Home Treatment
Cuts: Wet tobacco
Colds: Chicken soup; herb tea made from roots; alcohol concoctions; Vicks and hot towels
  on chest; lots of fluids, rest; Vicks, sulfur and molasses
Sore throat: Four onions and sugar steeped to heal and soothe the throat
Rashes: Burned linen and cornstarch

English, Episcopal

Health Maintenance
Thorough diet, vitamins
Enough sleep
Cod-liver oil
Home Treatment
Colds and sore throats: Camphor on chest and red scarves around chest

French (France), Catholic

Health Maintenance
Proper food; rest; proper clothing; cod-liver oil daily
Prevention
Every spring give sulfur and molasses for three days as a laxative to get rid of worms
Home Treatment
Colds: Rub chest with Vicks; honey

French Canadian, Catholic

Health Maintenance
Wear rubbers in the rain and dress warmly; take part in sports; active body; lots of sleep
Prevention
Sulfur and molasses in the spring to clear the system
Cod-liver oil in orange juice
No "junk foods"; play outside; walk; daily use of Geritol; camphor on clothes; balanced
  meals
Home Treatment
Colds: Brandy with warm milk; honey and lemon juice; hot poultice on the chest; tea,
  whiskey, and lemon
Back pain: Mustard packs
Rashes: Oatmeal baths
Sore throat: Wrap raw potatoes in sack and tie around neck; soap and water enemas
Warts: Rub potato on wart, run outside and throw it over left shoulder

German (United States), Catholic

Health Maintenance
Wear rubbers; never go barefoot; long underwear and stockings
Wash before meals; change clothes often
Take shots
Take aspirin
Good diet
Prevention
No sweets at meals
Drink glass of water at meals
Cod-liver oil

TABLE 3–1—Continued

Plenty of milk
Exercise
Spring tonic: sulfured molasses
Home Treatment
Coughs: Honey and vinegar
Earache: Few drops of warm milk in the ear; laxatives when needed
Swollen glands or mumps: Put pepper on salt pork and tie around the neck
Constipation: Ivory soap suppositories
Sore throat: Saltwater gargle
Sore back: Hot mustard plaster
Sty: Cold tea-leaf compress
Cramps: Ginger tea
Coughs: Honey and lemon; hot water and Vicks; boiled onion water, honey, and lemon
Fever: Mix whiskey, water, and lemon juice and drink before bed; causes person to per-
  spire and break fever
Headache: Boil a beef bone and break up toast in the broth and drink
Recovery diet: Boil milk and shredded wheat and add a dropped egg—first thing eaten
  after an illness

Iran (United States), Islam

Health Maintenance
Cleanliness
Diet
Prevention
Dress properly for the season and weather; keep feet from getting wet in the rain
Inoculations
Home Treatment
Sore throat: Gargle with vinegar and water
Cough: Honey and lemon
Indigestion: Baking soda and water
Sore muscles: Alcohol and water
Rashes: Apply corn starch

Irish (United States), Catholic

Health Maintenance
Good food, balanced diet
Vitamins
"Blessing of the throat"
Wear holy medals, green scapular
Dress warmly
Plenty of rest
Avoid "fast foods"
Attitudes were important: "Good living habits and good thinking"; "Eat breakfast—if late
  for school, eat a good breakfast and be a little later"; "Don't be afraid to spend on gro-
  ceries—you won't spend on the doctor later"
Keep clean
Keep feet warm and dry
Outdoor exercise, enjoy fresh air and sunshine
Brush teeth, if out of toothpaste use table salt, or ivory soap, or Dr. Lyon's Tooth Powder
Be clean, wear clean clothes
Early to bed ("Rest is the best medicine.")
Prevention
Clean out bowels with senna for eight days

(continued)

TABLE 3–1—Continued

Irish (United States), Catholic—Continued

Every spring, drink a mixture of sulfur and molasses to clean blood
Avoid sick people
Onions under the bed to keep nasal passages clear
During flu season, tie a bag of camphor around the neck
Never go to bed with wet hair
Eat lots of oily foods
Take Father John's Medicine every so often
Prevent evil spirits: Don't look in mirror at night and close closet doors
Drink senna tea at every vacation; cleans out the system
Maintain a strong family with lots of love
Be goal-oriented
Nurture a strong religious faith
Home Treatment
See doctor only in emergency
Fever: Spirits of niter on a dry sugar cube or mix with water; cold baths; alcohol rubdowns
Earache: Heat salt, put in stocking behind the ear
Colds: Tea and toast; chest rub; vaporizer; hot lemonade and a tablespoon of whiskey; mustard plasters; Vicks on chest; whiskey; Vicks in nostrils; hot milk with butter, soups, honey, hot toddies, lemon juice and egg whites; ipecac ("cruel but good medicine"); whiskey with hot water and sugar; soak feet in hot water and sip hot lemonade
Coughs: Cough syrup (available on stove all winter) made from honey and whiskey; Vicks on chest; mustard plaster on chest; onion-syrup cough medicine; steam treatment; swallow Vicks; linseed poultice on chest; mustard plaster on chest; flaxseed poultice on back, red flannel cloth soaked in hot water and placed on chest all night
Menstrual cramps: Hot milk sprinkled with ginger; shot of whiskey, glass of warm wine; warm teas; hot-water bottle on stomach
Splinters: Flaxseed poultice
Sunburn: Apply vinegar; put milk on cloth and apply to burn; a cold, wet tea bag on small areas such as eyelids
Nausea and other stomach ailments: Hot teas; castor oil; hot ginger ale; bay leaf; cup of hot boiled water; potato for upset stomach; baking soda; gruel
Sore throat: Paint throat with iodine, honey and lemon, Karo syrup; paint with kerosene oil internally with a rag and then tie a sock around the neck; paint with iodine or Mercurochrome and gargle with salt and water, honey, melted Vicks
Insect bites: Vaseline or boric acid
Boils: Oatmeal poultice
Cuts: Boric acid
Headaches: Hot poultice on forehead; hot facecloth; cold, damp cloth to forehead; in general, stay in bed, get plenty of rest and sleep, a glass of juice about once an hour, aspirin, and lots of food to get back strength
Sties: Hot tea bag to area

Italian (United States), Catholic

Health Maintenance
Hearty and varied nutritional intake; lots of fruit, pasta, wine (even for children), cheese, homegrown vegetables, and salads; exercise in form of physical labor; molasses on a piece of bread or oil and sugar on bread; hard bread (good for the teeth)
Pregnancy: Two weeks early: girl
Two weeks late: boy
Heartburn: baby with lots of hair
Eat (solved emotional and physical problems); fruit at end of meal cleans teeth; early to bed and early to rise
Prevention
Garlic cloves strung on a piece of string around the neck of infants and children to prevent colds and "evil" stares from other people, which they believed could cause headaches

TABLE 3-1—Continued

and a pain or stiffness in the back or neck (a piece of red ribbon or cloth on an infant served the same purpose)

Keep warm in cold weather

Keep feet warm

Eat properly

Never wash hair or bathe during period

Never wash hair before going outdoors or at night

Stay out of drafts

To prevent "evil" in the newborn a scissor was kept open under the mattress of the crib

To prevent bowlegs and keep ankles straight, up to the age of 6 to 8 months a bandage was wrapped around the baby from the waist to the feet

If infants got their nights and days mixed up, they were tied upside down and turned all the way around

Home Treatment

Chicken soup for everything from colds to having a baby

Boils: Cooked oatmeal wrapped in a cloth (steaming hot) applied to drain pus

Headache: Fill a soup bowl with cold water and put some olive oil in a large spoon; hold the spoon over the bowl in front of the person with the headache; while doing this, recite words in Italian and place index finger in the oil in the spoon; drop three drops of oil from the finger into the bowl; by the diameter of the circle the oil makes when it spreads in the water the severity of the headache can be determined (larger = more severe); after this is done three times the headache is gone

Kerchief with ice in it is wrapped around the head; mint tea

Upset stomach: Herb tea made with herbs sent from Italy

Sore throat: Honey; apply Vicks on throat at bedtime and wrap up the throat

Sprains: Beat egg whites, apply to part, wrap part up

Fever: Cover with blankets to sweat it out

Cramps: Creme de menthe

Poison ivy: Yellow soap suds

Colic: Warm oil on stomach

Acne: Apply baby's urine

Sucking thumb: Apply hot pepper to thumb

High blood pressure: In Italy for high blood pressure, colonies of blood suckers were kept in clay, where they were born; the person with high blood pressure would have a blood sucker put on his fanny, where it would suck blood; it was thought that this would lower his blood pressure; the blood suckers would then be thrown in ashes and would then throw up the blood they had sucked from the person. If the blood sucker died, it alerted the person to see a doctor because it sometimes meant that there was something wrong with the person's blood

Stomachache: Carnilla and maloa (herbs) added to boiled water

Colds: Boiled wines; coffee with anisette

Pimples: To draw contents, apply hot flaxseed

Toothache: Whiskey applied topically

Backache: Apply hot oatmeal in a sock; place a silver dollar on the sore area, light a match to it; while the match is burning put a glass over the silver dollar and then slightly lift the glass, and this causes a suction, which is said to lift the pain out

To build up blood: Eggnog with brandy; Marsala wine and milk

Muscle pain: Heat up carbon leaves (herb) and bundle in a hot cloth to make a pack (soothes any discomfort)

Norwegian (Norway), Lutheran

Health Maintenance

Cod-liver oil

Cleanliness

Rest

(continued)

TABLE 3–1—Continued

Norwegian (Norway), Lutheran—Continued

Prevention
Immunizations
Home Treatment
Colds and sore throat: Hot peppermint drink and Vicks

Nova Scotian, Catholic

Health Maintenance
Sleep; proper foods
Prevention
Cut up some onions and put them on back of stove to cook; feed them to all
Home Treatment
Colds: Boil carrots until jellied, add honey; as expectorant boil onions, add honey
Sore throat: Coat a tablespoon of molasses with black pepper
Earache: Put few drops of heated camphorated oil in ear; melted chicken fat and sugar, put in ear
Psoriasis: Hang a piece of lead around the neck
Earache with infection: To drain the infection, cut a piece of salt pork about 2 inches long and ¾-inch thick and insert it into the infected ear and leave for a few days
Cold in the back: Alcohol was put in a small metal container, a piece of cotton on a stick was placed in the alcohol, ignited, and put in a *banky* (a type of glass resembling a whiskey glass); this was put on the back where the cold was and left for half an hour and a hickylike rash would develop; it was believed that the rash would drain the cold
Skin ulcer and infection: A sharp blade was sterilized and used to make a small incision in the skin, and live blood suckers were placed in the opening; they would drain the infection out; when the blood sucker was full, it would fall to a piece of paper, be bled, placed in alcohol, and reused

Polish (United States), Catholic

Health Maintenance
Use of physician
Eating good, nutritious foods
Plenty of rest
Cod-liver oil
Prevention
Exercise; good diet; eat fresh, homegrown foods; work; good personal hygiene
Home Treatment
Headache: Take aspirin, hot liquids
Sore muscles: Heating pads and hot compresses
Colds: Drink hot liquids, chicken soup, honey

Swedish (United States), Protestant

Health Maintenance
Eat well-balanced meals
A lot of walking
Routine medical exams
Cod-liver oil
Prevention
Eat an apple a day
"I don't do a blooming thing"; eat well
Eat sorghum molasses for general all-round good health
Dress appropriately for weather
Blessing of the throats on St. Blaise Day

TABLE 3-1—Continued

Home Treatment
Cough: Warm milk and butter
Run-down and tired: Eat a whole head of lettuce
Sick: Lots of juices and decarbonated ginger ale; lots of rest
Upset stomach: Baking soda
Sore throat: Gargle with salt and take honey in milk; herringbone wrapped in flannel
   around the neck
Anemia: Cod-liver oil
Bee stings: Poultice
Lumbago: Drink a yeast mixture
Black eye: Leeches
Earache: Warm oil
Congestion: Steamy bathroom
Fever: Blankets to sweat it out

"CONSCIOUSNESS-RAISING"

Recognizing Similarities

In my experience, as the group discussion continues people realize that many personal beliefs and practices do in fact differ from what they are being taught in nursing education to accept as the "right" way of doing things. Participants begin to admit that they do not seek medical care when the first symptoms of illness appear; on the contrary, they usually delay seeking care and often elect to self-treat at home. They also recognize there are many preventive and health-maintenance acts learned in school they choose not to comply with. Sometimes they discover they are following an entire regimen for health-related problems, and are not seeking any outside intervention.

Another facet of a group discussion is the participants' exposure to the similarities that exist among them in terms of prevention and health maintenance. To their surprise and delight, they find many of their daily acts that are taken for granted directly relate to methods of maintaining health and preventing illness.

As is common in most large groups, students seem to be shy at the beginning of this exploration. However, as more and more members of the group are willing to share their experiences, other students feel more comfortable and share more readily. A classroom tactic I have used to break the ice is to reveal an experience I had upon the birth of my first child. My mother-in-law, a woman from Eastern Europe, drew a circle around the child's crib with her fingers and spat on the baby three times to prevent the evil spirits from harming him. Once such an anecdote is shared, other participants have less difficulty in remembering similar events that may have taken place in their own homes.

Students have a variety of feelings about the self-care practices of their families. One feeling discussed by many students is *shame*. A number of students express conflict in their attitudes: they cannot decide whether to believe these old ways or to drop them and adopt the more modern ones they are learning in nursing school. (This is an example of cognitive dissonance.) Many admit that this is the first time they have disclosed these beliefs and practices in public, and they are relieved and amazed to discover similarity with others. The acts may have different names or be performed in a slightly different manner, but the uniting thread among them is to prevent evil (illness) and to maintain good (health).

Transference to Clients

The effects of such a verbal catharsis are long remembered and often quoted or referred to throughout the remainder of a course. The awareness that we gain helps us to better understand the behavior and beliefs of our patients. Given this understanding, we are comfortable enough to ask patients how they interpret a symptom and how they think it ought to be treated. We begin to be more sensitive to people who delay in seeking health care or fail to comply with preventive measures and treatment regimens. We come to recognize that we do the same thing. I believe that the increased familiarity with home health practices and remedies helps us to project this awareness—and understanding—to the clients who are served.

When analyzed from a "scientific" perspective, the majority of these practices do have a sound basis. In the area of health maintenance (Table 3–1) one notes an almost universal adherence to activities that include rest, balanced diet, and exercise.

In the area of prevention there are various differences—ranging from visiting a physician to wearing a clove of garlic around the neck. While the purpose of wearing garlic around the neck is "to keep the evil spirit away," the act also forces people to stay away: what better way to cut down exposure to wintertime colds than to avoid close contact with people?!

One person remembered that during her childhood her mother forced her to wear garlic around her neck. Like most children, she did not like to be different from the rest of her schoolmates. As time went on, she began to have frequent colds, and her mother could not understand why this was happening. The mother followed her child to school some weeks later and discovered that she removed the garlic on her way to school—hiding it under a rock and then replacing it on the way home. There was quite a battle between the mother and daughter! The youngster did not like this method of prevention because her peers mocked her.

A discussion of home remedies is of further interest when each of the methods presented is analyzed for its possible "medical" analogy and also for its prevalence among ethnic groups. Many of these practices, to the surprise and relief of students, tend to run throughout ethnic groups but have different names or contain different ingredients.

In this day of computers and sophisticated medicine with transplants and intricate surgery, the most prevalent need expressed by people who practice folk medicine is to remove the "evil" that may be the cause of the health problem. As students we analyze and discuss a problem and its folk treatments and we begin to see how "evil" continues to be considered the cause of illness and how often the treatment is then designed to remove it.

Each person testifies to the efficacy of a given remedy. Many state that when their grandmothers and mothers shared these remedies with them, they experienced great feelings of nostalgia for the good old days when things seemed so simple. Some people may express a desire to return to these practices of yesteryear, whereas others openly confess that they continue to use such measures even now—sometimes in addition to what a physician tells them to use or often without even bothering to consult a physician.

The goal of this kind of consciousness-raising session is to reawaken the participant to the types of health practices within her own family. The other purpose of the sharing is to make known the similarities and differences that exist as part of a crossethnic phenomenon. At this point, a great deal of myth-debunking occurs. We are intrigued to discover the wide range of beliefs that exist among our peers' families. We had assumed that these people thought and believed as we did. For the first time, we individually and collectively realize that we *all* practice a certain amount of folk medicine, that we *all* have ethnically specific ways of treating illness, and that we, too, often delay in seeking professional health care. We learn that most people prefer to treat themselves at home, and that they have their own ways of treating a particular set of symptoms—with or without a prescribed medical regimen. The previously held notion that "everybody does it this way" is shattered.

REFERENCE

1. Frances Kennett, *Folk Medicine—Fact and Fiction: Age-Old Cures, Alternative Medicine, Natural Remedies* (New York: Crescent Books, 1976), p. 9.

UNIT II

Issues of Delivery and Acceptance of Health Care

Unit II covers topics that relate to the acquisition and use of health-care sources. The overall theme encompasses the problems that the client encounters.

Chapter 4 explores the health-care delivery system on the experiential level, rather than attempting to recite a synopsis of health-care delivery. Enlarging upon a theme introduced earlier, Chapter 5 explores culture and ethnicity—analyzing the impact that ethnic background may have on perception of health and illness. Chapter 6 discusses healing—both ancient and modern, with a number of illustrative examples.

Unit II should enable the reader to:

1. Understand the universal problems encountered in the use of the health-care system
2. Understand how organized medical practice serves as an institution of social control
3. Identify the alternative types of healing systems in contemporary society
4. Understand the interrelationships of culture, religion, and ethnicity relative to health and illness beliefs and practices

5. Identify religious beliefs related to both the prevention and healing of illness

Before you begin to read Chapter 4, please consider the following issues:

1. Who is the first person you turn to when you are ill?
2. Who do you go to and where do you go from there?
3. You have just moved to a new location. You do not know a single person in this community. How do you find health-care resources?
4. Call the county medical society in your area and request the name of a surgeon. Now make an appointment with this doctor. (Assume you have a health problem that requires surgery.)
5. Visit an emergency room in a large municipal hospital. Visit an emergency room in a small community hospital. Spend several hours quietly observing what occurs in each setting.
   a. How long do patients wait to be seen?
   b. Are patients called by name?
   c. Are relatives or friends allowed into the treatment room with the patient?

CHAPTER 4

The Delivery of Health Care

American medicine, the pride of the nation for many years, stands on the brink of chaos. To be sure, our medical practitioners have their great moments of drama and triumph. But, much of U.S. medical care, particularly the everyday business of preventing and treating illness, is inferior in quality, wastefully dispensed, and inequitably financed. Medical manpower and facilities are so maldistributed that large segments of the population, especially the urban poor and those in rural areas, get virtually no care at all, even though their illnesses are most numerous and, in a medical sense, often easy to cure.[1]

—John Knowles

The timeliness of this quotation is easily demonstrated with a presentation of data. Although there are some people today who maintain that, in fact, the health of the nation is no longer in crisis, one need only reflect on the material that follows* to conclude that Dr. Knowles' observations are still accurate.

1. Health resources for the Latino *barrio* (community) in Detroit are nonsystematic, haphazard, and of an acute or episodic nature. The underemployed or unemployed worker has little or no access to comprehensive health care. For these workers, a routine visit to a clinic can result in severe financial strain.[2]

2. Hispanic males aged 15 to 45 have horrifyingly high death rates compared with their contemporaries of other backgrounds. The infant mortality rate continues to be relatively higher among the Puerto Ricans in New York compared with the general population. It is reported that the "children from 6 to 11 who are from families with incomes under $3,000 per year average 3.5

---

*These data were presented at the American Public Health Association's Annual Meeting (Chicago) in November 1975 dental caries per year; however, children from families (other than Hispanic) with incomes over $15,000 per year average less than one carie per year."[3]

3. Three-fourths of the nation's retarded children are found in impoverished rural and urban slums. A child from a low-income family is 15 times more likely to be diagnosed as retarded than a child from a high-income family.[4]

4. A study in Santa Clara County, California, pointed out that, for the Latino population, motor-vehicle traffic accidents ranked as the fourth leading cause of death; cirrhosis of the liver was fifth; and diabetes was sixth. For the white population, traffic accidents and cirrhosis of the liver ranked eighth and ninth; diabetes did not even appear among the ten leading causes of death. In addition, deaths among Latino infants are nearly three times that of the white population.[5]

I believe that these examples graphically illustrate the words of Dr. Knowles. However, as mentioned, there are those who contend that the crises of health-care delivery and increasing costs that were feared in the early 1970s no longer exist. Dr. David E. Rogers and Dr. Robert J. Blendon have stated: "Things within the health care system have gotten better." They cite the following data to support their claims:

1. Physician care is less difficult to obtain; between 1969 and 1975, personal-physician visits rose by 20 percent.

2. There are indications that medical care is more available to the poor and to blacks; the pattern changed from 1965 to 1975, with the poor seeing physicians slightly more often than people of high income.*

3. Death rates have been falling for the last seven years.

4. Infant mortality rates have declined to 16.1 per 1000 live births in 1975 compared with 26 per 1000 live births in 1960.

Rogers and Blendon conclude their article with this statement: "These broad changes do not suggest an overall worsening in the health situation for those who live in the United States. We must be doing some things right, and there seems room for some cautious optimism about the future."[6]

COMMON PROBLEMS IN HEALTH-CARE DELIVERY

On the one hand, it is refreshing to read a report such as Rogers' and Blendon's. However, if we carefully examine the background information as well as the counter arguments, we are likely to be less op-

---

*Rogers and Blendon fail to mention the quality of care, the reason for seeking care, or the percentage of the black population that is included in this formulation.

timistic than Rogers and Blendon would like us to be. There are many problems within the health-care delivery system today. There are problems that affect all of us, and there are those that are specific to the poor and to minority populations. Statistics cannot hide these issues. Changes in death rates and infant mortality rates do not change morbidity rates. To say that people are seeing physicians more frequently in no way indicates that they are necessarily receiving quality care. If the frequency of going to a physician has increased, it may signify more illness rather than more use in general. It may mean that physicians are not treating patients properly, so that people must keep returning until the right combinations of treatments are found, presented, and followed.

The findings of a 1982 national survey of access to medical care revealed that:

1. There are now fewer people who see one particular physician as their regular source of health care;
2. Non-whites are still more likely than whites to use the emergency rooms or outpatient departments of hospitals for health care, rather than a regular family physician;
3. Farm dwellers, low-income people, and non-whites are more likely to not have health insurance;
4. People who do not have health insurance and who do not have a regular physician are less likely to have had elective preventive tests and procedures.[7]

The problems of access to health care continue to plague the health-care delivery system. On one hand we have a system that has made enormous strides. In just the year of 1984 we have seen the increased ability to perform transplants such as that of the heart and liver, the use of the artificial heart, and the transplant of a baboon heart into a human. Yet, on the other hand, problems related to limited access and the lack of health insurance and physician care continue and may well increase in the face of federal cut-backs in health-care-related expenditures.

It has been suggested that the health-care delivery system fosters and maintains a childlike dependence and depersonalized condition for the consumer.[8] The following sections describe problems experienced by most consumers of health care.

"Finding Where the Appropriate Care Is Offered at a Reasonable Price"

It may be difficult for even a knowledgeable consumer to receive adequate care. In the summer of 1976, I was on vacation with my 11-year-old daughter. She complained of a sore throat for two days and, when she did not improve on the third day, I decided to take her to a pediatrician and have a throat culture taken. She was running a low-grade fever, and I suspected a strep throat. I phoned the emergency room of a local teaching hospital for the name of a pediatrician, but I was instructed to "bring her in." I questioned the practicality of using an emergency room but the friendly voice on the other end of the line assured me: "If you have health insurance and the child has a sore throat, this is the best place to come." After a rather long wait, we were seen by an intern who was beginning his first day in pediatrics. To my dismay and chagrin, the young man appeared to have no idea of how to proceed. The resident entered and patiently demonstrated to the fledgling intern—using my daughter—how to go about doing a physical examination on a child. Since I had brought the child to the emergency room merely for a throat culture, I felt that what they were doing was unnecessary and said so. After much delay, the throat culture was taken; we were told we could leave and should call back in 48 hours for the report. As we left the cubicle, we had to pass another cubicle with an open curtain—where a woman was vomiting all over herself, the bed, and the equipment while another intern was attempting to pass a gastric tube. Needless to say, my daughter was distressed by the sight which she could not help but witness. The reward for this trial was a bill for $70. The hospital charged $25 for the use of the emergency room and $45 for the throat culture. I expressed shock and outrage at such an inflated bill.

Two days later I called back for the report. It could not be located. When it was finally "found," the result was negative. I took issue with this because it took 30 minutes for them to find the report. Perhaps this sounds a bit overstated; however, I had the feeling that they told me it was negative just to get me off the phone.

I have related this actual experience to bring out two major points. First, it is not easy to obtain what I, as a health-care provider, would consider to be a rather minor procedure. Second—and more important to those who may be down-and-out financially—it is expensive!

The average person who undergoes such an experience may very well have no idea of what is really going on in the surrounding environment. When health care is sought, one should have access to professionally given examinations and treatment. When one is seeking the results of a laboratory test, the results should be immediately available at the agreed-upon time and place instead of being lost in a jungle of bureaucracy.

"Finding One's Way Amidst the Many Available Types of Medical Care"

A friend's experience illustrates how hard it may be to find appropriate medical care. She had minor gastric problems from time to time and initially sought help from a family physician. He was unable to treat the problem adequately; therefore, she decided to go elsewhere. However, for many reasons—including anger, embarrassment, and fear of reprisal—she chose not to tell the family physician that she was dissatisfied with his care, nor did she request a referral. She was, for all intents and purposes, on her own in terms of securing an appointment with either a gastroenterologist or a surgeon. She very quickly discovered that no physician who was a specialist in gastroenterology would see her on a self-referral. In order to get an appointment, she had to ask her own general practitioner for a referral or else seek initial help from another general practitioner or internist. Since she had little money to spend on a variety of physicians, she decided to wait to see what would happen. In this instance, happily, she has been fortunate: she has had few further problems.

However, numerous people experience difficulty when seeking a second opinion or locating a new physician if they are dissatisfied with their current one. Most people, unlike my friend, are not lucky enough to have their problems resolve themselves and must go in search of additional medical advice.

As a teaching and learning experience, I ask students to describe how they go about selecting a physician and where they go for health care. The younger students in the class generally seek the services of their families' physicians. The older or married students often have doctors other than those with whom they "grew up." These latter students are generally quite willing to share the trials and tribulations that they have experienced. When given the freedom to express their actions and reactions, most admit to having a great deal of difficulty in getting what they perceive to be *good* health care. A number of the older students state that they select a physician on the staff of the institution where they are employed: they have had an opportunity to see him at work and can judge, first hand, whether he is "good" or "bad." One mother stated that she worked in pediatrics during her pregnancy solely to discover who was the best pediatrician. A newly married student stated that she planned to work in the delivery room to see which obstetrician delivered a baby with the greatest amount of concern for both the mother and the child.

That is all well and good for members of the nursing profession. But what about the average lay person who does not have access to this resource? This question alerts the students to the specialness of their personal situations and exposes them to the immensity of the problem that the average person experiences. After individual experiences are shared, the class can move on to work through a case study such as the following.

Ms B. is a new resident in this city. She discovered a lump in her breast and does not know where to turn. How does she go about finding a doctor? Where does she go? What does she do?

One initial course of action is to call the American Cancer Society for advice. From there, she is instructed to call the County Medical Society—the American Cancer Society is not allowed to give out physicians' names. During a phone call to the County Medical Society she is given the names of three physicians in her part of the city; from there she is on her own in attempting to get an appointment with one

of them. It is not unknown for a stranger to call a physician's office
and be told: (1) "The doctor is no longer seeing any additional new
patients"; (2) "There is a six-month wait"; or (3) "He sees no one without a proper referral."

The woman, of course, has another choice: She can go to an emergency room or a clinic. But then she discovers that the wait in the
emergency room is intolerable for her. She may rationalize that because a "lump" is not really an "emergency," she should choose another route. She may then try to secure a clinic appointment, and once
again she may experience a great deal of difficulty in getting an appointment at a convenient time. She may finally get one and then discover that the wait in the clinic is unduly long—which may cause her
to miss a day of work, and that will entail all sorts of explanations.

"Figuring Out What the Physician Is Doing"

It is not always easy for members of the health professions to understand what is happening to them when they are ill. Alas, what must
it be like for the average person who has little or no knowledge of
health-care routines and practices?

Pretend that you are a lay person who has just been relieved of
all your clothes and given a paper dress to put on. You are lying on a
table with strange eyes peering down at you. A sheet is thrown over
you, and you are given terse directions—"breathe," "cough," "don't
breathe," "turn," "lift your legs." You may feel without warning a
cold disk on your chest or a cold hand on your back. As the physical-
examination process continues, you may feel a few taps on the ribs,
see a bright light shining in your eye, feel a cold tube in your ear, and
gag on a stick probing the inside of your mouth. What is going on?
The jargon you hear is unfamiliar. You are being poked, pushed, prod-
ded, peered at and into, jabbed, and you do not know why. If you are
female and going for your first pelvic examination, you may have no
idea what to expect. Perhaps you have heard only hushed whisperings,
and your level of fear and discomfort is high. Insult is added to injury
when you experience the penetration of the cold, unyielding speculum:
"What is he doing now and why?"

These hypothetical situations are typical of the usual physical examinations that you may routinely encounter in a clinic or private physician's office. But suppose you have a more complex problem, such
as a neurologic condition, for which the diagnostic procedures may
indeed be painful and complicated. Have you ever had a spinal tap?
A myelogram? An angiogram? Quite often, those who deliver care have
not experienced the vast number of procedures that are done in diagnostic workups and in treatment; they have little awareness of what
the patient is thinking, feeling, and experiencing. Similarly, because
the names and the purposes of the procedures are familiar to health-
care workers—don't forget, this is *their* culture, *their* bailiwick, *their*

turf—they may experience a great deal of difficulty in appreciating why the patient cannot understand what is happening.

"Finding Out What Went Wrong"

What did you do the last time a patient asked to read the chart? Traditionally, you uttered an authoritative "tsk," turned abruptly on white-heeled shoes, and walked briskly away. Who ever heard of such nerve? A patient asking to read a chart! In recent years, a "patient's bill of rights" has evolved. One of its mandates is that the patient has the right to read the medical record. Experience, however, demonstrates that this right is still not granted. Suppose one enters the hospital for what is deemed to be a simple medical or surgical problem. All well and good, if everything goes according to routine. However, what happens when complications develop? The more determined the patient is to discover what the problem is or why there are complications, the more the patient believes that the health-care providers are trying to hide something. The cycle perpetuates itself, and a tremendous schism develops between provider and consumer. Quite often, "the conspiracy of silence" tends to grow as more questions are asked. This unpleasant situation may continue until the patient is locked inside his subjective world. It is rare for a person truly to understand unforeseen complications. Nurses all too often enter into this collusion and play the role of a silent partner with the physician and the institution.

"Overcoming the Built-in Racism and Male Chauvinism of Doctors and Hospitals"

Students tend to have little difficulty in describing many incidents of racism and male chauvinism: that they are mostly women suffices, and that they are nurses adds meaning to the problem. Classroom discussion helps to identify subtle incidents of racism and to identify them as such. For example, students may realize that black patients may be the last to receive morning or evening care, meal trays, and so forth. If this is a "normal" occurrence on a floor, it is an indictment in itself. However, such racism may take another tack. Is it an accident that the black person is the last patient to receive routine care, or has consciously been made to wait? Does the fact that the black person may have to wait longest for water or a pill demonstrate racism on a conscious level, or is it subliminal?

Nurses recognize the subtle patronization of both themselves and of female patients. Once the situation is probed and spelled out, the students adopt a much more realistic attitude toward the insensitivity of those who choose a racist or chauvinistic style of giving care. Students have noted that when they are aware of what is happening, they are better able to take steps to block future occurrences. Some have written letters to me after they have begun or returned to the practice of nursing, stating that knowing the phenomenon is universal helps them to project a stronger image in their determination to work for change.

PATHWAYS TO HEALTH SERVICES

When a health problem occurs, there is an established system whereby health-care services are obtained. The family is usually the first resource. It is in the domain of the family that the person seeks validation that what he is experiencing is indeed an illness. Once the belief is validated, health care outside of the home is sought. When one is dealing with the medical system in general, help is sought from a physician in one setting or another. It may be the private office of a general practitioner, internist, or pediatrician, or it may be in a hospital emergency room or clinic.* This is known as the level of first contact, or the *entrance* into the health-care system.[9]

The second level of care, if needed, is found at the specialist's level: in clinics, private practice, or hospitals. Obstetricians, gynecologists, surgeons, neurologists, and other specialists make up a large percentage of those who practice in medicine.[10]

The third level of care is delivered within hospitals that provide inpatient care and services. Care is determined by need, whether long-term (as in a psychiatric setting or rehabilitation institute) or short-term (as in the acute-care setting and community hospitals).[11]

An in-depth discussion of the different kinds of hospitals—voluntary or profit-making and nonprofit institutions—is more appropriate to a book dealing solely with the delivery of health care (see the annotated bibliography at the end of this book). In our present context, the issue is: What does the patient know about such settings, and what kind of care can he expect to receive?

To many students, the problems of the ward are far removed from the scope of practice they know from nursing school and from what they ordinarily see in a work setting (unless they choose to work in a city or county hospital). Many students assume that the care they observe and deliver in a suburban or community hospital is the universal norm. This is a fundamental error in experience and understanding, which can be corrected if students are assigned first to visit the emergency room of a city hospital and then the emergency room of a suburban hospital in order to compare and contrast the two mil-

---

*It is not unusual for a family to have a multitude of physicians providing its care, with limited or no communication between the attending physicians. Problems and complications erupt when a physician is not aware that there are other physicians caring for a patient. Let us not forget that in rural and remote areas, comprehensive health care is difficult to obtain. For patients who are forced to use the clinics of a hospital, there is certainly no continuity of care because intern and resident physicians come and go each July 1.

ieus. Unless students visit each setting, they fail to gain an appreciation of the major differences—how vastly such facilities differ in scope of treatment and in regard for patients. Students typically report that in the suburban emergency room the patients are called by name, their families wait with them, and every effort is made to hasten their visit. The contrast is astounding when they talk with people in urban emergency rooms who have waited for extended periods of time, are sometimes not addressed by name, and are not allowed to have family members come with them while they are examined. The noise and confusion are also factors that confront and dismay students who are exposed to big-city emergency rooms.

MEDICINE AS AN INSTITUTION OF SOCIAL CONTROL

The people of today's death-denying, youth-oriented society have unusually high expectations of the healers of our time. We expect a cure (or if not a cure, then the prolongation of life) as the normal outcome of illness. (The technology of modern health care dominates our expectations of treatment and our primary focus is on the *curative* aspects of medicine, not on prevention.)

As control over the behavior of a person has shifted from the family and church to a physician, "be good" has shifted to "take your medicine." The role that physicians play within society in terms of social control is ever-growing, so that there is frequent conflict between medicine and the law over definitions of accepted codes of behavior and the relative status of the two professions in governing American life.[12] The following examples serve to illustrate the "medicalization" of society.

"Through the Expansion of What in Life Is Deemed Relevant to the Good Practice of Medicine"
This factor is exemplified by the change from a specific etiologic model of disease to a multicausal one. The "partners" in this new model include greater acceptance of comprehensive medicine, the use of the computer, and the practice of preventive medicine. In preventive medicine, however, the medical person must get to the lay person before the disease occurs: clients must be sought out. Because of this, forms of social control emerge in an attempt to *prevent* disease: low-cholesterol diets, avoidance of stress, stopping smoking, getting proper and adequate exercise.

"Through the Retention of Absolute Control over Certain Technical Procedures"
This step is, in essence, the right to perform surgery and the right to prescribe drugs. In the life span of human beings, modern medicine can often determine life or death from the time of conception to old

age through genetic counseling, abortion, surgery, and technologic devices such as computers, respirators, and life-support systems. Medicine has at its command drugs that can cure or kill—from antibiotics to the chemotherapeutic agents used to combat cancer. There are drugs to cause sleep or wakefulness, to increase or decrease the appetite, to increase or decrease levels of energy. There are drugs to relieve depression and stimulate interest. (In the United States these mood-altering drugs are consumed at a rate higher than those medications prescribed and used to treat specific diseases). In addition, medicine can control what medications are available for legal consumption.

The controversy over Laetrile is an example of how the medical establishment is thwarting the popular consumption of a drug. In spite of the "scientific" evidence that this drug is worthless, there is no evidence to date that it is harmful, and there are a significant number of people who desire to use it in the prevention and treatment of cancer. The ongoing battle between the proponents and opponents of Laetrile is a fascinating study in the power of modern medical social control and the factions that are attacking this power. Since 1977, the proponents have made headway in lobbying for legalization of the drug in a number of states, and a Federal judicial ruling has permitted its use in individual cases.*

"Through the Retention of Near Absolute Access to Certain 'Taboo' Areas"

Medicine has almost exclusive license to examine and treat that most personal of individual possessions: the mechanics of mind and body. If it can be determined that some factor affects the body or the mind, that element can be interpreted as a medical problem; it falls into the hands of practitioners of medicine for treatment. Such situations currently include the normal processes of pregnancy and aging, as well as the human behavior problems of drug addiction and alcoholism.

"Through the Expansion of What in Medicine Is Deemed Relevant to the Good Practice of Life"

This expansion is illustrated by the use of medical jargon to describe a state of being—such as the "health" of the nation or the "health" of the economy. Any political or economic proposal or objective that enhances the "health" of those concerned wins approval.

There are numerous areas in which medicine, religion, and law overlap. One example is how, in public-health practice, law and medicine overlap in the creation of laws that establish quarantine and the

---

*In July of 1977, Laetrile was the focus of much attention. Since August 1977, more studies have been conducted seeking to prove its danger. On the other hand, Laetrile has been accepted by a number of additional states. Since this remains an ongoing issue, the reader should be aware that nothing has been settled as of the time these comments were written and that the situation may change at any time.

need for immunization. As another example, a child is unable to enter school without proof of having received certain inoculations. Medicine and law also merge in areas of sanitation, rodent control, and insect control. A legal-medical dispute can arise over the guilt or innocence of a criminal as determined by his "mental state" at the time of a crime.

There are diseases that carry a social stigma: one must be screened for tuberculosis before employment; a history of typhoid fever prevents a person from commercially handling food for life; venereal disease must be reported and treated; and even the ancient disease of leprosy continues to carry a stigma.

Abortion represents an area replete with conflict that involves politics, law, religion, and medicine. Those in favor of abortion believe that it is the right of the female to have an abortion and that the matter is confidential between the patient and her physician. Opponents argue on religious and moral grounds that abortion is murder. At the present time, the law sanctions abortion. In many states, however, Medicaid will no longer pay for an abortion unless the mother's life is in danger; this is making it increasingly difficult for the poor to obtain these services.

Another highly charged area of conflict involves the practice of euthanasia. With the burgeoning of technologic improvements, the definition of "death" has changed in recent years: it sometimes takes a major decision from the courts to "pull the plug," such as in the Karen Quinlan case.

Finally, one might ponder that although there are many daily practical activities we undertake in the name of health—taking vitamins, practicing hygiene, using birth control, engaging in dietary or exercise programs—the "diseases of the rich" (cancer, heart disease, and stroke) tend to capture more public attention and funding than the diseases of the poor (malnutrition, high maternal and infant death rates, sickle cell anemia, and lead poisoning).

FUNDING HEALTH SERVICES

On August 13, 1981, President Reagan signed into law legislation designed to reduce the high costs of federal government: much of this reform affected the funding mechanisms for the delivery of health care. This legislation contained the key reform of block grants. It was expected that these block grants would alter the way that taxpayers' dollars were spent for health and human services.[13] Prior to this legislation, there had been 25 separate health and human services spending programs, each having its own set of rules and regulations. With the creation of the blocks, the programs were consolidated into seven areas. The purpose of allocating funds in this manner was to achieve greater flexibility in the use of funds and to provide a more efficient use of tax dollars. The blocks went into effect in the fall of 1981. The establishment of the block grants was a major goal of President Reagan's long-held belief that cities and states ought to have more flexibility in spending allocated federal dollars and be relieved of burdensome regulatory requirements. Before this shift in funding, federal dollars allocated for health and human services had been funded through categorical grants.[14]

Types of Grants

Categorical. Categorical grants were federal monetary assistance programs in which funds were targeted for specifically designated activities. Categorical grant programs generally required applications and approvals to obtain funds from the federal agency administering the programs. As the number of categorical grants increased, programs were duplicated and the reporting requirements to Washington became onerous. In addition, it was charged that categorical programs could not be sufficiently responsive to the local needs of each state.[15]

Block. Block grants are broad federal monetary aid programs intended to give recipient states and local governments wider latitude in the use of grant funds within a designated broad area. The responsibility for administration and evaluation of the program under the grant is primarily the responsibility of the recipient of the grant. Generally, a state plan is required in order to receive the funds. With block grants, states can tailor their spending to meet their local needs. The federal regulations and reporting requirements are reduced to the minimum necessary to assure that the broad programs comply with the law and that funds are spent for the purposes intended by law.[16]

The following are noteworthy attributes of block grants:

1. The Department of Health and Human Services no longer directs spending, but retains power in most cases to withhold funds in order to keep them from being misused.
2. Independent audits of state programs are required.
3. Funding for a few essential services remains mandated.
4. Public reports and legislative hearings are required.
5. The states answer to their own citizens on spending decisions. (This aspect of block grants—bringing government decisions closer to those who are being served—is a most important principle.)
6. The states are in charge of block grants; they can prevent duplication of services and make linkages with the private and volunteer sectors to help deliver services at the lowest cost.[17]

Current Block Grants

Twenty-five health-related programs were consolidated into the following seven blocks:

1. Preventive Health
   This block contains preventive programs such as rodent con-

trol, home health, fluoridation, health education, emergency medical services, rape crises, and hypertension control.
2. Maternal and Child Health
   This block contains such programs as hemophilia, lead-based paint poisoning prevention, genetic disease prevention, adolescent health services, and sudden infant-death syndrome.
3. Alcohol, Drug Abuse, and Mental Health
   This block contains such programs as community mental health, drug abuse, and alcoholism.
4. Primary Care
5. Social Services
6. Community Services
7. Energy Assistance[18]

These programs were not only consolidated into blocks, but the amount of money allocated to the blocks and hence to the programs was drastically cut. This has placed an additional burden on the states to either continue to fund the programs or to dismantle them. Programs such as migrant health services, family planning, and immunization, have remained as categorical grants.

The block grants have been in effect since 1981. Many programs that once had been available to the poor have been eradicated in the effort not to duplicate programs. The budget funding health-related programs has shrunk and the available programs have dissipated. Obtaining health-care services has become more difficult rather than easier.

In addition to altering the mechanism for funding federal grant programs that are health related, the mechanism for funding reimbursement has also been altered. Funding has gone from a mechanism of retrospective reimbursement to one of prospective reimbursement, putting a strain on already tight health-care programs. In addition, severe fiscal cuts are threatened for Medicare programs, and "cost savings" are the goal of the Reagan administration.

Recipients and Costs of Health Services

Racial and ethnic minorities in the United States use medical services less often and may get lower-quality care than whites.[19] In addition, there are a greater number of health-care problems among minorities. Although federal health-care programs were developed to be ameliorative, and although the poorer quality of health care for minorities is known, services are being decreased. Another complicating factor is that institutions that once provided "free care," are currently restricted because they do not have sufficient resources to provide this care.

The costs of modern day health care continue to rise at an astonishing rate. People, however, continue to die and the morbidity rates remain high. One institution was forced in midyear to suspend its free-care program because the allocated funds had been overspent in order to pay for a neo-natal intensive-care unit.

TYPES OF HEALTH CARE

The Allopathic System

In preceding pages the dominant health-care system in the United States has been discussed: this system is called "allopathic." The word "allopathy" has two roots. One comes from Greek roots meaning "other than disease," because drugs are prescribed on a basis that has no consistent or logical relationship to the symptoms. The second definition for allopathy is derived from German roots and means "all therapies." Allopathy is a "system of medicine that embraces all methods of proven value in the treatment of diseases."[20] After 1855, the American Medical Association adopted the second definition of allopathy and has been exclusive in determining who can practice medicine in the United States. For example, in the 1860s the American Medical Association refused to admit women doctors to medical societies, practiced segregation, and demanded the purging of homeopaths. Today, allopaths show little tolerance or respect for such other providers of health care as homeopaths, osteopaths, and chiropractors and for such traditional healers as lay midwives, herbalists, and medicine men.[21]

Alternative Systems

There are other forms of healers in contemporary American society. These include homeopaths, chiropractors, osteopaths, Christian healers, and traditional healers who practice within ethnic groups. Chapter 6 describes Christian healers. Each chapter on ethnic groups discusses healers indigenous to that community. Chapter 12 gives as a case study the role of lay midwives.

Homeopathic Medicine. Homeopathic medicine was developed in 1810 by Samuel C. Hahnemann in Germany. Homeopathy, or homoeopathy, comes from the Greek words *homoios* ("similar") and *pathos* ("suffering"). In the practice of homeopathy, the person, not the disease, is treated. The practitioner treats a given person by using minute doses of plant, mineral, or animal substances. The medicines are selected upon the principle of the "law of similars." A substance that is used to treat a specific set of symptoms is the same substance that if given to a healthy person would cause the symptoms. The medicines are administered in extremely small doses. These medicines are said to provide a gentle but powerful stimulus to the person's own defense system and in turn to help the person heal.

Homeopathy was popular in nineteenth-century America and Europe because it was successful in treating the raging epidemics of those times. In 1900 20 percent to 25 percent of physicians were homeopaths. Following the allopathic efforts to wipe out the homeopaths, the movement has greatly dissipated. However, there is a small group of homeopaths in the United States, and there are larger practices in India, Great Britain, France, Greece, Germany, Brazil, Argentina, and Mexico.[22]

Osteopathic Medicine. Osteopaths are fully qualified physicians who can practice in all areas of medicine and surgery. They, like the medical doctor, have completed four years of medical school, one year of internship, and generally a further residency in a specialty area. They take the same course work as do medical doctors, often use the same textbooks, and often take the same licensing exams. There are 14 osteopathic medical schools in the United States and 214 hospitals. The lines of distinction between the medical doctor and the osteopath arise because the osteopath, in addition to using traditional forms of medical diagnosis and treatment, uses manipulation of the bones, muscles, and joints as therapy. Osteopaths also employ structural diagnosis and take into account the relationship between body structure and organic functioning when they determine a diagnosis. The osteopathic doctor has the same power to treat patients as a medical doctor.[23]

Chiropracty. Chiropracty is a controversial form of healing that has been in existence for well over eighty years. It, too, is a disease-theory and a method of therapy that differs from allopathy. It was developed as a form of healing in 1895 in Davenport, Iowa, by a storekeeper named Daniel David Palmer, also known as a "magnetic healer." Palmer's theory underlying the practice of chiropracty was that an interference with the normal transmission of "mental impulses" between the brain and body organs produced diseases. The interference is caused by misalignment or subluxation of the vertebrae of the spine, which decreases the flow of "vital energy" from the brain through the nerves and spinal cord to all parts of the body. The treatment consists of manipulation to eradicate the subluxation.

Chiropracty is practiced in two ways. One form is that of the "mixers" who use heat therapy, enemas ("colonic irrigation"), exercise programs, and other therapeutic practices. The other group, the "straight" chiropractors who use only manipulation, disapprove of the practices of the "mixers." They believe that the other techniques are a form of allopathic medicine.[24]

REFERENCES

1. John Knowles, "It's Time to Operate," *Fortune*, January 1970, p. 79.
2. Ruben G. Zamorano, "The Unemployed Detroit Latino Worker: A Health Resource Profile." Paper presented at the 103rd Annual Meeting of the American Public Health Association, Chicago, 16–20 November 1975, pp. 7, 17, 19.
3. Pedro Juan Lecca et al., "Profile of Health Resources among Unemployed

Puerto Ricans in the U.S." Paper presented at the 103rd Annual Meeting of the American Public Health Association, Chicago, 16–20 November 1975, pp. 6, 10.

4. Ibid., p. 10.
5. Simon Dominguiz with Hector B. Garcia, "Health Resources for Unemployed Latinos in the United States." Paper presented at the 103rd Annual Meeting of the American Public Health Association, Chicago, 16–20 November 1975, pp. 6–8.
6. David E. Rogers and Robert J. Blendon, "How Healthy Is America's Health Care?" *Boston Globe,* 10 July 1977.
7. Lu Ann Aday and Ronald M. Andersen, "The National Profile of Access to Medical Care: Where Do We Stand?" *American Journal of Public Health,* December 1984, p. 1337.
8. Barbara Ehrenreich and John Ehrenreich, *The American Health Empire: Power, Profits, and Politics* (New York: Random House, Vintage Books, 1971), p. 4–12. The following headings are quoted from this book.
9. John Fry, *Medicine in Three Societies* (London: Aylesbury (Bucks), MTP, 1969), p. 22.
10. Ibid.
11. Ibid., p. 23.
12. Irving Kenneth Zola, "Medicine as an Institution of Social Control," *Sociological Review* n. s. 20, no. 4, (November 1972): 487–504. The following headings are quoted from this book.
13. "Health and Human Services Department Block Grants," *HHS Fact Sheet* (Washington, D.C.: U.S. Government Printing Office, August 1981), p. 1.
14. D. Stone, director, State of Texas, Office of State-Federal Relations. *An Analysis of the Budget Reconciliation Act of 1981* (Austin, Texas, 1981), pp. i–ii.
15. HHS Fact Sheet, p. 1.
16. Ibid., p. 1.
17. Ibid., pp. 1–2.
18. Ibid., p. 3.
19. "Minorities Use Medical Services Less, Study Shows." Austin, Tex. *Austin American Statesman,* 13 March 1982.
20. Andrew Weil, *Health and Healing* (Boston: Houghton Mifflin, 1983), p. 17.
21. Ibid., pp. 22–25.
22. Homeopathic Educational Services, Berkeley, Calif. Educational pamphlet. (Reprint. Harrisburg, Pa.: Pennsylvania Osteopathic Association, 1979.)
23. Herb Denenberg, "Shopper's Guide to Osteopathic Physicians," pamphlet.
24. Ann Kuckelman Cobb, "Pluralistic Legitimation of an Alternative Therapy System: The Case of Chiropractic," *Medical Anthropology* 6, no. 4 (Fall, 1977): 1–23.

BIBLIOGRAPHY

Bullough, Bonnie, and Bullough, Vern L. *Poverty, Ethnic Identity and Health Care.* New York: Appleton-Century-Crofts, 1972.

This book boldly demonstrates and documents the ways in which the inadequacies of the health-care system affect the poor and members of minority groups.

Cornacchia, Harold J. *Consumer Health.* St. Louis: Mosby, 1976.

The consumer movement in the United States has made great strides in the area of protecting the public in the marketplace. The purpose of this book is to aid consumers in implementing the Bill of Rights. It describes various aspects and problems of the health-care system.

Crichton, Michael. *Five Patients.* New York: Knopf, 1970.

This interesting book explores the hospital treatment of five people. It demonstrates how hospital practice is changing in this age of technology.

Ehrenreich, Barbara, and Ehrenreich, John. *The American Health Empire: Power, Profits, and Politics.* New York: Vintage Books, 1972.

According to this team of authors, the health system is not in business for people's health. The book explores the economic aspects of health and health care and how various institutions evolve into "empires."

Freidson, Eliot. *Profession of Medicine.* New York: Dodd, Mead, 1971.

Freidson explores the word "profession." He sees it both as an "occupation" and as an "avowal or promise." He demonstrates how the medical profession is organized, how professional performance is organized, and how illness is socially constructed.

Illich, Ivan. *Medical Nemesis: The Expropriation of Health.* London: Marion Bogars, 1975.

This excellent study deals with the topics of clinical iatrogenesis, the epidemic of modern medicine, social iatrogenesis, the medicalization of life, the destruction of medical cultures, the killing of pain, and the politics of health.

————; Zola, Irving K.; McKnight, John; Caplan, Jonathan; and Shaiken, Harley. *Disabling Professions.* Salem, N.H.: Boyars, 1977.

The authors explore the various arguments relevant to the public debate about the power of the professions. Each explores various aspects of the growing dependency of people on the professional elite who dominate, institutionalize, and ritualize all aspects of our daily lives.

Kennedy, Edward M. *In Critical Condition: The Crises in America's Health Care.* New York: Simon and Schuster, 1972.

The many problems that people often encounter when they deal with the health-care delivery system are outlined.

Millman, Marcia. *The Unkindest Cut.* New York: Morrow, 1977.

This explosive book explores and analyzes the "back rooms" of American medicine. It examines what is done in the mortality review conferences, the emergency room, and various hospital staff meetings.

Rosenberg, Ken, and Schiff, Gordon. *The Politics of Health Care: A Bibliography.* Somerville, Mass.: New England Free Press, 1973.

A bibliographic listing, this work cites numerous books and articles that deal with the politics of health care. It can be ordered from Health Bibliography, c/o Ken Rosenberg, 48 Aldie Street, Allston, Mass. 02134.

Silver, George. *A Spy in the House of Medicine.* Germantown, Md.: Aspen Systems, 1976.

Why is health care so costly? How is health care delivered? What goes on in health care? These and other questions are probed in this account of health-care delivery.

FURTHER SUGGESTED READINGS

BOOKS

Aiken, Linda G. *Health Policy and Nursing Practice.* New York: McGraw-Hill, 1981.

Ashely, Joann. *Hospitals, Paternalism, and the Role of the Nurse.* New York: Teachers College Press, 1976.

Berman, Edgar. *The Solid Gold Stethoscope.* New York: Macmillan Co., 1976.

Davis, Fred, ed. *The Nursing Profession: Five Sociological Essays.* New York: Wiley, 1966.

Fry, John. *Medicine in Three Societies.* London: Aylesbury (Bucks), 1969.

Fuchs, Victor R. *Who Shall Live? Health, Economics and Social Choice.* New York: Basic Books, 1974.

Jonas, Steven. *Health Care Delivery in the United States.* 2nd. ed. New York: Springer, 1982.

Kotelchuck, David, ed. *Prognosis Negative.* New York: Vintage Books, 1976.

McKeown, Thomas. *The Role of Medicine: Dream, Mirage or Nemesis?* London: Nuffield Provincial Hospitals Trust, 1976.

Norman, John C., ed. *Medicine in the Ghetto.* New York: Appleton-Century-Crofts, 1969.

Redman, Eric. *The Dance of Legislation.* New York: Simon and Schuster, 1973.

Weil, Andrew. *Health and Healing.* Boston: Houghton Mifflin Co., 1983.

ARTICLES

There are numerous articles available on health-care delivery; the following are a mere sampling.

Aday, Lu Ann and Ronald M. Andersen. "The National Profile of Access to Medical Care: Where Do We Stand?" *American Journal of Public Health,* 74, no. 12 (December 1974) 1331–1339.

Adler, Herbert M., and Hammett, V. "The Doctor-Patient Relationship Revisited: An Analysis of the Placebo Effect." *Annals of Internal Medicine* 78 (1973): 595.

Chopoorian, Teresa and Craig, Margaret Malrey. "Nursing and Health Care Delivery." *American Journal of Nursing* (December 1976): 1988–91.

Knowles, John. "It's Time to Operate." *Fortune,* January 1970.

McDermott, Walsh. "Medicine: The Public Good and One's Own." *Cornell University Medical College Alumni Quarterly* 4 (Winter 1977): 15–24.

Milio, Nancy. "Values, Social Class, and Community Health Services." *Nursing Research* 16, no. 1 (Winter 1967): 26–31.

Orque, Modesta S. "Health Care and Minority Clients." *Nursing Outlook* 24, no. 5 (May 1976): 313–16.

Perkins, Sister Mary Rose. "Does Availability of Health Services Ensure Their Use?" *Nursing Outlook* 22, no. 8 (August 1984): 496–98.

Roemer, Milton I. "Health Care Financing and Delivery around the World." *American Journal of Nursing* (June 1971): 1158–63.

White, Kerr L.; Murnaghan, Jane G.; and Gaus, Clifton R. "Technology and Health Care." *New England Journal of Medicine* 287, no. 24 (14 December 1972): 1223–26.

Zola, Irving Kenneth. "Medicine as an Institution of Social Control." *Sociological Review* n. s. 20, no. 4 (November 1972): 487–504.

CHAPTER 5

Culture, Health, and Illness

Culture is a unified whole even unto psychosis and death.
—Jules Henry, *Culture Against Man*

In the fall of 1983 a young Hispanic man collapsed and died while playing football. The police, who took his mother to the hospital, did not tell her the seriousness of the injury, and she was informed of his death when she arrived at the hospital. The mother requested to see her son's body so that she could verify his death and perform certain religious rituals, such as washing him and annointing the body with oil. She was not allowed to see the body—the reason given was that it could not be touched because of the pending autopsy. Subsequently, the mother believed that the autopsy was the cause of her son's death. To add insult to injury, the mother was assisted to a Catholic Church that was not of her ethnocultural background and did not hold worship services in her language.[1]

In the mid-1960s a social explosion in the United States resulted in a surge of group consciousness. Blacks first, then Hispanics, Asian-Americans, Native Americans, and white ethnic groups began to assert their cultural group identity. The rejuvenation of ethnic identity eroded both the "melting pot" myth and the belief that an "American Culture" would decrease group awareness.[2]

Immigrants and their descendants comprise most of the population of the United States. All Americans who are not themselves immigrants have ancestors who came from elsewhere. The only people considered "native" are the American Indians, the Aleuts, and the Eskimos, for they migrated here thousands of years before the Europeans.[3]

Immigrants came to the United States seeking economic, religious, and other opportunities.[4] The life of the immigrant was fraught with difficulties—going from an "old" to a "new" way of life, learning

---

TEST YOUR ETHNIC KNOWLEDGE

1. What three nations provided the greatest numbers of immigrants to the U.S. from 1820–1975?

2. Immigrants from what nation are the *most educated?*

3. What ethnic group has the best job status in America?

4. Who are the richest Indians in the U.S.?
   Who are the poorest Indians in the U.S.?

5. What is the largest Indian tribe?

6. Who claimed to have invented the telephone?

7. Who were the "original" Siamese twins?

8. What do these names mean?
   a. Chattanooga
   b. Kalamazoo
   c. Milwaukee
   d. Poughkeepsie
   e. Yosemite

9. Who are (a) Belle Silverman, (b) Anna Maria Italiano, (c) Concetta Ignolia, and (d) Rocco Barbella?

10. How many different peoples in the world believe in the "evil eye"?

11. What are "leapers"?

Answers at end of chapter

---

a new language, and adapting to a new climate, new foods, and a new culture. Socialization of immigrants occurred in American public schools and "Americanization" became for some a process of "vast psychic repression."[5] In part, the concept of the melting pot was created in schools where children learned English, rejected family traditions, and attempted to take on the values of the dominant culture and "pass" as "Americans."[6] Furthermore, Greeley describes the immigrant ethnic group as a combination of European cultural backgrounds, American acculturation experiences, and common political, social, and economic interests. Greeley also argues that different origins produce cultural differences and that diverse experiences in America reinforced the old differences between ethnic groups and created new ones.[7] Jordan and Jordan describe the immigrant's life as very hard and lonely.[8]

Every immigrant group brought cultural attitudes toward health, health care, and illness and within each of these groups widely varying health and illness beliefs and practices exist.[9]

ACCULTURATION AND HERITAGE CONSISTENCY

Health and illness can be interpreted and explained in terms of personal experience and expectations. There are many ways in which we can define our own health or illness and determine what these states mean to us in our daily lives. We learn from our own cultural and ethnic backgrounds *how* to be healthy, *how* to recognize illness, and *how* to be ill. Furthermore, the meanings attached to the notions of health and illness are related to the basic, culture-bound values by which we define a given experience and perception.[10]

To understand and appreciate differences in health and illness beliefs and practices that may be culturally determined, it is necessary to analyze theories relating to the "Americanization" of beliefs. This chapter presents two theories. The first relates to acculturation and the quasi creation of a melting pot or some other common threads that are part of an American whole. The second and opposite theory analyzes the degree to which people have maintained their traditional heritage. It then becomes possible to analyze health beliefs by determining a person's ties to the traditional heritage and culture rather than to signs of acculturation. The assumption is that there is a relationship in people between strong identities—either with one's heritage or the level at which one is acculturated into the American culture—and their health beliefs and practices. Support-group needs and networks may also be related to the degree one is identified with the traditional heritage. The concept of heritage consistency is a new one in traditional health-care provider circles. The following discussion focuses on both acculturation and heritage consistency.

Acculturation

Acculturation refers to cultural or behavioral assimilation and may be defined as the changes of one's cultural patterns to those of the host society. In the United States, people assume that the usual course of acculturation takes three generations: hence, the adult grandchild of the immigrant is fully "Americanized." Acculturation, may also be referred to as assimilation. It can be described as a collection of subprocesses: a process of inclusion through which a person gradually ceases to conform to any standard of life that differs from the dominant-group standards and, at the same time, a process through which someone learns to conform to all the dominant-group standards. The process of assimilation is considered complete when the foreigner is fully merged into the dominant cultural group.[11]

There are four forms of assimilation: cultural, marital, primary structural, and secondary structural. One example of cultural assimilation is the ability to speak excellent American-English. It is interesting to note that there are over 13 million households where a language other than English is spoken.[12] Marital assimilation occurs when members of one group intermarry with members of another group. The third and fourth forms of assimilation, those of structural assimilation, determine the extent to which there is social mingling and friendships between groups. In primary structural assimilation the relationships between people are warm, personal interactions between group members in the home, the church, and in social groups. In secondary structural assimilation there is nondiscriminatory sharing, often of a cold impersonal nature, between different groups in settings such as schools and workplaces.[13]

The concept of assimilation, or acculturation, is complex and sensitive. There are expectations within the dominant society that all persons we encounter are in the process of assimilation and that the world view that we share as health-care practitioners is commonly shared by our clients. Because we live in a pluralistic society, however, there are multiple variations of health beliefs and practices.

There are ongoing debates between those who believe that America is a melting pot and that all groups of immigrants must be acculturated to an "American norm," and those who dispute theories of acculturation and believe that the various groups are maintaining their own identities within the American whole. The concept of "heritage consistency" is one way of exploring whether people are maintaining their traditional heritage and of determining the depth of a person's traditional cultural heritage.

Heritage Consistency

Heritage consistency is a concept developed by Estes and Zitzow in 1980 to describe "the degree to which one's lifestyle reflects his/her respective tribal culture."[14] The theory has been expanded in an attempt to study to what degree a person's life-style reflects the traditional culture, whether European, Asian, African, or Hispanic.[15] The values indicating heritage consistency exist on a continuum and a person can possess value characteristics of both a consistent heritage (traditional) and an inconsistent heritage (acculturated). The concept of heritage consistency includes a determination of one's cultural, ethnic, and religious background (Fig. 5–1).

Culture. Fejos describes culture as "the sum total of socially inherited characteristics of a human group that comprises everything which one generation can tell, convey, or hand down to the next; in other words, the non-physically inherited traits we possess."[16] Another way of understanding the concept of culture is to picture it as the "luggage" that each of us carries around for our lifetime. It is the sum of beliefs, practices, habits, likes, dislikes, norms, customs, rituals, and so forth that we have learned from our families during the years of socialization. In turn, we transmit cultural "luggage" to our own chil-

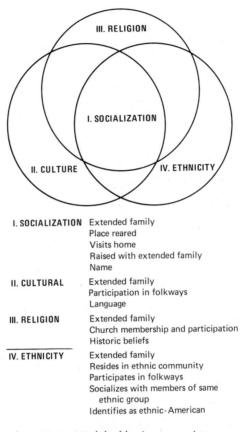

I. SOCIALIZATION	Extended family
	Place reared
	Visits home
	Raised with extended family
	Name
II. CULTURAL	Extended family
	Participation in folkways
	Language
III. RELIGION	Extended family
	Church membership and participation
	Historic beliefs
IV. ETHNICITY	Extended family
	Resides in ethnic community
	Participates in folkways
	Socializes with members of same
	ethnic group
	Identifies as ethnic-American

Figure 5-1. Model of heritage consistency.

dren. The society in which we live—and other forces, political, economic, and social—tend to alter the way in which some aspects of a particular culture are transmitted and maintained. Many of the essential components of a given culture do pass, however, from one generation to the next unaltered. Consequently, much of what we believe, think, and do, both consciously and unconsciously, is determined by our cultural background. In this way, culture and ethnicity are handed down from one generation to another.

Ethnicity. Cultural background is a fundamental component of one's ethnic background. At this point, a definition of terms is called for so that we can proceed from the same point of reference:

Ethnic: adj. 1. of or pertaining to a social group within a cultural and social system that claims or is accorded special status on the basis of complex, often variable traits including religious, linguistic, ancestral, or physical characteristics. 2. Broadly, characteristic of a religious, racial, national, or cultural group. 3. Pertaining to a people not Christian or Jewish; heathen; pagan: "These Are Ancient Ethnic Revels of a Faith Long Since Forsaken." (Longfellow)[17]

The term *ethnic* has for some time aroused strongly negative feelings and is often rejected by the general population. One can speculate that reasons for the upsurge in the use of the term are the recent interest of people in discovering their personal backgrounds, as well as appeals of politicians made when they overtly court "the ethnics." Paradoxically, in a nation as large and comprised of as many different peoples as is the United States—with the American Indians being the only true native population—we find ourselves still reluctant to speak of ethnicity and ethnic differences. This stance stems from the fact that most foreign groups that came to this land often shed the ways of the "old country" and quickly attempted to assimilate themselves into the mainstream, or the so-called melting pot.[18] We also need to clarify other terms:

Ethnicity: n. 1. The condition of belonging to a particular ethnic group. 2. Ethnic pride.

Ethnocentrism: n. 1. Belief in the superiority of one's own ethnic group. 2. Overriding concern with race.

Xenophobe: n. A person unduly fearful or contemptuous of strangers or foreigners, especially as reflected in his political or cultural views.

Xenophobia: A morbid fear of strangers.[19]

The behavioral manifestations of these phenomena occur in response to people's needs, especially when they are foreign born and must find a way to function (1) before they are assimilated into the mainstream and (2) in order to accept themselves. These people cluster together against the majority, who in turn may be discriminating against them.

Indeed, the phenomenon of ethnicity is "complex, ambivalent, paradoxical, and elusive."[20] Ethnicity is indicative of the following characteristics a group may share in some combination:

1. Common geographic origin
2. Migratory status
3. Race
4. Language and dialect
5. Religious faith or faiths
6. Ties that transcend kinship, neighborhood, and community boundaries
7. Shared traditions, values, and symbols
8. Literature, folklore, and music
9. Food preferences

10. Settlement and employment patterns
11. Special interest with regard to politics in the homeland and in the United States
12. Institutions that specifically serve and maintain the group
13. An internal sense of distinctiveness
14. An external perception of distinctiveness.[21]

There are at least 106 ethnic groups and more than 170 Native-American groups in the United States that meet many of these criteria.[22] People from every country in the world have immigrated to this country and now reside here. Some nations, such as Germany, England, Wales, and Ireland are heavily represented; other nations, such as Japan, the Philippines, and Greece have smaller numbers of people living here. According to Chrisman and Kleinman, ethnic groups within this country often believe in and practice their original health-care system and continue their ancestral or traditional practices. People continue to immigrate to the United States, and the present influx comes from Viet Nam, Laos, Cambodia, Cuba, Haiti, Mexico, and South and Central American countries.

Table 5–1 shows the national origins of the American people.

Religion. The third major component of heritage consistency is religion. Religion, "the belief in a divine or superhuman power or powers to be obeyed and worshipped as the creator(s) and ruler(s) of the universe; and a system of beliefs, practices, and ethical values," is a major reason for the development of ethnicity.[23] The practice of religion is revealed in numerous cults, sects, denominations, and churches. Ethnicity and religion are clearly related and one's religion is quite often

TABLE 5–1. NATIONAL ORIGINS OF THE AMERICAN POPULATION

Country of Origin	Percentage	Country of Origin	Percentage
Germany	22.4	Czechoslovakia	1.5
England and Wales	14.7	Austria	1.3
Ireland	10.2	Denmark	1.1
Africa	8.8	Finland	1.1
Italy	6.1	Hungary	1.1
Scotland	3.9	Spain	0.8
Poland	3.0	Puerto Rico	0.8
Canada	2.4	Switzerland	0.6
Netherlands	2.4	West Indies	0.6
France	2.3	Japan	0.4
Russia	2.0	Philippines	0.4
Mexico	2.0	China	0.4
Norway	1.9	Greece	0.3
Sweden	1.8	All others	6.0
		Total	100.3%

Source: 1977 NORC General Social Survey. From Stephen Thernstrom, ed., Harvard Encyclopedia of American Ethnic Groups *(Cambridge: Harvard University Press, 1980).*

the determinent of the ethnic group. Religion gives the person a frame of reference and a perspective with which to organize information. Religious teachings—vis-à-vis health—help to present a meaningful philosophy and system of practices within a system of social controls having specific values, norms, and ethics. These are related to health in that adherence to a religious code is conducive to spiritual harmony and health. Illness may well be seen as the punishment for the violation of religious codes and morals.

The United States census has resisted asking questions about religion. However, data of religious affiliations are available from the 1976 Survey Research Center American National Election Study. Table 5–2 lists religious affiliations in the United States.

Examples of Heritage Consistency

The factors that constitute heritage consistency are listed in Table 5–3. The following are examples of each factor:

1. The person's childhood development occurred in the person's country of origin or in an immigrant neighborhood in the United States of like ethnic group. For example, the person was raised in a specific ethnic neighborhood, such as an Italian, black, Hispanic, or Jewish one, in a given part of a city and was only exposed to the culture, language, foods, and customs of that particular group.

TABLE 5–2. RELIGIOUS AFFILIATIONS IN THE UNITED STATES

Group	Percentage	Group	Percentage
Protestant		Nontraditional Christian	
Methodist	10.95	Latter-Day Saints	1.53
Baptist	9.38	All other[b]	1.40
Southern Baptist	8.51		
Lutheran	8.27	Catholic[c]	24.80
Presbyterian	4.36		
Episcopalian	2.34	Jewish	2.37
Pentacostal	2.16	Other religions[d]	1.26
Church of Christ	1.88		
Primitive Baptist	1.74	Agnostic, atheistic, or no	
Congregational	1.53	religious preference	6.38
Church of God	0.73		
All other[a]	10.39	Total	99.98

Notes:
[a]All other Protestant denominations and sects, each representing less that 1 percent of the total.
[b]Includes Christian Scientists, Unitarians, Jehovah's Witnesses, Quakers, and Universalists.
[c]Includes Roman Catholics and Greek Rite Catholics.
[d]Includes Eastern Orthodox, Muslims, Buddhists, Hindus, Bahai, and others.
Source: 1976 Survey Research Center American National Election Study. From Stephen Thernstrom, ed.: Harvard Encyclopedia of American Ethnic Groups (Cambridge: Harvard University Press, 1980).

TABLE 5-3. FACTORS INDICATING HERITAGE CONSISTENCY

1. Childhood development occurred in the person's country of origin or in an immigrant neighborhood in the United States of like ethnic group.
2. Extended family members encouraged participation in traditional religious or cultural activities.
3. Individual engages in frequent visits to country of origin or to the "old neighborhood" in the United States.
4. Family homes are within the ethnic community.
5. Individual participates in ethnic cultural events such as religious festivals or national holidays, sometimes with singing, dancing, and costumes.
6. Individual was raised in an extended family setting.
7. Individual maintains regular contact with the extended family.
8. Individual's name has not been "Americanized."
9. Individual was educated in a parochial (nonpublic) school with a religious or ethnic philosophy similar to the family's background.
10. Individual engages primarily in social activities with others of the same ethnic background.
11. Individual has knowledge of the culture and language of origin.
12. Individual possesses elements of personal pride about his heritage.

2. Extended family members encouraged participation in traditional religious and cultural activities. For example, the parents sent the person to religious school and most social activities were church related.

3. The individual engages in frequent visits to the country of origin or returns to the "old neighborhood" in the United States. The desire to return to the "old country" or to the old neighborhood is generally prevalent in many people; however, there are many who for various reasons cannot return. The people who have come here to escape religious persecution or whose families were slaughtered during either World War or the holocaust may not want to return to European homelands. Other reasons why people may not return to their native country include political conditions in the original homeland or no existing relatives or friends in that land.

4. Their family's home is within the ethnic community of which they are members. For example, as an adult the person has elected to live with family in an ethnic neighborhood.

5. The individual participates in ethnic cultural events such as religious festivals or national holidays, sometimes with singing, dancing, and costumes.

6. The individual was raised in an extended family setting. For example, when the person was growing up, there may have been grandparents living in the same household, or aunts and uncles living in the same house or close by. The person's social frame of reference was the family.

7. The individual maintains regular contact with the extended family. For example, the person maintains close ties with members of the same generation, the surviving members of the older generation, and members of the younger generation.

8. The individual's name has not been "Americanized." For example, the person has restored the family name to its European original if it had been changed by immigration authorities at the time the family immigrated or if the family changed the name at a later time in an attempt to more fully assimilate.

9. The individual was educated in a parochial (nonpublic) school with a religious or ethnic philosophy similar to the family's background. The person's education plays an enormous role in socialization and the major purpose of education is to socialize a given person into the dominate culture. It is in the schools where children learn English and the customs and norms of American life. In the parochial schools, they not only learn English, but are also socialized in the culture and norms of the particular religious or ethnic group that is sponsoring the school.

10. The individual engages primarily in social activities with others of the same religious or ethnic background. For example, the major portion of the person's personal time is spent with primary structural groups.

11. The individual has knowledge of the culture and language of origin. The person has been socialized in the traditional ways of the family and expresses this as a central theme of life.

12. The individual expresses pride in his heritage.[24] For example, the person may identify as ethnic-American and be supportive of ethnic activities to a great extent.

It is not possible to isolate the aspects of culture, religion, and ethnicity that shape a person's world view. Each is part of the other and all three are united within the person. When one writes of religion, one cannot eliminate culture or ethnicity but descriptions and comparisons can be made. Referring to Figure 5–2 to assess heritage consistency can help determine ethnic group differences in health beliefs and practices. It can go a long way to help enhance the health-care providers' understanding of the needs of patients and their families and the support systems that people may have or need.

CULTURE AND HEALTH-CARE PROVIDERS

The United States was once considered a melting pot of diverse ethnic and cultural groups. One aspect of the American dream was that all of these diverse groups would blend into one common whole. This did not really occur, and today there are many groups that cling to and identify with their ethnic heritage. In fact, among the third-, fourth-, or in some cases subsequent-generation Americans, there are those who desire to know where they come from (who they are). The phenomenon of seeking one's heritage is widespread in today's society:[25] a fine example of this is Alex Haley's book and movie, which document his search for his family's *Roots*.

Because the melting pot—which carried with it the dream of assimilation into a common culture—has proved to be a myth and faded, it is now time to identify and both accept and appreciate the differences among people. It is suggested that this be done not to change people so that they are all alike, but to better understand both one's own ethnic culture and the ethnic culture of other people living in this society. Within the health professions, this is mandatory: because health-care providers learn from their culture the why and the how of being healthy or ill, it behooves them to treat each *client* with deference to *his* own cultural background.

Health-care professionals who have been socialized into a given culture and subsequently resocialized into what I define as the *provider culture* come into intimate contact with people who may choose to maintain their traditional perceptions and beliefs regarding health and illness. Here lies the paradox: one culture may believe, for example, that people should starve a cold and feed a fever; another may believe the opposite. Thus there are "elopements" from clinics, broken appointments, and failures to follow prescribed regimens.

The Health-Care Provider's Culture

The providers of health care—physicians, nurses, social workers, dietitians, laboratory and departmental professionals—are socialized into the "culture" of their profession. Professional socialization teaches the student a set of beliefs, practices, habits, likes, dislikes, norms, and rituals (components already described as factors that comprise a given culture). This newly learned information regarding health and illness differs in varying degrees from that of the individual's background. As students become more and more knowledgeable, they usually move farther and farther from their past belief systems and, indeed, farther from the population at large in terms of its understanding and beliefs regarding health and illness. How often people have stated: "I have no idea what the nurses and doctor are saying!" "They speak a foreign language!" "What they are doing is so strange to me."

In light of these ideas, health-care providers can be viewed as a foreign culture or ethnic group. They have a social and cultural system; they experience "ethnicity" in the way they perceive themselves in relation to the health-care consumer. Even if they deny the reality of the situation, health-care providers must understand that they are ethnocentric. Not only are they ethnocentric, but many of them are also xenophobic. In order to appreciate this critical issue, one must

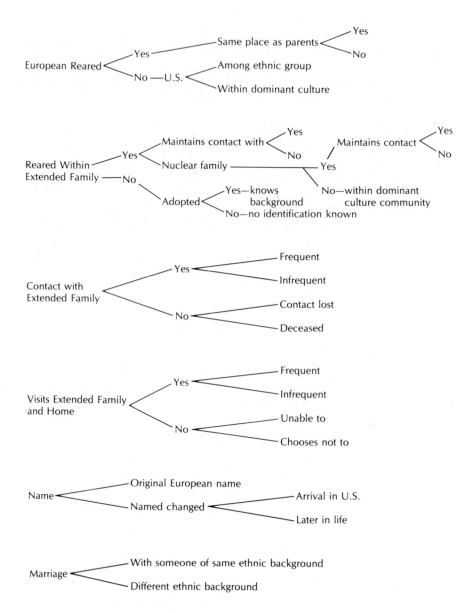

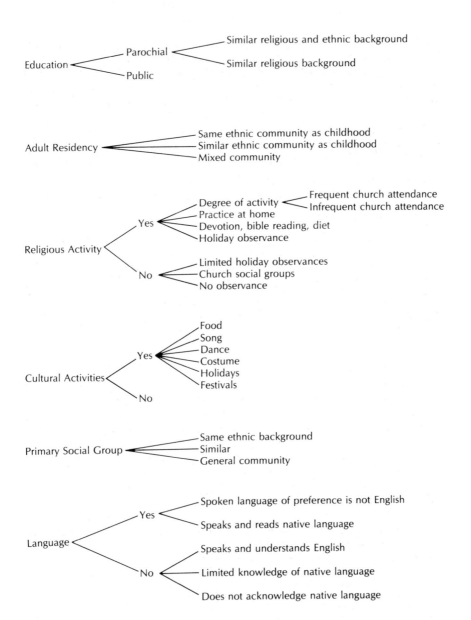

Figure 5-2. Matrix of heritage consistency.

consider the following. A principal reason for the difficulty experienced between the health-care provider and the consumer is that health-care providers, with few exceptions, adhere rigidly to the Western system of health-care delivery. With few exceptions they do not publicly sanction any methods of prevention or healing other than "scientifically proved" ones. They ordinarily fail to recognize or use any sources of medication other than those that have been "proved" to be effective by scientific means. The only types of healers that are sanctioned are those that have been educated and certified according to the requirements of this culture.

What happens, then, when people of one belief system encounter people who have other beliefs regarding health and illness (either in prevention or in treatment)? Is the provider able to meet the needs as perceived and defined by the patient? More often than not, there is a wall of misunderstanding between the two. At this point, there occurs what is commonly referred to as a "breakdown in communications"— and we know who ends up on the short end of the situation: the *consumer.*

Providers think that they comprehend all facets of health and illness. Granting that, by training and education, they are at a significant distance from the consumer-patient, I nevertheless suggest and *insist* that it is entirely appropriate for them to explore alternative ideas regarding health and illness and to adjust their approach to coincide with the needs of the specific client. In the past, health-care providers have tried to force Western medicine on one and all, come what may. It is time that health care coincided with the needs of the client instead of inducing additional conflict.

The following list outlines the more obvious aspects of the health-care provider's culture. In connection with later chapters, it can be referred to as a framework of comparison with various other ethnic and cultural beliefs and practices.

1. Beliefs
   a. Standardized definitions of health and illness
   b. The omnipotence of technology
2. Practices
   a. The maintenance of health and the prevention of disease through such mechanisms as the avoidance of stress and the use of immunizations
   b. Annual physical examinations and diagnostic procedures such as Pap smears
3. Habits
   a. Charting
   b. The constant use of jargon
   c. Use of a systematic approach and problem-solving methodology

4. Likes
   a. Promptness
   b. Neatness and organization
   c. Compliance
5. Dislikes
   a. Tardiness
   b. Disorderliness and disorganization
6. Customs
   a. Professional deference and adherence to the "pecking order" found in autocratic and bureaucratic systems
   b. "Hand-washing"
   c. Employment of certain procedures attending birth and death
7. Rituals
   a. The physical examination
   b. The surgical procedure
   c. Limiting visitors and visiting hours

Culture and Epidemiology

Another area in which culture plays a broad role is in the interpretation of the causation of illness, or *epidemiology*. The science is inherent in the health-care educational process. In the study of epidemiology, the relationships among the host, agent, and environment are explored. The modern approach attributes the cause of disease (the agent) to bacteria, viruses, chemical carcinogens, pollutants, and so forth. The disorders have names such as pneumonia, meningitis, influenza, polycystic kidney disease. Unless the student delves further into study of the field, he may well never become familiar with more traditional theories of epidemiology. For example, the concepts of "soul loss," "spirit possession," and "spells" are rarely, if ever, described and discussed during the educational process of health-care providers.[26] Yet these ideas, too, contribute to people's perceptions of the cause of a given disease.

I have found many students who were familiar with concepts such as "evil eye," and in some instances they took precautions to protect themselves. As discussed in Chapter 3, they often were forced to take these precautions because of the beliefs of their mothers or grandmothers. After much thought, the acquisition of new facts, and further learning, many of the students chose to shed such beliefs and not *consciously* practice what they had been taught by their families. However, others admitted to still holding such beliefs—but were constantly experiencing conflict. This group of students can be viewed as a microcosm of the larger society. It is known that there are many people who cling to familiar belief systems, a fact that lends comfort to them. (In what other way can some of the hardships of life be explained in a more satisfactory or acceptable manner?)

Another facet of epidemiology that one does not ordinarily encounter in academia is that of the causative agent's being another person and not a microbe. The idea of another person making someone ill
by the use of witchcraft or voodoo (or some other form of magic) is an
unusual subject within the constraints of a traditional curriculum. If
the student is to study the cultural perceptions of health and illness,
however, some knowledge of a belief in magic is important. The environment that fosters the use of these agents is one in which hate,
envy, or jealousy may exist. The way of preventing illness thus caused
involves not provoking the wrath of one's friends, neighbors, and enemies. A victim of disease may believe that his success provoked the
envy of his friends, that it called the attention of a "witch" to him, or
that someone was jealous of a new possession and put a "hex" on him.
In the minds of people who still believe and practice traditional health
beliefs, these contributing factors are as real as the bacteria and viruses of modern epidemiology are to health-care providers. Regardless
of the provider's belief system, the provider needs to keep an open
mind in order to provide *useful* care to consumers who retain traditional beliefs.

Culture and Response to Pain

- "Mr. Smith in room 222 is the ideal patient. He never has a
  single complaint of pain."
- "Mrs. Cohen in room 223 is a real complainer. She is constantly
  asking for pain medication and putting on her light."
- "Mrs. O'Mally in room 224 is an ideal patient. She never complains about pain. For that matter, she never complains."
- "Mr. Chen in room 225 says nothing, I often wonder what he
  is feeling."
- "Mrs. Petrini in room 226 dramatically cries every time I look
  at her and complains of pain at every opportunity."

These statements (however stereotypic) are descriptions of behaviors observed concerning patients' responses to the subjective feeling of pain. Social scientists, health-care researchers, and other professionals maintain that the phenomenon is culture bound: how pain
and discomfort—or, for that matter, most emotions—are presented
varies among cultures. A person raised in one cultural background
may be allowed the free and open expression of his feelings, whereas
a person from another culture may have been taught that (for a multitude of reasons) he must never reveal his true feelings.

Let us say that the above statements were all made by the same
nurse. Let us go one step further and say that each patient had the
same operation on the same day. It would not be unusual, within the
limits of general expectations, to see the different patients from differing cultures and ethnic groups exhibit the behaviors described. The

fact that culture plays a role in behavior during illness was aptly demonstrated and strongly documented by Mark Zborowski in his study on pain.[27] Briefly, his findings were that Jewish and Italian patients generally responded to pain in an emotional fashion, and they tended to exaggerate the response; "old American Yankees" tended to be more stoic; and the Irish tended to ignore pain.[28] Presentation of this type of data can often lead to a major problem: *stereotyping*. I want strongly to emphasize that such descriptions are *general*; the results of one study do not indicate a universal truth. Even within my own clinical experiences, however, I have observed events such as those described by the quotations. It is preferable to include and discuss such material rather than to ignore it—particularly inasmuch as there are numerous studies in anthropology, sociology, psychology, and social psychology to support these data, such as findings reported by David Mechanic[29] in 1963, by Edward Suchman in 1964[30] and 1965,[31] and Irving Zola in 1966.[32]

REFERENCES

1. M. Winerip, "Youth's Death: Sports System 'Broke Down,'" *New York Times,* 22 November 1983, pp. B1, B4.
2. Joseph Giordano and Grace P. Giordano, *The Ethno-Cultural Factor in Mental Health* (New York: Institute of Pluralism and Group Identity, 1977) p. 1.
3. Stephen Thernstrom, ed., *Harvard Encyclopedia of American Ethnic Groups* (Cambridge: Harvard University Press, 1980), p. vii.
4. Dale McLemore, *Racial and Ethnic Relations in America* (Boston: Allyn and Bacon, 1980), p. 1.
5. Andrew Greeley, *Why Can't They Be Like Us? America's White Ethnic Groups* (New York: E. P. Dutton, 1975).
6. Novak, Michael, "How American Are You if your Grandparents Came from Serbia in 1888?" in *The Rediscovery of Ethnicity: Its Implications for Culture and Politics in America,* ed. S. Te Selle (New York: Harper and Row, 1973).
7. Greeley, *Why Can't They Be Like Us?*
8. G. L. Jordan and T. G. Jordan, *Ernst and Li Sette Jordan: German Pioneers in Texas* (Austin: Von Blockman-Jones Co., 1971).
9. Leonel J. Castillo, "Keynote Address—'Communicating with Mexican-Americans—por su buena salud,'" (Houston: Baylor College of Medicine, 1979).
10. Jules Henry, *Culture Against Man* (New York: Random House, 1963), p. 323; Eric Bermann, *Scapegoat—The Impact of Death-fear on an American Family* (Ann Arbor: University of Michigan Press, 1973), pp. 2-4.
11. McLemore, *Racial and Ethnic Relations,* p. 4.
12. U.S., Department of Commerce, Bureau of the Census, *1980 Census of Population—Detailed Population Characteristics* (Washington, D.C.: Government Printing Office, 1981).
13. McLenore, *Racial and Ethnic Relations,* p. 39.

14. George Estes and Daryl Zitzow, "Heritage Consistency as a Considera-
    tion in Counseling Native Americans" (Paper read at the National Indian
    Education Association Convention, Dallas, Texas, November 1980).
15. Rachel E. Spector, "A Description of the Impact of Medicare on Health-
    Illness Beliefs and Practices of White Ethnic Senior Citizens in Central
    Texas." Ph.D. diss., University of Texas at Austin School of Nursing,
    1983; Ann Arbor, Mich.: University Microfilms International, 1983.
16. Paul Fejos, "Man, Magic, and Medicine," in *Medicine and Anthropology*,
    ed. Iago Goldston (New York: International University Press, 1959),
    p. 43.
17. *American Heritage Dictionary of the English Language*, s.v. "ethnic."
18. Novak, "How American Are You?"
19. *American Heritage Dictionary*, s.v. "ethnicity," "ethnocentrism," "xen-
    ophobe."
20. Clarince Senior, *The Puerto Ricans: Strangers Then Neighbors*. (Chicago:
    Quandrangle Books, 1965), p. 21.
21. Thernstrom, *American Ethnic Groups*, p. vii.
22. Ibid.
23. Harold J. Abramcon, "Religion," in *Harvard Encyclopedia of American
    Ethnic Groups*, ed. Stephen Thernstrom (Cambridge: Harvard University
    Press, 1980), pp. 869–75.
24. Spector, *Impact of Medicare*, pp. 62–67.
25. Sallie Te Selle, ed., *Rediscovery of Ethnicity: Its Implications for Culture
    and Politics in America* (New York: Harper and Row, 1973).
26. Irving Kenneth Zola, "The Concept of Trouble and Sources of Medical
    Assistance: To Whom One Can Turn, with What and Why," *Social Sci-
    ence and Medicine* 6 (1972): 673–79.
27. Mark Zborowski, "Cultural Components in Responses to Pain," *Journal
    of Social Issues* 8 (1952): 16–30.
28. Mark Zborowski, *People in Pain* (San Francisco: Jossey-Bass, 1969).
29. David Mechanic, "Religion, Religiosity, and Illness Behavior: The Special
    Case of the Jews," *Human Organization* 22 (1963): 202–8.
30. Edward A. Suchman, "Sociomedical Variations Among Ethnic Groups,"
    American Journal of Sociology 70 (1964): 319–31.
31. Edward A. Suchman, "Social Patterns of Illness and Medical Care," *Jour-
    nal of Health and Human Behavior* 6 (1965): 2–16.
32. Irving K. Zola. "Culture and Symptoms: An Analysis of Patients Pre-
    senting Complaints," *American Sociological Review* 31 (October 1966):
    615–630.

BIBLIOGRAPHY

Bermann, Eric. *Scapegoat.* Ann Arbor: University of Michigan Press, 1973.
    This book deals not only with the impact of fear of death on an American
    family but also with the role of culture in facing this event.
Galdston, Iago, ed. *Medicine and Anthropology.* New York: International
    Universities Press, 1959.
    Excellent background reading, this anthology explores the relation of an-
    thropology to medicine in a number of outstanding articles.
Newman, Katharine, D. *Ethnic American Short Stories.* New York: Pocket
    Books, 1975.

Numerous short stories that depict the literary perceptions and "laws" of various American ethnic groups are presented.

Rude, Donald, ed. *Alienation: Minority Groups.* New York: Wiley, 1972.

This book explores the values and goals of people who have sought to reshape American society. It examines the paradox in today's society that awards the expression of individuality but casts out those who by race, sex, politics, or mores are "different." It includes essays, poetry, and photography by those who are victims of oppression.

Ryan, William. *Blaming the Victim.* New York: Vintage Books, 1971.

Ryan demonstrates how the victims of poverty are blamed for their condition rather than the real villain—the inequality of American society.

Te Selle, Sallie, ed. *The Rediscovery of Ethnicity: Its Implications for Culture and Politics in America.* New York: Harper and Row, 1973.

How "American" are we? This book attempts to answer this question with a number of outstanding contributions by writers such as Michael Novak, Arthur V. Shostack, and Rudolph J. Vecoli.

Zborowski, Mark. *People in Pain.* San Francisco: Jossey-Bass, 1969.

Zborowski examines the feeling of pain as a cultural experience for different peoples with unique histories.

FURTHER SUGGESTED READINGS:

BOOKS

Bernardo, Stephanie. *The Ethnic Almanac.* Garden City, N.Y.: Doubleday, 1981.

Elling, Ray H. *Socio-Cultural Influences on Health and Health Care.* New York: Springer Co., 1977.

Finney, Joseph C., ed. *Culture Change, Mental Health and Poverty.* New York: Simon and Schuster, 1969.

Gelfond, D. E., and Kutzik, A., eds. *Ethnicity and Aging: Theory, Research and Policy.* New York: Springer, 1979.

Giordano, Joseph, and Giordano, Grace Pineiro. *The Ethno-Cultural Factor in Mental Health.* New York: Institute of Pluralism and Group Identity, 1977.

Glazer, N., and Moynihan, D., eds. *Ethnicity: Theory and Experience.* Cambridge: Harvard University Press, 1975.

Greeley, Andrew. *Why Can't They Be Like Us? America's White Ethnic Groups.* New York: E. P. Dutton, 1975.

Harney, Robert F., and Troper, Harold. *Immigrants: A Portrait of Urban Experience 1890–1930.* Toronto: Van Nostrand Reinhold, 1975.

Harwood, Alan, ed. *Ethnicity and Medical Care.* Cambridge: Harvard University Press, 1981.

Hecker, M. *Ethnic American, 1970–1977.* Dobbs Ferry, N.Y.: Oceana Publications, 1979.

Henderson, George, and Primeaux, Martha, eds. *Transcultural Health Care.* Menlo Park, Calif.: Addison-Wesley, 1981.

Howe, Irving. *World of Our Fathers.* New York: Harcourt Brace Jovanovich, 1976.

Klein, Judith Weinstein. *Jewish Identity and Self-Esteem: Healing Wounds through Ethnotherapy.* New York: Institute on Pluralism and Group Identity, 1980.

Landy, David, ed. *Culture, Disease and Healing.* New York: Macmillan, 1977.
Leininger, Madeleine. *Nursing and Anthropology: Two Worlds to Blend.* New York: Wiley, 1970.
———. *Transcultural Nursing: Concepts, Theories and Practices.* New York: Wiley, 1978.
McGoldrick, Monica; Pearce, John K.; and Giordano, Joseph. *Ethnicity and Family Therapy.* New York: Guilford Press, 1982.
McLemore, S. Dale. *Racial and Ethnic Relations in America.* Boston: Allyn and Bacon, 1980.
Marsella, A. B., and Pedersens, P. B., eds. *Cross Cultural Counseling and Psychotherapy.* New York: Pergamon, 1981.
Mindel, C. H., and Habenstein, R. W., eds. *Ethnic Families in America.* New York: Elsevier, 1976.
Morley, Peter, and Wallis, Roy, eds. *Culture and Curing.* Pittsburgh: University of Pittsburgh Press, 1978.
Novak, Michael. *The Rise of the Unmeltable Ethnics.* New York: MacMillan, 1972.
Orque, Modesta Soberano; Block, Bobbie; and Monrray, Lidia S. Ahumada. *Ethnic Nursing Care: A Multi-Cultural Approach.* St. Louis: C. V. Mosby, 1983.
Poynter, F. N. L., ed. *Medicine and Culture.* London: Wellcome Institute of the History of Medicine, 1969.
Read, Margaret. *Culture, Health and Disease,* London: Javistock Publications, 1966.
Sowell, T. *Ethnic America.* New York: Basic Books, 1981.
Spector, Rachel E. "A Description of the Impact of Medicare on Health-Illness Beliefs and Practices of White Ethnic Senior Citizens in Central Texas." Ph.D. diss. University of Texas at Austin School of Nursing, 1983; Ann Arbor, Mich.: University Microfilms International, 1983.
Thernstrom, Stephen, ed. *Harvard Encyclopedia of American Ethnic Groups.* Cambridge: Harvard University Press, 1980.
Thomas, Clarke. *They Came to Pittsburgh.* Pittsburgh: *Post-Gazette,* 1983.
Warren, N., ed. *Studies in Cross-Cultural Psychology.* New York: Academic Press, 1980.

ARTICLES

Blaylock, Jerry. "The Psychological and Cultural Influences on the Reaction to Pain." *Nursing Forum* 7 (1968).
Bush, Mary T.; Ullom, Jean A.; and Osborne, Oliver H. "The Meaning of Mental Health: A Report of Two Ethnoscientific Studies." *Nursing Research* 24, no. 2 (March-April 1975): 130–38.
Davitz, Lois J.; Sameshima, Yasuko; and Davitz, Joel. "Suffering as Viewed in Six Different Cultures." *American Journal of Nursing,* August 1976, pp. 1296–97.
Hogan, Rosemarie Mihelich. "Influences of Culture on Sexuality." *Nursing Clinics of North America* 17, no. 3 (September 1982): 365–76.
Kellert, Stephen R. "A Sociocultural Concept of Health and Illness." *Journal of Medicine and Philosophy* 1, no. 3 (March 1976): 222–28.
Leininger, Madeleine. "The Cultural Concept and Its Relevance to Nursing." *Journal of Nursing Education* 6 (April 1967): 27.

MacGregor, F. C. "Uncooperative Patients: Some Cultural Interpretations." *American Journal of Nursing* 67 (January 1967): 88–91.

Muecke, Marjorie, A. "Overcoming the Language Barrier." *Nursing Outlook*, April 1970, pp. 53–54.

LaFarque, Jane P. "Role of Prejudice in Rejection of Health Care." *Nursing Research* no. 1 (January-February 1972): 53–58.

Long, Rosemary. "A Tale of Two Cultures." *Nursing Times*, 4 August 1977, pp. 1215–16.

Parker, Marguerite. "Culture and Preventive Health Care." *JOGN Nursing*, November-December 1978, pp. 40–46.

Ragucci, Antionette T. "The Etnographic Approach and Nursing Research." *Nursing Research* 21, no. 6 (November-December 1972): 485–90.

Sheebin, Seymour. "Nursing Patients from Different Cultures." *Nursing 80*, June 1980, pp. 78–81.

"Symposium on Cultural and Biological Diversity and Health Care." *Nursing Clinics of North America* 12 (March 1977): 1.

Zola, Irving Kenneth. "The Concept of Trouble and Sources of Medical Assistance: To Whom One Can Turn, With What and Why." *Social Science and Medicine* 6 (1972): 673–79.

––––––. "Culture and Symptoms: An Analysis of Patients Presenting Complaints." *American Sociological Review* 31 (October 1966): 615–630.

Answers

1. Germany . . . . . . 6,954,160; Italy . . . . . . 5,269,992; Great Britain . . . . . . 4,851,806 (p. 474)

2. Russian-Americans between 25 and 34 (p. 483)

3. WASPS (p. 482)

4. a. The Aguas Calientes of California (p. 11)
   b. The Sesseton Sioux of South Dakota (p. 12)

5. Navaho—96,743 (p. 13)

6. Antonia Meucci (p. 27)

7. Chang and Eng (1871–1874), two Chinese men (p. 164)

8. a. "rock rising to a point"
   b. "boiling pot"
   c. "gathering place by the river"
   d. "at the bottom of the water fall"
   e. "killer grizzly bear"
   (These are all Indian names.)
   (p. 167)

9. a. Beverly Sills
   b. Ann Bancroft
   c. Connie Stevens
   d. Rocky Graziano

10. 67 different peoples—over 36% of the world's population (p. 244)

11. Mexican jumping beans (p. 50)

From Bernardo, S. The Ethnic Almanac, Garden City, N.Y.: Doubleday, 1981.

CHAPTER 6

Healing

Health-care providers have the opportunity to observe the most incredible phenomenon of life: the recovery from illness. In today's society, the healer is the physician, and the other members of the health team all play a significant role in the prevention, detection, and treatment of disease. Yet human beings have existed, some sources suggest, for 2 million years. How, then, did the species *Homo sapiens* survive before the advent of modern technology? It is quite evident that numerous forms of healing existed long before the methodologies that we apply today.

In the natural course of any illness, the stricken individual can expect to experience the following set of events: he becomes ill; the illness may be acute, with concomitant symptoms or signs such as pain, fever, nausea, bleeding. On the other hand, the illness may be insidious, with a gradual progression and worsening of symptoms, which might encompass slow deterioration of movement or an often soul-deadening intensification of pain.

If the illness is mild, the person relies on self-treatment or, as is often the case, does nothing and gradually the symptoms disappear. If the illness is more severe or is of longer duration, the person experiencing the symptoms may consult expert help from a healer of one type or another, usually from a physician.

The person recovers, or expects to recover. As far back as historians and interested social scientists can trace in the history of humankind, this phenomenon of recovery has occurred. In fact, it made very little difference what mode of treatment was used; recovery was usual. It is this occurrence of natural recovery that has given rise to all forms of "healing" that attempt to explain a phenomenon that is natural. That is, one may choose to rationalize the success of a "healing" method by pointing to the patient's recovery. Over the generations, natural healing has been attributed to all sorts of rituals, including trephining, cupping, magic, leeching, and bleeding. From medicine man to sorcerer,[1] the art of healing has passed through succeeding generations. People knew the ailments of their time and devised treatments for them. In spite of ravaging plagues, natural disasters, and pandemic and epidemic diseases, human beings as a species have survived!

This chapter explores a number of healing methods, both ancient and modern. In addition, a historical overview is included on how such methods evolved, their purpose, and their practice. The relation of these healing practices to current religions is demonstrated by listing the types of beliefs and practices found in a number of religions in the United States. A description of various types of healers and remedies found and used in today's society concludes the chapter.

RELIGION AND HEALING

Religion plays a vital role in one's perception of health and illness. Just as culture and ethnicity are strong determinants in an individual's interpretation of the environment and the events within the environment, so, too, is religion. In fact, it is often difficult to distinguish between those aspects of a person's belief system arising from a religious background and those that stem from an ethnic and cultural heritage. Some people may share a common ethnicity and yet be of different religions; a group of people can share the same religion and yet have a variety of ethnic and cultural backgrounds. It is never safe to assume that all individuals of a given ethnic group practice or believe in the same religion. The point was embarrassingly driven home when I once asked a Chicano woman if she would like me to call the priest for her while her young son was awaiting a critical operation. The woman became angry with me. I could not understand why until I learned that she was a Methodist and not a Catholic. I had made an assumption, and I was wrong. She later told me that all Chicanos are not Catholic. After many years of people making this assumption, she had learned to react with anger.

Religion strongly affects the way people interpret and respond to the signs and symptoms of illness. Today, just as it did in antiquity, religion also plays a role in the rites surrounding both birth and death. So pervasive is religion that the diets of many people are determined by their religious beliefs. Religion and the piety of a person determine not only the role that faith will play in the process of recovery, but in many instances the response to a given treatment and to the healing process. Each of these threads—religion, ethnicity, and culture—weave the fabric of each response of a particular person to treatment and healing.

Ancient Rituals
Many of the rituals that we observe at the time of birth and death have their origins in the practices of ancient human beings. Close your

eyes for a few moments and picture yourself living thousands and thousands of years ago. There is no electricity, no running water, no bathroom, no plumbing. The nights are dark and cold. The only signs of the passage of time are the changing seasons and the apparent movement of the various planets and stars through the heavens. You are prey to all the elements, as well as to animals and the unknown. How do you survive? What sort of rituals and practices assist you in maintaining your equilibrium within this often hostile environment? It is from this milieu that many of today's practices sprang.

Generally speaking, there are three critical moments in the life of almost every human being: birth, marriage, and death.[2] One needs to examine the events and rites that were attendant on birth and death in the past and to demonstrate how many of them are not only relevant to our lives today but are also still practiced.

In the minds of early human beings, the number of evil spirits far exceeded the number of good spirits, and a great deal of energy and time was devoted to thwarting these spirits. They could be defeated by the use of gifts or rituals. Or, when the evil spirits had to be removed from a person's body, redemptive sacrifices were used. Once these evil spirits were expelled, they were prevented from returning by various magical ceremonies and rites. When a ceremony and incantation were found to be effective, they were passed on through the generations. It has been suggested and supported by scholars that, from this primitive beginning, organized religion came into being. Today, many of the early rites have survived in altered forms, and we continue to practice them.[3]

The power of the evil spirits was believed to endure for a certain length of time. The third, seventh, and fortieth days were the crucial days in the early life of the child and new mother; hence it was on these days, or the eighth day, that most of the rituals were observed. It was believed that during this period the newborn and the mother were at the greatest risk from the power of supernatural beings and thus in a taboo state. "The concept underlying taboo is that all things created by or emanating from a supernatural being are his, or are at least in his power."[4] The person was freed from this taboo by certain rituals, depending on the practices of a given community. When the various rites were completed and the forty days were over, both the mother and child were believed to be redeemed from evil. The ceremonies that freed the person had a double character: they were partly magic and partly religious.

I have deliberately chosen to present the early practices of the Semitic peoples because their beliefs and practices evolved into the Judaic, Christian, and Islamic religions of today. Because the newborn baby and mother were considered vulnerable to the threats of evil spirits, many rituals were developed to protect them. For example, in some communities, the mother and child were separated from the rest of the community for a certain length of time, usually forty days. Various

people performed precautionary measures such as rubbing the baby
with different oils or garlic, swaddling the baby, and lighting candles.[5]
In other communities, the baby and mother were closely watched for
a certain length of time, usually seven days. (During this time span,
they were believed to be intensely susceptible to the effects of evil—
hence, close guarding was in order.) Orthodox Jews still refer to the
seventh night of life as the "watch night."[6]

The birth of a male child was considered more significant than
that of a female, and many rites were practiced in observance of this
event. One ritual sacrifice was cutting off a lock of the child's hair,
and then sprinkling his forehead with sheep's blood. This ritual was
performed on the eighth day of life.[7] In other Semitic countries, when
a child was named a sheep was sacrificed and asked to give protection
to the infant. Depending on regional or tribal differences, the mother
might be given parts of the sheep. It was believed that if this sacri-
ficial ritual was not performed on the seventh or eighth day of life the
child would die.[8] The sheep's skin was saved, dried, and placed in the
child's bed for three or four years as protection from evil spirits.

Both the practice of cutting a lock of the child's hair and the sacrifice of an animal served as a ceremony of redemption. The child could
also be redeemed from the taboo state by giving silver—the weight of
which equaled the weight of the hair—to the poor.[9] Although not universally practiced, these rites are still observed, in some form, in some
communities of the Arab world.[10]

Circumcision is closely related to the ceremony of cutting the
child's hair and offering it as a sacrifice. Some authorities hold that
the practice originated as a rite of puberty: a body mutilation performed to attract the opposite sex.[11] (Circumcision was practiced by
many peoples throughout the ancient world; Alex Haley's *Roots* describes it as a part of initiating boys into manhood in Africa.) Other
sources attribute circumcision to the concept of the sanctity of the
male organ and claim that it was derived from the practice of ancestor
worship. The Jews of ancient Israel, as today, practiced circumcision
on the eighth day of life.[12] The Moslems of Palestine circumcise their
sons on the eighth day in the tradition that Mohammed established.
In other Moslem countries, the ritual is performed anywhere from the
tenth day to the seventh year of life.[13] Again, this sacrifice redeemed
the child from being taboo in his early stages of life; once the sacrifice
was made, the child entered the period of worldly existence. The rite
of circumcision was accompanied by festivals of varying durations.
Some cultures and kinship groups feasted for as long as a week.

The ceremony of baptism is also rooted in the past. It, too, sym-
bolically expels the evil spirits, removes the taboo, and is redemptive.
It is practiced mainly among members of the Christian faith, but the
Yezidis and other non-Christian sects also perform the rite. Water was
thought to possess magical powers and was used to cleanse the body
from both physical and spiritual maladies, which included evil pos-

session and other impurities. Usually, the child was baptized on the fortieth day of life. In some communities, however, the child was baptized on the eighth day. The fortieth (or eighth) day was chosen because the ancients believed that—given performance of the particular ritual—this day marked the end of the evil spirits' influence.[14]

There were also rituals that involved the new mother. For example, not only was she (along with her infant) removed from her household and community for forty days, but in many communities she had to practice ritual bathing before she could return to her husband, family, and community. Again, these practices were not universal and they varied in scope and intensity from people to people.

As to death, it was believed that the work of evil spirits and the duration of their evil—whether it was seven or forty days—surrounded the person, family, and community at the time. Rites evolved to protect both the dying and dead person and his remaining family from the evil spirits. The dying person was cared for in specific ways, such as ritual washing, and his grave was prepared in set ways—such as storing food and water for his journey. Further rituals were performed to protect the deceased's survivors from the harm believed to be rendered by the deceased's ghost: it was believed that this ghost could return from the grave and, if not carefully appeased, gravely harm his surviving relatives.[15]

Extensions of Rituals to Today's Practices

Early human beings, in their quest for survival, strove to appease and prevent the evil spirits from interfering with their lives. Their beliefs seem simple and naive, yet the rituals that began in those years have evolved into those that exist today. Attacks of the evil spirits were warded off with the use of amulets, charms, and the like. People recited prayers and incantations.[16] Because survival was predicated on people's ability to appease evil spirits, the prescribed rituals were performed with great care and respect. Undoubtedly, this accounts in part for the longevity of many of these practices through the ages. For example, circumcision and baptism still exist, even when the belief that they are being performed to release the child from a state of being taboo may not continue to be held. It is interesting also that adherence to a certain "timetable" is maintained. For example, as stated, the Jewish religion mandates that the ritual of circumcision be performed on the eighth day of life.

The practice, too, of closely guarding the new mother and baby through the initial hours after birth is certainly not foreign to us. The mother is closely watched for hemorrhage and signs of infection; the infant initially is watched for signs of choking or respiratory distress. This form of observation is very intense. Could factors such as these have been what our ancestors watched for? If early human beings believed that evil spirits caused the frequent complications that surrounded the birth of a baby, then it stands to reason that they would seek to control or prevent these complications by adhering to astute observation, isolation, and rituals of redemption.

TRADITIONAL ETIOLOGY

The prevention and treatment of illness rests in the ability to understand the cause of a given illness or set of symptoms. Among those who hold traditional health and illness beliefs, there are beliefs regarding the causation of illness that are vastly different from the modern model of etiology. Here illness is most often attributed to the "evil eye." The evil eye is primarily a belief that someone can project harm by gazing or staring at another's property or person.[17]

The belief in the evil eye is probably the oldest and most widespread of all superstitions and it is found to exist in many parts of the world such as Southern Europe, the Middle East, and North Africa.[18]

It is thought by some to be merely a superstition but what is seen by one person as superstition may well be seen by another as religion. Various evil-eye beliefs were carried to this country by immigrant populations. These beliefs have persisted and may be quite strong among newer immigrants and heritage-consistent peoples.[19]

The common beliefs in the evil eye assert that:

1. The power emanates from the eye (or mouth) and strikes the victim.
2. The injury, be it illness or other misfortune, is sudden.
3. The person that casts the evil eye may not be aware of having this power.
4. The afflicted person may or may not know the source of the evil eye.
5. The injury caused by the evil eye may be prevented or cured with rituals or symbols.
6. This belief helps to explain sickness and misfortune.[20]

The nature of the evil eye is defined differently by different populations. The variables include how it is cast, who can cast it, who receives it, and the degree of power that it has. In the Philippines the evil is cast through the eye or mouth; in the Mediterranean it is the avenging power of God; in Italy it is a malevolent force like a plague and is prevented by wearing amulets.

In various parts of the world, various people cast it: in Mexico— strangers, Iran—kinfolk, and in Greece—witches. Its power varies and in some places such as the Mediterranean, it is seen as the "devil." In the Near East it is seen as a diety and among Slovak-Americans as a chronic but low-grade phenomenon.[21]

Among Germans the evil eye is known as *Abberglobin* or *Aberglaubisch* and causes preventable problems such as evil, harm, and illness. Among the Polish, the evil eye is known as *Szatan.* There are "evil spirits" that are equated with the devil and can be prevented by praying to a patron saint or guardian angel. *Szatan* is also prevented by prayer and repentence and the wearing of medals and scapulars. These serve as reminders of the "Blessed Mother and the Patrons in Heaven" and protect the wearer from harm. The evil eye is known in Yiddish as *Kayn Aynhoreh*. The expression *Kineahora* is recited by Jews after a compliment or when a statement of luck is made to prevent the casting of an evil spell on another's health. Often the speaker spits three times after uttering the word.[22]

Agents of disease may also be "soul loss," "spirit possession," "spells," and "hexes." Here prevention becomes a ritual of protecting oneself and one's children from these agents; treatment requires the removal of these agents from the afflicted person.[23]

Illness can also be attributed to people who have the ability to make others ill, for example, witches and practitioners of voodoo.[24] The ailing person attempts to avoid these people to prevent illness and to identify them as part of the treatment. Other "agents" to be avoided are "envy," "hate," and "jealousy." A person may practice prevention by avoiding situations that could provoke the envy, hate, or jealousy of a friend, acquaintance, or neighbor. The evil-eye belief contributes to this avoidance.

Another source of evil can be of human origin, and occurs when a person is temporarily controlled by souls not their own. In the Jewish culture, this control is known as *dybbuk*. The word comes from the Hebrew word meaning "cleaving" or "holding fast." A dybbuk is portrayed as a "wandering, disembodied soul which enters another person's body and holds fast."[25]

TRADITIONAL METHODS OF PREVENTION

Among people who believe in traditional ways, illness is often attributed to the evil eye, *envidia,* and "witches."[26] In these instances, illness may be prevented by external controls such as the avoidance of people who can bring it about by the "evil eye"; the avoidance of *envidia,* that is, by not provoking the envy of others; and the avoidance of witches or others who can cast spells and other forms of evil.

Traditional practices used in the prevention of illness consist of:

1. The use of protective objects—worn, carried, or hung in the home.
2. The use of substances that are ingested in certain ways and amounts or eliminated and substances worn or hung in the home.
3. The practices of religion, such as the burning of candles, the rituals of redemption, and prayer.

Protective Objects that Prevent Illness
Amulets are objects, such as charms, worn on a string or chain around the neck, wrist, or waist to protect the wearer from the evil eye or the evil spirits that could be transmitted from one person to another, or could have supernatural origins. For example, Figure 6-1 shows (1) *Malocchio,* worn by people of Italian origin to prevent the evil eye. The *Mano Milagroso* (2) is worn by many people of Mexican origin for luck and the prevention of evil. A *Mano Negro* (3) is placed on babies of Puerto Rican descent to prevent the evil eye. The *Mano Negro* is placed on the baby's wrist on a chain or pinned to the diaper or shirt and is worn throughout the early years of life. Both the Hand of God, (4), Israeli, and the Thunderbird (5), Hopi Indian, are worn for protection and to bring good luck. The *Milagros* (6) are worn by some people of Mexican background to ward off evil.

Bangles (7) are worn by people originating from the West Indies. The silver bracelets are open to "let out evil," yet closed to prevent evil from entering the body. They are worn from infancy, and as the person grows they are replaced with larger bracelets. These bracelets tend to tarnish and leave a black ring on the skin when a person is becoming ill. When this occurs, the person knows it is important to rest, to improve the diet, and to take other needed precautions. Many people believe they are extremely vulnerable to evil, even to death, when these bracelets are removed. Some people wear numerous bangles. When they move an arm, the bracelets tinkle. It is believed that this sound frightens away the evil spirit. Nurses should realize that when these bracelets are removed the person experiences a great deal of anxiety.

In addition to amulets, there are talismans (8). A talisman is believed to possess extraordinary powers and may be worn on a rope around the waist or carried in a pocket or purse. The talisman illustrated in Figure 6-1 is a marionette and it protects the wearer from evil. *It is recommended that people who wear amulets or carry a talisman be allowed to do so in health-care institutions.*

Substances that Prevent Illness
The second practice employs diet to prevent illness and consists of many different observances. Figure 6-2 shows some food substances that can be ingested to prevent illness. People from many ethnic backgrounds eat raw garlic or onions (9) in an effort to prevent illness. Garlic or onions may also be worn on the body or may be hung in the Italian, Greek, or Native-American home. *Chachayotel* (10), a seed, may be tied around the waist by a Mexican person to prevent arthritic pain. Among traditional Chinese people, thousand-year-old eggs (11) are eaten with rice to keep the body healthy and to prevent illness. The Ginsing root (12) is the most famous of Chinese medicines. It has

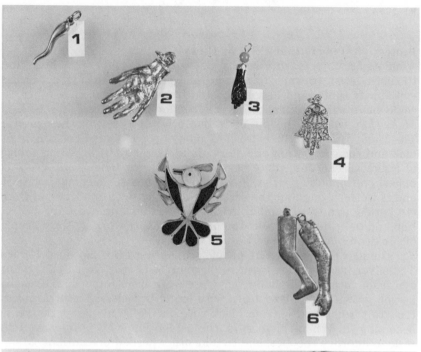

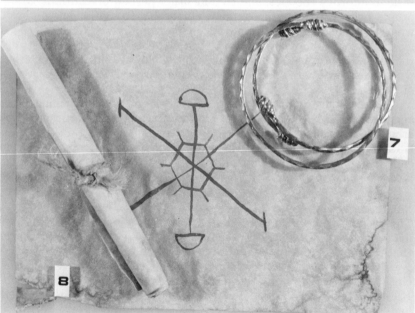

Figure 6-1. Objects that prevent illness. (1) *Malocchio;* (2) *Mano Milagroso;* (3) *Mano Negro;* (4) "Hand of God"; (5) Thunderbird; (6) *Milagros;* (7) Bangles; (8) Talismen. (From collection of the author; photograph by R. Schadt, 1984.)

Figure 6-2. Substances that prevent illness. (9) Garlic and Onion; (10) *Chachay-otel;* (11) Thousand-year-old Egg; (12) Ginsing Root. (From collection of the author; photograph by R. Schadt.)

universal medicinal applications and is used preventively to "build the blood" especially after childbirth. Tradition states that the more the root looks like a man, the more effective it is. Ginsing is also native to the United States and is used in this country as a restorative tonic. Another substance that is ingested is *Nervo Forza* (13), a vitamin tonic from Guatemala (Fig. 6-3) .

Diet regimens are also used to prevent illness. It is believed that the body is kept in balance or harmony by the type of food that one eats.

Traditionalists have strong beliefs about diet and foods, and their relationship to the prevention of illness. The rules of the kosher diet practiced among Jewish people mandate the elimination of pig products and shellfish. Only fish with scales and fins are allowed, and only certain cuts of meat from animals with a cleft hoof and that chew the cud can be consumed. Examples of this kind of animal are cattle and sheep. Many of these dietary practices are also adhered to by Muslims, such as the avoidance of pig products. Jews also believe that milk and meat must never be mixed and eaten at the same meal.[27]

In traditional Chinese homes a balance must be maintained be-

Figure 6-3. A tonic for health. (From collection of the author. Photograph by R. Schadt.)

tween foods that are yin or yang. These are eaten in specified proportions. In Hispanic homes, foods must be balanced as to "hot" and "cold." These foods too, must be eaten in the proper amounts, at certain times, and in certain combinations.

Religious Practices that Prevent Illness
A third traditional approach toward illness prevention centers around religion. Religion strongly affects the way people choose to prevent illness and it plays a strong role in rituals associated with health protection. It dictates social, moral, and dietary practices that are designed to keep a person in balance and healthy. Many people believe that illness and evil are prevented by strict adherence to religious codes, morals, and religious practices. They view illness as a punishment for breaking a religious code. One example of a religious practice is the "Blessing of the Throats" on Saint Blaise Day, performed to prevent sore throats and choking.[28] Another example is the Virgin of Guadalupe, the patron saint of Mexico, who is pictured on medals that

people wear or in pictures hung in the home (Fig. 6-4). She is believed
to protect the person and home from evil and harm and she serves as
a figure of good hope. Other religious practices include baptism as a
ritual of cleansing that prevents evil from harming the person, and
circumcision as a redemptive practice, again to prevent illness and
harm.

Religion can therefore help to provide the believer with an ability
to understand and interpret the events of the environment and life.

BELIEFS THAT CAN AFFECT THERAPY

Ancient Forms of Healing

The crises of birth and death were certainly not the only ones to affect
our ancestors. Illness also caused crises. Just as the people of ancient
times developed ways of dealing with the events that surrounded birth
and death, they evolved elaborate systems of healing. The cause of an
illness, once again, was attributed to the forces of evil, which originated either within or outside of the body. Early forms of healing dealt
with the removal of evil. Once a method of treatment was found ef-

Figure 6-4. The Virgin of Guadalupe. (From collection of the author; photograph by R. Schadt.)

fective, it was passed down through the generations in slightly altered forms.

The people who healed were often those who received the gift of healing from a "divine" source. They frequently received this gift in a vision, and were unable to explain to others how they knew what to do. Other healers learned their skills from their parents. Most of the healers with acquired skills were women, who subsequently passed their knowledge on to their daughters. People who used herbs and other preparations to remove the evil from the sick person's body were known as herbalists. Other healers included bone setters and midwives, and although early humankind did not separate ills of the body from ills of the mind, there were healers who were more adept at solving problems by using early forms of "psychotherapy."

The use of natural products—such as wild herbs and berries accessible to the healers—developed into today's science of pharmacology. Early humankind had a wealth of knowledge with respect to the medicinal properties of the plants, trees, and mushrooms in their environment. They knew how to prepare concoctions from the bark and roots of trees and from berries and wild flowers. As an example, purple foxglove was the "digitalis" of yesteryear: it slowed the heart rate.

If the source of sickness-causing evil was within the body, treatment involved drawing the evil out of the body. This may have been accomplished through the use of purgatives that caused either vomiting or diarrhea, or by blood-letting: "bleeding" the patient or "sucking out" blood. (The barbers of medieval Europe did not originate this practice; bleeding was done in ancient times.) Leeching was another method used to remove corrupt humors from the body, and the reader may recall that in Chapter 3 leeching was mentioned by a student whose grandmother had treated illness by that method.

If the source of the evil was outside the body, there were a number of ways to deal with it. One source of "external" evil was witchcraft. In a community, there were often many people (or a single person) who were "different" from the other people. Quite often, when an unexplainable or untreatable illness occurred, it was these people (or person) who were seen as the causative agents. In such a belief system successful treatment depended on the identification and punishment of the person believed responsible for the disease. (Certainly the practice of scapegoating is in part derived from this belief.) By removing or punishing the guilty person from the community the disease would be cured. In some communities, the healers themselves were seen as witches and the possessors of evil skills. How easy it was for ancient humankind to turn things around and blame the person with the skills to treat the disease for causing the disease!

Various rituals were involved in the treatment of ill people. Often the sick person was isolated from the rest of the family and community. In addition, it was customary to chant special prayers and incantations on the invalid's behalf; sacrifices and dances were often performed in an effort to cure the ills. Often the rituals of the healer involved reciting incantations in a language foreign to the ears of the general population ("speaking in tongues") and using practices that were strange to the observers. Small wonder, then, as superstition abounded, that at times the healers themselves were ostracized by the population.

Another cause of illness was believed to be the *envy* of people within the community. The best method, consequently, of preventing such an illness was to avoid provoking the envy of one's friends and neighbors. The treatment was to do away with whatever was provoking the envy—even though the act might have prevented a person from accomplishing a "mission in life," and the fear of being "responsible" may have been psychologically damaging.

Today we tend to view the healing methods of ancient people as primitive. Yet to fully appreciate their efficacy, we need only make the simple observation that these methods in many forms exist today and have aided the survival of humankind!

Religious Beliefs and Healing
There are far too many religious beliefs and practices related to healing to include in this chapter. A discussion of religious healing beliefs from the Judeo-Christian background, however, is possible.

The Old Testament does not focus on healing to the extent the New Testament does. God is seen to have total power over life and death and is the healer of all man's woes. God is the giver of all good things and of all misfortune, including sickness. Sickness represented a break between God and man. In Exodus 15:26 God is proclaimed the supreme healer ("I will put none of the diseases upon you which I put upon the Egyptians; for I am the Lord, your healer.") and in another passage from Deuteronomy 32:39 it is stated "I kill, and I make alive. I have wounded and I heal." The traditionalist Jew believes that the "healing of illness comes from God through the mediation of His 'messenger,' the doctor." The Jew who is ill combines hope for a cure with faith in God and faith in the doctor.[29]

The healing practices of the Roman Catholic tradition include a variety of beliefs and numerous practices, both of a preventive and healing nature. For example, the saint known for the prevention of sore throats is Saint Blase. He was an Armenian bishop who died in 316 A.D. as a martyr. The blessing of the throats on his feast day (February 3) derives from the tradition that he miraculously saved the life of a boy by removing a fishbone that he swallowed.

The saints concerned with other aspects of illness include the following:[30]

Saint	Problem
St. Anthony of Padua	Barren women
St. Odilia	Blindness
Our Lady of Lourdes	Bodily ills

Saint	Problem
St. Peregrine	Cancer patients
St. Francis de Sales	Deafness
St. Joseph	Dying
St. Vitus	Epilepsy
St. Raymond Nonnatus	Expectant mothers
St. Lucy	Eye diseases
St. Teresa of Avila	Headache sufferers
St. John of God	Heart patients
St. Roch	Invalids
St. Dymphna	Mentally ill
St. Bruno	Possessed

Many more saints could be included. I refer you to other sources for information and I also recommend that you ask patients for information.

In the United States people make pilgrimages to a number of shrines in search of special favors and petitions.

The oldest is the Shrine of Our Lady of La Leche, located in St. Augustine, Florida (Fig. 6-5A). This shrine was founded in 1620 by Spanish settlers as a sign of their love for the Mother of Christ. The shrine is visited by thousands of mothers to ask for the blessings of motherhood, a safe and happy delivery, a healthy baby, and holy children. There are countless letters to be read at the shrine that attest to the powers of Our Lady of La Leche.[31]

Another shrine is that of Our Lady of San Juan (Fig. 6-5B) located in San Juan, Texas. This shrine houses a statue of the Virgin that was brought to Mexico by the Spanish missionaries in 1623. The statue was responsible for causing a miracle and devotion to "La Virgen de San Juan" spread. The statue was brought to Texas in the 1940s after a woman claimed to have seen an image of the Virgin in the countryside around San Juan. The statue presently is housed in a beautiful new church and pilgrims arrive daily to ask for healing and other favors. Again, there are countless letters displayed that attest to the healing powers of this statue.[32]

A third shrine is that of St. Peregrine for Cancer Sufferers (Fig. 6-6) located at the Old Mission San Juan Capistrano in California. This statue is housed in a small grotto in the shrine. St. Peregrine was born in Italy in 1265 and died in 1345. He was believed to have miraculous powers against sickness and could cure cancer. This won for him the title "Official Patron for Cancer Victims." Ten years ago a woman was afflicted with cancer and a lady gave her a prayer to St. Peregrine. The woman prayed for a period of six months and her cancer was arrested. In gratitude for this, the woman had a statue of the saint placed in the mission. Today, the belief in this saint has spread, and, again, countless documents attesting to his healing powers are on display in the mission.[33]

A.

B.

Figure 6–5A. Our Lady of La Leche Shrine and Mission. **B.** Our Lady of San Juan Shrine. (From collection of the author.)

94

Figure 6-6. Saint Peregrine Shrine. (From collection of the author.)

Table 6-1 summarizes the beliefs of people from some religions with respect to health and healing.[34]

Healing and Today's Beliefs

It is not an accident or coincidence that today, more so than in recent years, we are not only curious but vitally concerned about the ways of healing that our ancestors employed. There are those who choose to condemn the health system, with more vociferous critics such as

TABLE 6-1. BELIEFS THAT CAN AFFECT THERAPY

Baptist Bodies (27 bodies)

Birth
Opposed to infant baptism. Only believers should be baptized, and it must be done by immersion.
Death
Clergy seeks to minister by counsel and prayer with patient and family.
Health crisis
Some Baptists believe and practice healing by the "laying on of hands."
Diet
Some groups condemn coffee and tea.
Beliefs
Supreme authority of Bible in all matters of faith and practice. Many Baptists condemn what the American Baptist Association terms "so-called modern science." Although the practical expression of this view is largely confined to opposition to Darwinism, resistance to medical therapy may be encountered. Most, however, believe that God works through the physician. Some who believe in predestination respond passively to care.

Church of Christ, Scientist (Christian Scientist)

Health crisis
They deny the existence of health crises; sickness, sin, and death are errors of the human mind and can be destroyed by altering thoughts, not by drugs or medicines. They do not allow hypnotism or any form of psychotherapy which alters the "Divine Mind." A Christian Science Practitioner can be called to administer spiritual support; the *Christian Science Journal* contains a directory of Christian Science nurses available to help bandage wounds, set bones, etc.
Diet
Alcohol, coffee, tobacco are seen as drugs, so not used.
Beliefs
Disease is a human mental concept that can be dispelled by "spiritual truth." Many Christian Scientists adhere to this belief to the extent that they refuse all medical treatment, but each individual may decide whether he wishes to rely completely on Christian Science. Many adherents desire the services of a Practitioner or Reader. The Church operates several nursing homes that rely solely on such "spiritual" means of health maintenance. They do not use drugs or blood transfusions, accept vaccines only when required by law, and do not seek biopsies or physical examinations.

Church of Christ (Temple Lot)

Birth
No baptism until a minimum of 8 years, then baptism by immersion.
Death
No last rites.

(continued)

TABLE 6–1—Continued

Church of Christ (Temple Lot)–Continued

Health crisis

Communion offered only to members of this church. Belief in the anointing with oil and "laying on of hands" by the ministry for healing of sick. Blood transfusions are acceptable and all normal medical practice. Ministers (elders) will visit any who desire.

Beliefs

No objection to "modern science" or therapy *per se*, but a simple recognition of human limitations to wisdom and understanding. Sunday is observed as the Sabbath but no objection to medical care on Sunday.

Church of Jesus Christ of Latter-Day Saints (Mormon)

Birth

Baptism by immersion at 8 years or older.

Death

Believe it proper to bury in ground; cremation is discouraged. Baptism of the dead is held essential, though a living person may serve as a proxy. Preaching the Gospel to the dead is also practiced.

Health crisis

Devout adherents believe in divine healing through the "laying on of hands," though many do not prohibit medical therapy. The Church maintains an extensive and well-funded welfare system, including financial support for the sick.

Diet

Prohibits alcoholic beverages, tobacco, hot drinks (tea, coffee), or any other substance which may be injurious to the body. Encourages sparing use of meats but prohibits none outright.

Beliefs

There is a strong tradition of revelation through visions. A special undergarment is often worn. Patients may desire to have a Church Priesthood holder administer the sacrament to them while in the hospital. This would be on Sunday.

Eastern Orthodox Churches

(Turkey, Egypt, Syria, Romania, Bulgaria, Cyprus, Albania, Poland, Czechoslovakia)

Birth

Generally, these denominations believe in infant baptism by total immersion, followed immediately by confirmation.

Death

Last rites obligatory if death is impending.

Health crisis

Anointing of the sick is a form of healing by prayer.

Diet

Restrictions dependent on particular sect.

Episcopalian

Birth

Infant baptism is mandatory and especially urgent if prognosis is grave, although aborted fetuses and stillborns are not baptized.

Death

Last rites (Rite for the Anointing of the Sick) is not mandatory for all members.

Health crisis

Some believe in spiritual healing.

Diet

Some abstain from meat on Fridays and some fast before receiving Holy Communion, which may be daily.

Beliefs

Many practice confession of sins and absolution.

TABLE 6–1—Continued

Friends (Quakers)

Birth
Do not baptize—at birth, an infant's name is recorded in official books.
Death
Do not believe in life after this life.
Beliefs
Are pacifists and conscientious objectors in wartime. Believe in plain speech and dress and refusal of tithes, oaths. Believe God is in every man and can be approached directly—religion inward, personal.

Greek Orthodox Church

Birth
Baptism is significant. Prefer to baptize the child at least 40 days from birth. If it is not possible to baptize by sprinkling or immersion, the church allows the child to be baptized "in the air" by moving the child in the form of the sign of the cross as appropriate words are said.
Death
Last rites are the administration of the Sacrament of Holy Communion. The priest should be called early enough so that the patient is still conscious.
Health crisis
In most cases, each of these health-crisis situations must be handled by an ordained priest, though a Deacon of the Church may also serve in some cases. Usually a priest administers Holy Communion in the hospital room in a procedure that takes only a few minutes. Some patients may also want the Sacrament of Holy Unction, which the Priest can conduct in the hospital room in a brief time in an abbreviated service.
Diet
The Church usually prescribes a fast period, which means avoidance of meat and, in many cases, dairy products. These rules need not be enforced in cases of illness, especially when they may be of some harm to the health of the patient. Sometimes Orthodox patients will insist upon fasting even when in the hospital. If decision and desire to fast in the hospital do not interfere with medical procedures, there would be no reason for this to be refused. However, if this would adversely influence the medical condition of the patient, a priest should be called to convince the patient to forego fasting until his health is restored. The usual fasting days are Wednesday, Friday, and Lent.

Hindu

Death
Certain prescribed rites are followed after death: The priest may tie thread around neck or wrist to signify blessing; the thread should not be removed. Immediately after death the priest will pour water into the mouth of the corpse; the family washes the body. They are particular about who touches their dead, and the bodies are cremated.
Diet
There are many dietary restrictions that conform to individual sect doctrine. The patient should be questioned when admitted.

Islamic (Muslim/Moslem)

Birth
The fetus before 130 days is treated as any other discarded tissue; after 130 days it must be treated as a fully developed human being.
Death
The patient must confess sins and beg forgiveness before death, and the family should be present. The family washes, prepares, and places body facing Mecca. Only relatives or friends touch the body and unless required by law, there should be no postmortem; no body part should be removed.

(continued)

98

TABLE 6-1—Continued

Islamic (Muslim/Moslem)–Continued

Health crisis

In pathologic conditions, faith healing is not acceptable unless the psychological condition of the patient is deteriorating. Then it is done for the patient's morale.

Diet

All pork products are proscribed. Ninth month (Ramadan) daylight fasting is practiced.

Beliefs

Older or more conservative Muslims often have a fatalist view that can militate against ready compliance with therapy.

Jehovah's Witnesses

Birth

No infant baptism.

Death

No last rites.

Health crises

Adherents are generally absolutely opposed to blood transfusion, though individuals can sometimes be persuaded in emergencies. When parents refuse consent for a child's transfusion, it is often possible to obtain a court order appointing some key hospital official temporary guardian of the child. The official may then legally consent to the transfusion.

Beliefs

The sect opposes the "false teachings" of other sects; opposition often extends to modern science, including medicine. Some are pacifists and conscientious objectors in wartime; conversion of others is important. They don't participate in nationalistic ceremonies or celebrate holidays by gift giving.

Lutheran

Birth

Baptize (only living) persons at 6–8 weeks following birth by pouring, sprinkling, or immersing.

Death

Last rites are optional.

Health crisis

If the prognosis is grave, the patient may request the anointing and blessing of the sick.

Beliefs

Accept developments of science and technology but would raise objections if such techniques are administered unjustly or are clearly contrary to Christian theology.

Methodist

Birth

Baptism for children or adults.

Death

Believe in divine judgment after death. Good will be rewarded and evil punished.

Health crisis

Communion may be requested prior to surgery or similar crisis.

Beliefs

Ministers counsel but do not hear confession. Donation of one's body or part of body at death is encouraged.

Pentecostal (Assembly of God, Four-square Church)

Birth

Water baptism by complete single immersion after age of accountability.

TABLE 6-1—Continued

Death
No last rites.
Health crisis
No inhibitions against blood transfusions or medical care. Believe in possibility of divine healing through prayer. Anointing with oil may be practiced with laying on of hands.
Diet
Abstain from alcohol, tobacco, eating blood and strangled animals. Individual may resist pork.
Beliefs
Some insist illness is divine punishment but most consider illness an intrusion of Satan. Deliverance from sin and sickness are provided for in atonement. Pray for divine intervention in health matters and seek to reach God in prayer for themselves and others when ill.

This table was developed from responses to questionnaires sent to 32 religious denominations throughout the United States. The material is presented with the recognition that within each religion there are individuals and sects whose beliefs and teachings differ from those described here. (Reprinted with the permission of Nursing Update, July 1975. Copyright © 1975, Miller and Fink Corporation, Darien, Conn. All rights reserved.)

Illich citing its failure to create a utopia for humankind.[35] It is obvious to those who embrace a more moderate viewpoint that diseases continue to occur and that they outflank our ability to cure or prevent them. Once again, many people are seeking the services of people who are knowledgeable in the arts of healing and folk medicine. Many patients may elect, at some point in their lives, and more specifically during an illness, to use modalities outside the medical establishment. It is important to understand these treatment methods.

For example, the current popularity of "health foods" has given rise to the popular use of various diets to prevent illness. In addition, health-food stores make available a number of medicinal teas and herbs. (A listing of commonly used herbs is presented in Table 6-2.) Almost 100 herbal teas are listed in a small paperback entitled *Herbal Tea Book*.[36] The herbs are alphabetically listed, and the source and use of each are given. An even larger listing is given in *Herbs: Medicine and Mysticism*[37] by Sybil Leek, who is known as one of the "world's foremost astrologers and witches." This book has a wide audience.

As discussed in Chapter 4, Laetrile is considered by some to be a cure for cancer. Apart from numerous political ramifications within the health-care system, Laetrile creates another dilemma. If it has healing powers—even if limited to making people feel a little better until they die—then one can appreciate its usefulness.[38] But if Laetrile does not live up to what its proponents claim it is able to do, the public is falling prey to a pseudomedical hoax.

It is difficult to sort out which aspects of folk medicine have merit and which are a hoax. From the viewpoint of the consumer—if he has faith in the efficacy of an herb, a diet, a pill, or a healer—it is not a hoax. From the viewpoint of the medical establishment, jealous of its territorial claim, this same herb, diet, pill, or healer is indeed a hoax if it is *ineffective* and *prevents* the person from using the method of treatment that the physician-healer believes is effective.

TABLE 6–2. COMMONLY USED HERBS

Herb	Action	Use	Administration
Alfalfa (or Lucerne)	Stimulant; nutritive	Arthritis; weight gain; strength-giving	1 oz. herb to 1 pint water; drink 1 cupful as tea
Anise (seed used)	Stimulant; aromatic; relaxant	Flatulence; dry coughs	2 tsp. of seed to ½ pint water; dose—1-3 tsp. often
Bayberry (bark used)	Astringent; stimulant; emetic	Sore-throat gargle; cleanses stomach; douche; rinse for bleeding gums	1 oz. powdered bark to 1 pint water; drink as tea
Blessed thistle	Diaphoretic; stimulant; emetic	Reduces fevers; breaks up colds; digestive problems	1 oz. herb to 1 pint water; small doses as desired.
Bugleweed	Aromatic; sedative; tranquilizer; astringent	Coughs; relieves pulmonary bleeding, increases appetite	1 oz. herb to 1 pint water; drink by glassful often
Catnip (leaves)	Diaphoretic; tonic; antispasmodic	Helpful in convulsions; produces perspiration	1 oz. leaves to 1 pint water (measured by teaspoonful); tsp.
Cayenne pepper (fruit and seed)	Stimulant; toxic	Purest and most positive stimulant in herbal medicine; healing of burns and other wounds; relieves toothaches	Powder in small doses; by mouth or topical
Chestnut, Horse (bark and fruit)	Astringent; narcotic; tonic	Bark used for fevers; fruit to treat rheumatism	Bark: 1 oz. to 1 pint water, tsp. 4 times per day; fruit: tincture 10 drops twice per day
Chicory (root)	Diuretic; laxative	Liver enlargement; gout; rheumatic complaints	1 oz. root to 1 pint water; take freely
Corn silk	Diuretic; mild stimulant	Irritated bladder; urinary stones; trouble with prostate gland	2 oz. in 1 pint water; take freely
Dandelion (root)	Diuretic; tonic	Used in many patent medicines; general body stimulant; used chiefly with kidney and liver disorders	Roasted roots are ground and used like coffee; small cup once or twice per day
Ergot (fungus)	Uterine stimulant; sedative; hemostatic	Menstrual disorders; stops hemorrhage	Liquid extract 10-20 minims by mouth
Eucalyptus	Antiseptic; antispasmodic; stimulant	Inhale for sore throat; apply to ulcers and other wounds	Local application or fluid extract in small doses by mouth

Herb (part)	Properties	Uses	Preparation/Dosage
Fennel (seeds)	Aromatic; carminative (expels air from bowels)	Gas; gout; colic in infants; increases milk in nursing mothers	Pour water (½ pint) on 1 tsp. of seeds; take freely
Garlic (juice)	Diaphoretic; diuretic; stimulant; expectorant	Treats colds; diuretic; antiseptic	Juice, 10-30 drops
Goldenrod (leaves)	Aromatic; stimulant	Sore throat; general pain; colds; rheumatism	1 oz. leaves to 1 pint water; small dose often
Hollyhock (flowers)	Diuretic	Chest complaints	1 oz. flowers to 1 pint water; drink as much as needed
Ivy (leaves)	Cathartic; diaphoretic	Poultices on ulcers and abscesses	As a poultice
Ivy, poison (leaves)	Irritant; stimulant; narcotic	Rheumatism; sedative for the nervous system	Liquid extract 5-30 drops
Juniper berries	Diuretic; stimulant	Bladder and kidney problems; gargles; digestive aid	Oil of berries 1-5 drops
Licorice (root)	Demulcent	Coughs; prevents thirst	Powdered root
Lily of the valley (flower)	Cardiac; diuretic; stimulant	Headaches	½ oz. of flowers to 1 pint water; tbsp. doses
Marigold (flowers and leaves)	Diaphoretic; stimulant	Flowers and leaves made into a salve for skin eruptions; relieves sore muscles; amenorrhea	1 oz. herbs and petals to 1 pint water; tbsp. on mouth or topical application
Mistletoe (leaves)	Nervine; antispasmodic; tonic; narcotic	Epilepsy and hysteria; painful menstruation; induces sleep	2 oz. to ½ pint water; 1 tbs. often
Mustard (leaves)	Cooling; sedative	Hoarseness (excellent aid in recovering the voice)	Liquid extract; small doses
Nightshade, deadly (poison) (leaves and root)	Narcotic; diuretic; sedative; antispasmodic	Eye diseases; increases urine; stimulates circulation	Powdered leaves and root; small amounts
Papaya leaves	Digestive	Digestive disorders; fresh leaves; dry wounds	Papain; small doses
Rosemary (leaves) (herb)	Astringent; diaphoretic; tonic; stimulant	Prevents baldness; cold; colic; nerves; strengthens eyes	1 oz. herb to 1 pint water; small doses
Saffron (flower pistils)	Carminative; diaphoretic	Amenorrhea; dysmenorrhea; hysteria	1 drachm flower pistils in 1 pint water; teacup doses
Thyme (dried herb)	Antiseptic; antispasmodic; tonic	Perspiration; colds; coughs; cramps	1 oz. herb to 1 pint water; tbs. doses often

Source: Sybil Leek, Herbs: Medicine and Mysticism (Chicago: Henry Regnery, 1975) pp. 73–235.

There are numerous healers in the general population, some of whom are legitimate and some of whom are not. They range from housewives and priests to gypsies and "witches." Many people seek their services. I have had occasion to meet with several of these folk healers. Without attempting to make a value judgment, I will merely report on their skills and methods.

One healer has an office in a community near to where I live. He charges a nominal fee for consultation with either groups or individuals and then gives advice on how to solve a problem. He does not see physically ill people but prefers to help people who have moderate emotional and practical problems. His primary objective is to help people solve these problems. This man tends to be quite popular with young adults in the area, as he lends a "willing ear" and is "not too expensive." He does not keep his clients waiting long, and often the brief wait proves to be interesting because the waiting room is always the scene of an open discussion about his talents.

Another healer I knew was a young college student. He believed that he possessed certain spirits and skills that enabled him to heal. He had visions that interpreted for him the problems and ills of his clients. This young man maintained a special altar in his room, where he prayed to the "spirits." At that time, he did not charge for his services because he had just received the "message," and the art of healing was new to him. He admitted that he had formerly been a drug addict, but was now enrolled in college and hoped to use his education and healing skills to make life better for the people of the streets.

The third healer I am personally acquainted with is a Catholic priest; he is extremely reluctant to call himself a "healer." Yet he does claim to have witnessed and participated in numerous healings. He conducts prayer meetings in his parish. He comes to my classes and lectures to the students on healing and the charismatic movement within the Catholic Church.[39] He defines healing as the "satisfactory response to crises by a group of people, individually or corporately." "Healing," as he explains it, "is applied in a broad, holistic approach; that is, body, mind, and spirit are not separated." His vision of reality is that of a man being full of the spirit of God. According to this priest, the healer has the ability to *heal* but not really to *cure*. He further explains that there are "three types of illness: spiritual, physical, and mental." In this context, faith is the underlying basis of healing, although he questions whether faith is the only component. Healing becomes a living process whereby that which is wounded or broken becomes whole.

A review of healing and spiritual literature reveals there are four types of healing.

Spiritual Healing.   When a person is experiencing an illness of the spirit spiritual healing applies. The cause of suffering is personal sin. The treatment method is repentence, which is followed by a natural healing process.

Inner Healing.   When a person is suffering from an emotional (mental) illness inner healing is used. The root of the problem may lie in the person's conscious or unconscious mind. The treatment method is to heal the person's memory. The healing process is delicate and sensitive, and exposure takes considerable time and effort.

Physical Healing.   When a person is suffering from a disease or has been involved in an accident that resulted in some form of bodily damage physical healing is appropriate. Laying on of hands and speaking in tongues usually accompany physical healing. The person is prayed over by both the "leader" and members of a prayer group (Fig. 6-7).

The priest referred to above related an incident in which one of the members of the group was experiencing difficulty with ulcers and was not responding to conventional medical treatment. The man, who initially was embarrassed by the idea, allowed the prayer group and the priest to pray over him. In a short time, to his surprise, he recovered from his ulcers.

Deliverance or Exorcism.   When the body and mind are the victims of evil from the outside exorcism is used. In order to effect treatment, the person must be delivered or exorcised from the evil. The popularity of films such as *The Exorcist* gives testimony to the return of these beliefs. Incidentally, the priest who has lectured in my classes stated that he does not, as yet, lend credence to exorcisms; however, he was guarded enough not to discount it either.

Other Forms of Healing

Auric Healing.   Another form of treatment is "auric healing." John Richard Turner of Waltham, Massachusetts, explains that "from the moment of birth until the last breath is taken, a person has a bioenergetic field surrounding his body." This field of energy is known as an "aura." If strong enough, it is believed to be transmittable and to have healing powers. By the use of touch, the person with the auric powers is able to effect cure for an ill person.[40] Mr. Turner, who is fairly well known in the Boston area, also claims to be quite popular in California. He states that he visits patients in the hospital along with the physician and that he has been quite successful in treating people in that setting.

Pilgrimages.   There is also a film available that demonstrates how some people relate to folk healers. The film, *We Believe in Nino Fidencio,* is a documentary on folk curing and penitent pilgrimages in northern Mexico. Shot in October 1971 in northern Mexico by Dr. and Mrs. Jon Olson (who were in Mexico doing file research), the film is concerned with:

> . . . the belief system and ceremonies surrounding a folk curer, Fidencio Constantino, who practiced in Nuevo Leon from the early 1920's until

church of saint ignatius of loyola

Liturgy

of

Anointing

THE CHURCH OF ST. IGNATIUS WILL PRAY FOR THE SICK AND ELDERLY IN THE PARISH ON THE FEAST OF CHRIST THE KING, NOVEMBER 20th AT THE LITURGY FOR ANOINTING AT 9:30 A.M.. AREA RESIDENTS, ESPECIALLY THOSE WHO ARE SICK, DISABLED OR ELDERLY, ARE WELCOME TO TAKE PART. EACH PERSON WHO DESIRES IT WILL BE BLESSED OR ANOINTED WITH HOLY OIL.

Figure 6–7. Sample of an announcement for a Mass to be said for the sick. (From collection of the author.)

his death in 1938, and who is presently the central figure in a widespread curing cult. Twice each year, upon the anniversaries of his birth and death, Espinazo (a town of about 300 population) is inundated by 10,000 to 15,000 people from Mexico and the United States who make pilgrimages in hopes of a cure and/or help from the Nino. It was during one of these celebrations that the film was made.

Believers combine elements of traditional ⊂atholicism, Indian dances, herbology, and laying-on-of-hands in effecting cures. It is believed that certain individuals receive the Nino's power to heal. They are called "Cajitas" or "Materias" (women), and "Cajones" (men)—"receptacles" of the Nino's power—and they cure in the name of Nino Fidencio and God. During the celebrations they roam Espinazo curing all who wish a cure-blessing. There are several "holy places" in Espinazo where curing is conducted: Fidencio's tomb, "temple," and death bed, two trees, a cemetary hill, the hill of the bell, and the "charco" or mudpond, where Fidencio conducted baptisms to cure his patients.

The film includes references to other curing alternatives, and attempts to present some of the reasons why the believers continue to select this curing method in the face of modern medical alternatives in nearby towns and cities.

As previously stated, Dr. Olson first learned about this cult in 1968-1969 while doing field research in Mina, a community in the same county as Espinazo. It was during this time that the Olsons met members of the cult (in Mina and Espinazo) including the local "materia," Cayetana, who appear in the film. The narration of the film is based on information and actual recorded interviews given by participants in the cult. Jon Olson is presently an Assistant Professor of Anthropology at California State University at Los Angeles.

Extensive study of the Nino Fidencio complex has been done by Professor June Macklin (Connecticut College).[41]

This chapter is no more than an *overview* of the topics introduced; the amount of relevant knowledge could fill many books. The issues raised here are those that, I think, have special meaning to the practice of nursing, medicine, and health-care delivery. We must be aware (1) of what people may be thinking that may differ from our own thoughts and (2) that sources of *help* exist outside the traditional medical community. As the beliefs of ethnic communities of color are explored in later chapters, I shall attempt to delineate who are specifically recognized and used as healers by the members of the community, and I shall describe some of the forms of treatment employed by each community.

REFERENCES

1. Joyce Leeson, "Paths to Medical Care in Lasaka, Zambia" (Master's thesis, University of Manchester, England; preliminary findings, 12 July 1967), p. 14.
2. Julian Morgenstern, *Rites of Birth, Marriage, Death and Kindred Occasions among the Semites* (Chicago: Quadrangle Books, 1966), p. 3.

3. Ibid., p. 5.
4. Ibid., p. 31.
5. Ibid., pp. 22–30.
6. Ibid.
7. Ibid., p. 36.
8. Ibid., p. 87.
9. Ibid., p. 46.
10. Ibid., p. 47.
11. Ibid., p. 48.
12. Ibid., p. 58.
13. Ibid., p. 53.
14. Ibid., p. 82.
15. Ibid., p. 117–60.
16. Ibid., p. 186.
17. Clarence Maloney, ed., *The Evil Eye* (New York: Columbia University Press, 1976), p. 14.
18. Ibid., p. vi.
19. Ibid., p. vii.
20. Ibid.
21. Ibid., p. xv.
22. Rachel E. Spector, "A Description of the Impact of Medicare on Health-Illness Beliefs and Practices of White Ethnic Senior Citizens in Central Texas." Ph.D. diss. University of Texas at Austin School of Nursing, 1983; Ann Arbor, Mich.: University Microfilms International, 1983, p. 126–27.
23. Irving K. Zola, "The Concept of Trouble and Sources of Medical Assistance to Whom One Can Turn With What," *Social Science and Medicine* 6 (1972): 673–79.
24. Robert Tallant, *Voodoo in New Orleans* (New York: Collier Books, 1946).
25. Gershon Winkler, *Dybbuk* (New York: Judaica Press, 1981), pp. 8–9.
26. Zola, "Concept of Trouble."
27. Milton Steinberg, *Basic Judaism* (New York: Harcourt, Brace and World, 1947), pp. 125–26.
28. *Monthly Missalette* 15, no. 13 (February 1980): 38.
29. Nathan Ausubel, *The Book of Jewish Knowledge* (New York: Crown Publishers, 1964), pp. 192–95.
30. F. A. Foy, ed., *Catholic Almanac* (Huntington, Ind.: Our Sunday Visitor, 1980), pp. 305–13.
31. Information obtained during a visit to this shrine, July 1983.
32. Information obtained during a visit to this shrine, November 1981.
33. Information obtained during a visit to this shrine, March 1984.
34. Summary Table 6–1 developed from larger tables in the first edition of this book, pages 114–23.
35. Ivan Illich, *Medical Nemesis: The Expropriation of Health* (London: Marion Bogars, 1975).
36. Ann Adrian and Judith Dennis, *Herbal Tea Book* (San Francisco: Health Publishing Co., 1976).
37. Sybil Leek, *Herbs: Medicine and Mysticism* (Chicago: Henry Regnery, 1975).
38. John A. Richardson and Patricia Griffin, *Laetrile Case Histories* (New York: Bantam, 1977).
39. Francis MacNutt, *Healing* (Notre Dame, Ind.: Ave Maria Press, 1974);

Morton T. Kelsey, *Healing and Christianity* (New York: Harper and Row, 1973).

40. John Richard Turner, notes from a lecture delivered at a meeting of the World's Future Society held at Boston College, 16 March 1977.

41. Flyer on the film *We Believe in Nino Fidencio* (Jon and Natalie Olson, P.O. Box 14914, Long Beach, Calif. 90814).

BIBLIOGRAPHY

Belgum, David, ed. *Religion and Medicine.* Ames: Iowa State University Press, 1967.
  This book explores two dimensions of healing: religion and medicine. The essays it contains explore the nature of humankind and its problems in sickness and health.

Kelsey, Morton T. *Healing and Christianity.* New York: Harper and Row, 1973.
  Kelsey presents a comprehensive history of the sacrament of healing in the Christian church from Biblical times to the present.

Leek, Sybil. *Herbs: Medicine and Mysticism.* Chicago: Henry Regnery, 1975.
  Many herbs and their uses are described—both those in current use among the general population and those used among the Hopi Indian tribes.

MacNutt, Francis. *Healing.* Notre Dame, Ind.: Ave Maria Press, 1974.
  This book explores the charismatic movement in the Catholic Church. It describes in great detail the multiple forms of healing within the Church.

_____. *The Power to Heal.* Notre Dame, Ind.: Ave Maria Press, 1977.
  In this book, Father MacNutt further describes his experiences within the healing ministry. He addresses such topics as "Healing through Touch," "Soaking Prayer," "Suffering and Death," and "When and When Not to Pray."

Montgomery, Ruth, *Born to Heal.* New York: Coward, McCann and Geoghegan, 1973.
  This is the story of a dynamic man and his seemingly miraculous cures of tragic ailments, which run the gamut of human suffering. Mr. A. first devoted himself to healing in 1941 and experienced conflict with the traditional health system.

Morgenstern, Julian. *Rites of Birth, Marriage, Death, and Kindred Occasions among the Semites.* Chicago: Quadrangle Books, 1966.
  Morgenstern presents a fascinating history of the rites that preceded today's religions. It is hard to follow, because the author tends to jump back and forth, but it is well worth the effort because its content is quite interesting.

Scott, W. Richard, and Volkhart, Edmund H. *Medical Care Readings in the Sociology of Medical Institutions.* New York: Wiley, 1966.
  This anthology explores such topics as the varieties of healers, the relationships between healers and patients, and relationships between patients and hospitals.

FURTHER SUGGESTED READINGS

BOOKS

Adrian, Ann, and Dennis, Judith. *Herbal Tea Book.* San Francisco: Health Publishing Co., 1976.

Ausubel, Nathan. *The Book of Jewish Knowledge.* New York: Crown Publishers, 1964.

Bishop, G. *Faith Healing: God or Fraud?* Los Angeles: Shervourne Press, 1967.

Buxton, John. *Religion and Healing in Mandari.* Oxford: Clarendon Press, 1973.

Calhoun, Mary, *Medicine Show.* New York: Harper and Row, 1976.

Cassell, Eric J. *The Healer's Art: A New Approach to the Doctor-Patient Relationship.* Philadelphia: Lippincott, 1976.

Cramer, M. E. *Divine Science and Healing.* Denver: Colorado College of Divine Science, 1923.

Densmore, Frances. *How Indians Use Wild Plants for Food, Medicine, and Crafts.* New York: Dover, 1974.

Donin, Hayim Halevy. *To Be a Jew.* New York: Basic Books, 1972.

Elworthy, R. T. *The Evil Eye: The Origins and Practices of Superstition.* N.Y.: Julian Press, 1958. (originally published by John Murray, London, 1915)

Ford, P. S. *The Healing Trinity: Prescriptions for Body, Mind, and Spirit.* New York: Harper and Row, 1971.

Foy, F. A., ed. *Catholic Almanac.* Huntington, Ind.: Our Sunday Visitor, 1980.

Hand, Wayland D. *American Folk Medicine: A Symposium.* Berkeley: University of California Press, 1973.

Hutchens, Alma R. *Indian Herbalogy of North America.* Windsor, Ont.: Meico, 1973.

Hutton, J. Bernard. *The Healing Power.* London: Leslie Frewin, 1975.

Jarvis, D. C. *Folk Medicine: A Vermont Doctor's Guide to Good Health.* New York: Henry Holt and Co., 1958.

Kiev, Ari, ed. *Magic, Faith, and Healing: Studies in Primitive Psychiatry Today.* New York: Free Press of Glencoe, 1969.

Kordel, Lelord. *Natural Folk Remedies.* New York: G. P. Putnam's Sons, 1974.

Kreiger, Dolores. *The Therapeutic Touch.* Englewood Cliffs, N.J.: Prentice-Hall, 1979.

Krippner, Stanley, and Villaldo, Alberto. *The Realms of Healing.* Millbrae, Calif.: Celestial Arts, 1976.

McGill, O. *The Mysticism and Magic of India.* South Brunswick, N.J. and New York: A. S. Baines and Co., 1977.

Malinowski, Bronislaw. *Magic, Science and Religion.* Garden City, New York: Doubleday and Co., Inc., 1954.

Maloney, C. ed. *The Evil Eye.* New York: Columbia University Press, 1976.

Ortez y Pino, Jose, III. *The Herbs of Galisteo and Their Powers.* Santa Fe, N.M.: Vergara, 1972.

Russell, A. J. *Health in His Wings.* London: Methuen and Co., 1937.

S., E. M. *The House of Wonder—A Romance of Psychic Healing.* London: Rider and Co., 1927.

Saunders, Ritt. *Healing through the Spirit Agency.* London: Hutchinson and Co., 1927.

Shaw, W. *Aspects of Malaysian Magic.* Kuala Lumpur, Malaysia: Naziabum Nigara, 1975.

Steinberg, Milton. *Basic Judaism,* New York: Harcourt, Brace and World, 1947.

Sweet, Muriel. *Common Edible and Useful Plants of the West.* Healdsbury, Calif.: Naturegraph, 1962.

Wheelright, Edith Grey. *Medicinal Plants and Their History.* New York: Dover, 1974.

Winkler, Gershon. *Dybbuk*. New York: Judaica Press, 1981.
Young, James H. *The Medical Messiahs*. Princeton: Princeton University Press, 1967.
Zolla, Elemire. *The Writer and the Shaman*. New York: Harcourt Brace Jovanovich, 1969.

ARTICLES

Grad, Bernard. "Some Biological Effects of the 'Laying on of Hands': A Review of Experiments with Animals and Plants." *Journal of the American Society for Psychical Research* 59 (1965): 94–127.
Kleinman, Arthur M.: "Some Issues for a Comparative Study of Medical Healing." *International Journal of Social Psychiatry* 19 (1973): 159–65.
Krieger, Dolores. "Therapeutic Touch: The Imprimatur of Nursing." *American Journal of Nursing* 75 (1975): 784–87.
Leeson, Joyce. "Paths to Medical Care in Lusaka, Zambia." Master's thesis, University of Manchester, England; preliminary findings, 12 July, 1967.

UNIT III

Traditional Views of Health and Illness

The chapters in this unit will enable the reader to:

1. Develop a level of awareness of the background and health problems of both ethnic people of color and white ethnics
2. Understand some traditional beliefs of ethnic people with respect to health and illness
3. Understand the traditional pathways to health care and the relationship between these pathways and the American health-care system
4. Understand certain manpower problems of each of the communities discussed
5. Be more familiar with the available literature regarding each of these communities

The following exercises are appropriate to all chapters in Unit III:

1. Familiarize yourself with some literature of the ethnic community. That is, read literature, poetry, or a biography of a member of each of these communities. (See Bibliographies for Chapters 7–12.)
2. Familiarize yourself with the history and sociopolitical background of each of these communities.

The questions that follow should be thoughtfully considered:

1. What are the traditional definitions of health and illness in each of these communities?
2. What are the traditional methods of maintaining health?
3. What are the traditional ways of preventing illness?
4. What are the traditional ways of treating an illness?
5. What are traditionally thought to be the causes of an illness?
6. Who are the traditional healers? What functions do they perform?

The final unit of this book explores the traditional health and illness beliefs, practices, and problems of ethnic people, both white and of color. The ethnic people of color of the United States are Asians and Pacific Islanders; blacks; Native Americans, Eskimos, and Aleuts. Persons of Spanish origin, according to the 1980 census, may be of any race (Fig. III–1). According to the 1980 census the population of the United States was 226,504,825. Whites numbered 188,340,790, or 83.2 percent of the population. The breakdown of whites by ancestry will be included in the chapter describing health beliefs and practices among white ethnics. The ethnic/racial minorities constituted 16.8 percent of the population. The following charts and comments are introductory material to provide the reader with a brief overview of the demographic and economic backgrounds of the American population.

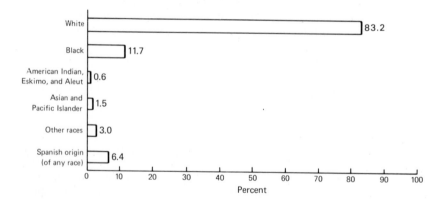

Figure III–1. Percent distribution of the population by race and Spanish origin: 1980. (U.S. Department of Commerce, Bureau of the Census, *United States Summary: General Population Characteristics,* Washington, D.C.: Government Printing Office, 1980.)

TOTAL POPULATION CHARACTERISTICS

The 1980 census figure for the United States population was 226,504,825. The population has increased by more than 24 million people since the 1970 census. The young-adult and the elderly populations have seen the greatest gains (Figs. III-2, III-3) with the 25 to 34 age group growing from 25.2 million persons in 1970 to 39 million in 1980. This represents a growth of 12.3 percent of the total population to 17 percent. The 65-and-over population has increased from 20 million to 26.3 million persons or from 9.8 percent to 11.4 percent

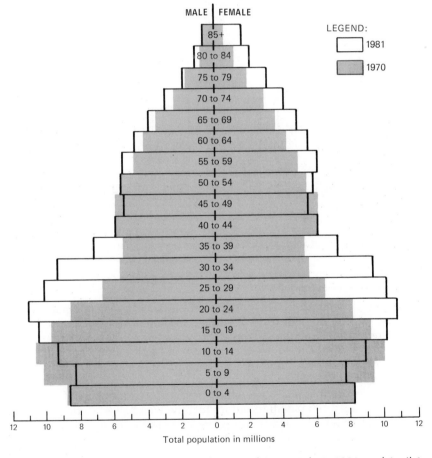

Figure III–2. Age and sex structure of the United States: July 1, 1981, and April 1, 1970. (U.S. Department of Commerce, Bureau of the Census, *Population Profile of the United States: 1981,* Washington, D.C.: Government Printing Office, 1982, p. 16.)

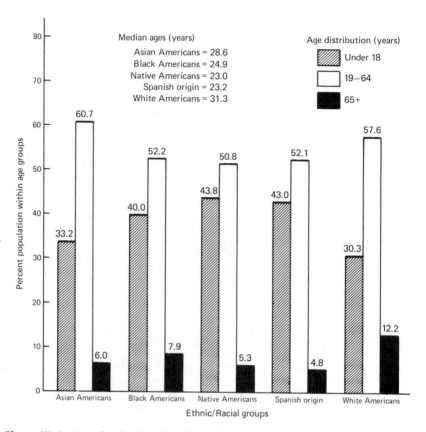

Figure III-3. Age distributions by ethnic/racial groups: 1980. (Data from U.S. Department of Commerce, Bureau of the Census, Washington, D.C.: Government Printing Office.)

of the total population. The population under 15 years of age dropped from 58 million in 1970 to 51.2 million in 1980. The median age of the total population increased from 27.9 years in 1970 to 30.0 years in 1980. The percentage of people 15 years old and older who completed high school was 63.5, and 13.4 percent of this population completed four or more years of college.[1]

There were 59,190,133 families, with an average size of 3.27 persons per family. The median family income was $19,917 and the mean income was $23,092. The percentage of persons below the specified poverty level in 1979 was 12.4.[2]

Asian and Pacific Islander Population
The Asian and Pacific Islander population (Fig. III-4) numbered 3,500,636 persons, 1.5 percent of the total population. Of this total, 806,027 are Chinese; 774,640, Filipino; 700,747, Japanese; 361,544,

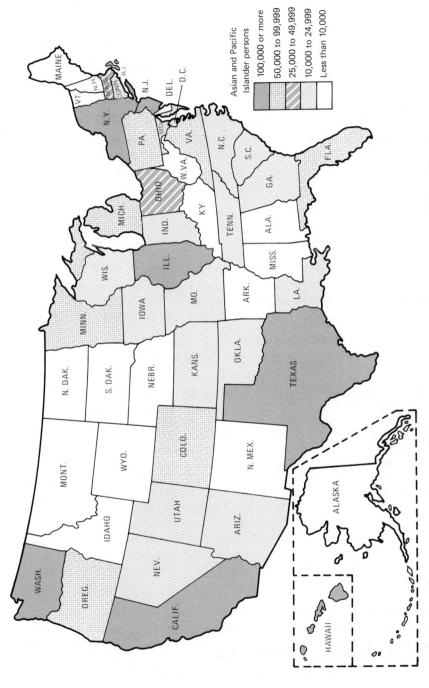

Figure III-4. Number of Asian and Pacific Islander persons by state: 1980. (U.S. Department of Commerce, Bureau of the Census, *United States Summary: General Population Characteristics*, Washington, D.C.: Government Printing Office, 1982, p. 1–14.)

Asian and Pacific
Islander persons

- 100,000 or more
- 50,000 to 99,999
- 25,000 to 49,999
- 10,000 to 24,999
- Less than 10,000

Asian Indian; 354,529, Korean; 261,714, Vietnamese; 167,253, Hawaiian; 42,050, Samoan; and 32,132, Guamanians.[3] The greatest percentage of this population (60.7 percent) falls between the ages of 20 and 64, while 33.2 percent are below 20 years of age and 6.0 percent are 65 and over. The percentage of this population, 15 years and older, that completed high school was 71.1 and 27.1 percent have completed four or more years of college.[4]

There were 818,029 families, with an average size of 3.75 persons per family. The median income was $22,713 and the mean income, $26,439. The percentage of people from this population group below the specified poverty level in 1979 was 13.1.[5]

Black Population
The black population in the United States (Fig. III-5) numbered 188,340,790 persons or 11.7 percent of the population. The greatest percentage (52.2 percent) of this population falls between the ages of 20 to 64, while 40 percent are below 20 years of age and 7.9 percent are 65 years old and older. The percentage of this population 15 years and over that has completed high school is 49.6 and 6.5 percent of the population have completed four or more years of college.[6]

There were 6,105,698 families, with an average size of 3.69 persons per family. The median income was $12,598, and the mean income was $15,684. The percentage of people who fell below the specified poverty level in 1979 was 29.9.[7]

Native American, Eskimo, and Aleut Population
The Native American, Eskimo, and Aleut population in the United States (Fig. III-6) numbered 1,418,195 persons, 0.6 percent of the total population. Of this total, 1,361,869 were American Indians; 42,149 were Eskimos; and 14,177 were Aleuts. The greatest percentage (50.8) of this population falls between the ages of 20 to 64; while 43.8 percent are below 20 years of age and 5.3 percent are 65 and over. The percentage of this population 15 years and older that has completed high school is 51.0 and 5.6 percent have completed four or more years of college.[8]

There were 341,401 families, with an average size of 3.83 persons per family. The median family income was $13,724 and the mean income was $16,643. The percentage of people who fell below the specified poverty level in 1979 was 27.5.[9]

Spanish-Origin Population
The Spanish-origin population numbered 14,605,283 persons, 6.4 percent of the population (Table III-1). However, Spanish-origin people may be of any race (e.g., black or white), so this percentage figure is not accurate. The greatest numbers of the Spanish-origin population are from the following types of Spanish origin (in thousand):[10]

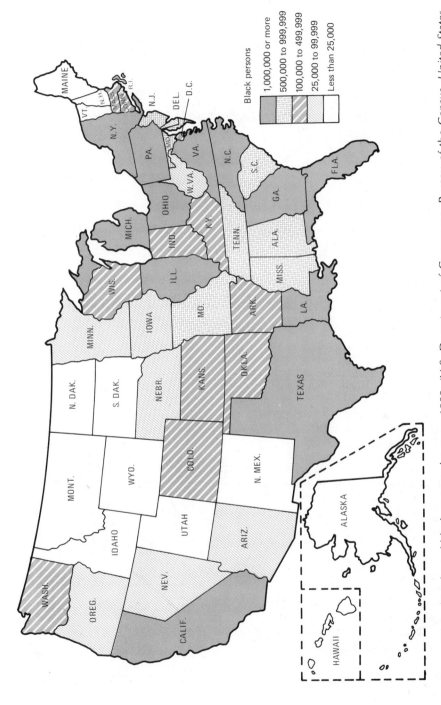

Figure III-5. Number of black persons by state: 1980. (U.S. Department of Commerce, Bureau of the Census, *United States Summary: General Population Characteristics*, Washington, D.C.: Government Printing Office, 1980.)

Black persons

1,000,000 or more
500,000 to 999,999
100,000 to 499,999
25,000 to 99,999
Less than 25,000

117

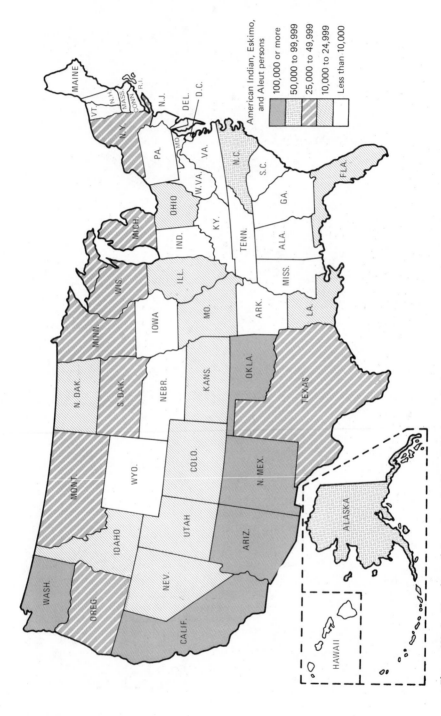

Figure III-6. Number of American Indian, Eskimo, and Aleut persons by state: 1980. (U.S. Department of Commerce, Bureau of the Census, *United States Summary: General Population Characteristics*, Washington, D.C.: Government Printing Office, 1980.)

American Indian, Eskimo, and Aleut persons

100,000 or more
50,000 to 99,999
25,000 to 49,999
10,000 to 24,999
Less than 10,000

Mexican	7,693
Spanish/Hispanic	2,687
Puerto Rican	1,444
Cuban	598
Dominican	171
Colombian	156
Spaniard	95
Ecuadoran	88
Salvadoran	85

For further clarification, see Figures III-7 and III-8.

The greatest percentage (52.1) of this population falls between the ages of 20 to 64, while 43 percent of the population are younger than 20 years and 4.8 percent of the population are 65 and over (Table III-2). The percentage of the population, 15 years and older, that has completed high school is 42.4 and 5.8 percent have completed four or more years of college.[11]

There were 3,273,728 families with an average size of 3.87 persons

TABLE III-1. RACE AND SPANISH ORIGIN, FOR THE UNITED STATES: APRIL 1, 1980, AND APRIL 1, 1970[a]

			Percent Distribution	
United States	*1980*	*1970*	*1980*	*1970*
Total	226,504,825	203,211,926	100.0	100.0
White	188,340,790	177,748,975	83.2	87.5
Black	26,488,218	22,580,289	11.7	11.1
American Indian, Eskimo, and Aleut	[c]1,418,195	[d]827,268	0.6	0.4
Asian and Pacific Islander	[e]3,500,636	[f]1,538,721	1.5	0.8
Other[g]	[b]6,756,986	[h]516,673	3.0	0.3
Persons of Spanish origin[i]	14,605,883	9,072,602	6.4	4.5
Persons not of Spanish origin	211,898,942	194,139,324	93.6	95.5

[a]Resident population.
[b]Of the 6,756,986 persons of other races in 1980, 5,840,648 were identified as Spanish in the separate origin question. In 1980, 56 percent of persons of Spanish origin were classified as white, compared with 93 percent in 1970. If, for comparative purposes, 93 percent of the 5.8 million (or 5.4 million) are included with white, the white population would have been about 194 million in 1980.
[c]Comprises 1,361,869 American Indians, 42,149 Eskimos and 14,177 Aleuts.
[d]Comprises 792,730 American Indians and in Alaska only, 28,186 Eskimos and 6,352 Aleuts.
[e]Comprises 806,027 Chinese, 774,640 Filipinos, 700,747 Japanese, 361,544 Asian Indians (classified as white in 1970), 354,529 Koreans, 261,714 Vietnamese, 167,253 Hawaiians, 42,050 Samoans, and 32,132 Guamanians.
[f]Comprises 591,290 Japanese, 435,062 Chinese, Filipinos, and excluding Alaska, 100,179 Hawaiians, and 69,130 Koreans.
[g]Includes Asian and Pacific Islander groups not specifically identified in footnotes e and f.
[h]Includes Eskimos and Aleuts outside Alaska.
[i]Persons of Spanish origin may be of any race.
Source: U.S. Bureau of the Census, 1980 Census of Population, Press Release CB81-32 (February 23, 1981), and Supplementary Report, PC80-S1-1 (May 1981); and 1970 Census of Population, Supplementary Report, PC(S1)-104 (December 1975).

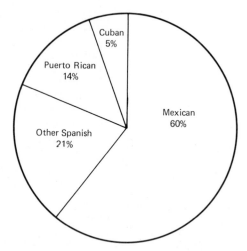

Figure III-7. Percent distribution of persons of Spanish origin by type of Spanish origin: 1980. (U.S. Department of Commerce, Bureau of the Census, *United States Summary: General Population Characteristics,* Washington, D.C.: Government Printing Office, 1982, p. 1–14.)

per family. The median family income was $14,712 and the mean family income was $17,263. The percentage of people below the specified poverty level in 1979 was 23.5.[12]

White Population

The white population in the United States numbered 226,504,825 persons, 83.2 percent of the total population. This percentage decreased from 87.5 percent of the population in 1970. The greatest percentage (57.6) of this population falls between the ages of 20 to 64 years; while the population under 20 is 30.3 percent, the lowest of all groups; and the population 65 and over is 12.2 percent, the highest. The percentage

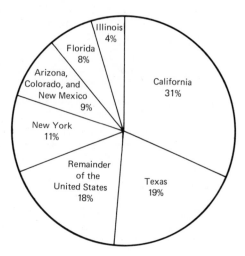

Figure III-8. Percent distribution of persons of Spanish origin by residence in selected states: 1980. (U.S. Department of Commerce, Bureau of the Census, *United States Summary: General Population Characteristics,* Washington, D.C.: Government Printing Office, 1980.)

TABLE III-2. RACE AND SPANISH ORIGIN, BY AGE AND SEX, FOR THE UNITED STATES: APRIL 1, 1980[a]

Age	Total	Race[b]					Persons of Spanish Origin[c]
		White	Black	American Indian, Eskimo, and Aleut	Asian and Pacific Islander	Other	
			Number				
All ages	226,504,825	188,340,790	26,488,218	1,418,195	3,500,636	6,756,986	14,605,883
Under 5 years	16,344,407	12,631,197	2,435,915	149,003	293,470	834,822	1,662,792
5 to 9 years	16,697,134	13,031,017	2,489,947	146,364	302,296	727,510	1,536,895
10 to 14 years	18,240,919	14,460,283	2,672,908	155,731	279,849	672,148	1,474,837
15 to 19 years	21,161,667	16,957,541	2,983,440	170,061	288,550	762,075	1,605,827
20 to 24 years	21,312,557	17,283,385	2,724,355	148,985	320,129	835,703	1,585,651
25 to 34 years	37,075,629	30,625,328	4,208,892	231,775	740,415	1,269,219	2,503,876
35 to 44 years	25,631,247	21,584,367	2,708,418	153,226	497,583	687,653	1,566,200
45 to 54 years	22,797,367	19,612,854	2,271,182	109,589	338,702	465,040	1,185,746
55 to 64 years	21,699,765	19,210,785	1,907,335	78,673	227,808	275,164	775,274
65 to 74 years	15,577,586	13,905,249	1,339,974	48,142	137,765	146,456	457,114
75 to 84 years	7,726,826	6,994,079	586,991	20,794	60,215	64,747	202,841
85 years and over	2,239,721	2,044,705	158,861	5,852	13,854	16,449	48,830
Median age (years)	30.0	31.3	24.9	23.0	28.6	22.8	23.2

(continued)

TABLE III-2—Continued

Age	Total	Race[b]					Persons of Spanish Origin[c]
		White	Black	American Indian, Eskimo, and Aleut	Asian and Pacific Islander	Other	
				Percent			
All ages	100.0	100.0	100.0	100.0	100.0	100.0	100.0
Under 5 years	7.2	6.7	9.2	10.5	8.4	12.4	11.4
5 to 9 years	7.4	6.9	9.4	10.3	8.6	10.8	10.5
10 to 14 years	8.1	7.7	10.1	11.0	8.0	9.9	10.1
15 to 19 years	9.3	9.0	11.3	12.0	8.2	11.3	11.0
20 to 24 years	9.4	9.2	10.3	10.5	9.1	12.4	10.9
25 to 34 years	16.4	16.3	15.9	16.3	21.2	18.8	17.1
35 to 44 years	11.3	11.5	10.2	10.8	14.2	10.2	10.7
45 to 54 years	10.1	10.4	8.6	7.7	9.7	6.9	8.1
55 to 64 years	9.6	10.2	7.2	5.5	6.5	4.1	5.3
65 to 74 years	6.9	7.4	5.1	3.4	3.9	2.2	3.1
75 to 84 years	3.4	3.7	2.2	1.5	1.7	1.0	1.4
85 years and over	1.0	1.1	0.6	0.4	0.4	0.2	0.3
Sex							
Male	110,032,295	91,669,626	12,515,932	701,007	1,693,342	3,452,388	7,278,259
Female	116,472,530	96,671,164	13,972,286	717,188	1,807,294	3,304,598	7,327,624
Sex ratio (males per 100 females)	94.5	94.8	89.6	97.7	93.7	104.5	99.3

[a]Resident population.
[b]See footnotes for Table III-1.
[c]Persons of Spanish origin may be of any race.

Source: U.S Bureau of the Census, 1980 Census of Population, Supplementary Report, PC80-S1-1 (May 1981).

of the population, 15 years and older, that has completed high school is 65.9, while 14.3 percent of the population have completed four or more years of college.[13]

There were 50,644,862 families, with a size of 3.19 persons. The median income was $20,835 and the mean income was $24,166. The percentage of people who fell below the specified poverty level in 1979 was 9.4.[14]

New Immigrants

Between 1972 and 1981, more than 10 million people were legally admitted to this country as immigrants. The people have come from all over the world, with the greatest numbers coming from Mexico and other Latin American countries, and Southeast Asia. In 1978 alone, over 88,000 people immigrated from Vietnam.[15] In addition to those who have immigrated here legally there are those who are here as undocumented workers, or illegal aliens. It is not possible to present a precise number of people living here illegally, but it is estimated that the range is between 2 to 12 million.[16] Much of this migration has been from Mexico and other countries in Central and South America,[17] although there are also undocumented people here from Europe, Asia, and Canada. At the present time, there has not been a law passed to change the immigration policies and the fate of the undocumented people is still in limbo.

This book does not delve specifically into the health-related issues of the people with this background. However, the bibliographies of Chapters 7, 9, and 12 do contain specific reference materials.

BACKGROUND INFORMATION: ETHNIC GROUP'S VIEWS ON HEALTH AND ILLNESS

In the discussion of the health and illness beliefs and practices of each ethnic group the following information is included:

- Traditional definitions of health
- Traditional forms of epidemiologic beliefs
- Traditional names and symptoms of a given disease
- Traditional sources of "medical" assistance
- Traditional remedies
- Problems the group encounters in dealing with the health-care system
- The current health-care provider manpower

It must be kept in mind that this information is general and not universal. It is *not* specific to any one person. However, a person's health care and behavior during illness may well have roots in that person's traditional belief system. If we are caring for a person from one of the ethnic or racial minority groups and we find that there are problems in our interactions or with the patient's compliance, an understanding of traditional beliefs may be helpful. If we understand that these beliefs may well differ from our own, this can help us as well as the consumer to resolve the problems that occur. In addition, the tendency to disrespect a person who does not practice his personal health care as we think he should can be dissipated when we understand the underlying reasons for that individual's behavior.

Among all people there is agreement that good health is essential for survival. If we are sick, we cannot work, we cannot provide food for ourselves, and we cannot survive and reproduce. Satisfactory health is mandatory for our existence. Yet the definition of health and the means of preserving it vary from people to people. It has been demonstrated earlier in this book that there is great disagreement among health workers as to what health is. Yet professionals expect other people to accept *their* "nondefinition."

As there are differences in the meaning of health, so are there differences in the meaning of illness. What does illness mean to others? Is it simply the symptoms of a disease, or is it more? What causes illness from a traditional viewpoint? Who are the native, traditional healers, and what methods do they use to treat and heal disorders? How do native healers differ from physicians? What resources are available to a person when he seeks traditional health care?

Research carried out by medical sociologists and anthropologists in the area of health and illness beliefs has been done to discover and understand these folkways. There is currently much criticism among ethnic groups who have been studied. They question the meaning of these studies and the interpretations of the researchers. Despite these criticisms, however, the work of sociologists and anthropologists is helpful if used as a stepping stone. In this unit results of these studies will be looked at from a specific standpoint. They will be referred to and recommended for further examination in order to *help* health-care providers understand the behaviors and attitudes of the people for whom they care. In addition, I include bibliographic resources that have been recommended by the members of a given community.

It is important to note that much of the literature regarding the health and illness beliefs of any group of people is contradictory. One research report will indicate that a given group of people view health as a reward for good behavior. Another will state that people of the same cultural background believe that health is a matter of chance—something that may be here today, and luck will determine how long it will remain. Yet another study will indicate that some illnesses are believed to be caused by witchcraft and others by natural elements.

In no way do I wish to imply that (a) any of these findings are universally accurate, or (b) all health care should be based on them. What is important to note about these studies is that they do give, in part, some understanding as to *why* there may be two (or more) conflicting viewpoints between provider and consumer regarding a diagnosis and treatment regimen.

Statements about the health practices of chosen ethnic communities are based not only on the existing literature, as noted, but also on:

1. Data collected from surveys of students, including ethnic students of color, over a five-year period
2. Information shared by guest lecturers who are both health-care providers and members of the communities under discussion
3. Data collected from the author's interviews with health-care consumers and providers over a period of 15 years
4. Intense research in both community-based consumer groups and provider groups

REFERENCES

1. U.S. Department of Commerce, Bureau of the Census, *1980 Census of Population: Detailed Population Characteristics* (Washington, D.C.: Government Printing Office, 1981), p. 1–47.
2. Ibid., pp. 1–505 and 1–549.
3. U.S. Department of Commerce, Bureau of the Census, *1980 Census of the Population: Population Profile of the United States: 1981* (Washington, D.C.: Government Printing Office, 1982), p. 20.
4. U.S., Bureau of the Census, *Detailed Population Characteristics*, p. 1–49.
5. Ibid., pp. 1–505 and 1–557.
6. Ibid., p. 1–45.
7. Ibid., pp. 1–505 and 1–553.
8. Ibid., p. 1–47.
9. Ibid., pp. 1–505 and 1–555.
10. U.S., Department of Commerce, Bureau of the Census, *1980 Census of the Population: Ancestry of the Population by State: 1980* (Washington, D.C.: Government Printing Office, 1983), p. 3.
11. U.S., Bureau of the Census, *Detailed Population Characteristics*, p. 1–51.
12. Ibid., pp. 1–505 and 1–559.
13. Ibid., p. 1–43.
14. Ibid., pp. 1–505 and 1–551
15. U.S. Department of Justice, Immigration and Naturalization Service, *1981 Statistical Yearbook: Advance Copy*. Statistical Analysis Branch, July, 1984.
16. Luis B. Steizner. "Precis of Wayne Cornelius's 'Mexican Migration to the United States: Causes, Consequences, and United States Responses,' " in Robert S. Landmann, ed., *The Problem of the Undocumented Worker*. Albuquerque, N.Mex.: Latin American Institute, University of New Mexico, 1981, p. 15.
17. Ibid., p. 15.

CHAPTER 7

Health and Illness in the Asian-American Community

The members of the Asian-American community have their origins in China, Hawaii, the Philippines, Korea, and Japan. This chapter will focus on the traditional health and illness beliefs and practices of the Chinese-Americans because those of other Asians derive in part from the Chinese.

BACKGROUND

The Chinese immigration to the United States began over 100 years ago. In 1850, there were only 1,000 Chinese inhabitants in this country; in 1880, there were well over 100,000. This rapid increase arose in part from the discovery of gold in California and in part from the need for cheap labor to build transcontinental railroads: these immigrants were laborers who met the needs of the dominant society. Like many early immigrant groups, they came here intending only to stay as temporary workers. Mainly men came. They clung closely to their customs and beliefs and stayed together in their own communities. The hopes they had for a better life when they came to the United States did not materialize. Subsequently, many of the workers and their kin returned to China before 1930. Part of the disharmony and disenchantment occurred because these immigrants were not white and did not have the same culture and habits as whites. For these reasons, they were not welcomed, and many jobs were not open to them. For example, Chinese immigrant workers were excluded from many mining, construction, and other hard-labor jobs even though the transcontinental railroad was constructed mainly by Chinese laborers. Between 1880 and 1930, the Chinese population declined by nearly 20 percent. Another factor that added to and helped perpetuate this decline in population was a series of exclusion acts that halted further immigration. The people who remained behind were relegated to menial jobs such as cooking and dishwashing. The Chinese workers first took these jobs in the West, and later they moved eastward throughout the United States. They tended to move to cities where they were allowed to let their entrepreneurial talents surface—their main pursuits included running small laundries, food shops, and restaurants.

The people settled in tightly knit groups in urban neighborhoods that took the name "Chinatown." Here they were able to maintain the ancient traditions of their homeland. They were hard workers and, in spite of the dull, menial jobs that were usually available to them, they were able to survive.

Both immigration laws of the United States and political problems in China had an effect on the nature of today's Chinese population. When the exclusion acts were passed, many men were left alone in this country without the possibility of their families joining them. For this reason, a great majority of the men spent many years alone. In addition, the political oppression experienced by the Chinese in the United States was compounded when, at a time immigration laws were relaxed here after World War II, people were unable to return to or leave China because of that country's restrictive new regulations. By 1965, however, a large number of refugees who had relatives here were able to come to this country. They settled in the Chinatowns of America, causing the population of these areas to swell: the rate of increase since 1965 has been 10 percent per year.

One outstanding problem being faced in the nation's Chinatowns is that of elderly men who are sick and alone. Men have always outnumbered women in Chinatown because, as stated earlier, so many of them came to the United States without their families and then were unable to send for them.[1]

TRADITIONAL DEFINITIONS OF HEALTH AND ILLNESS

Chinese medicine teaches that health is a state of spiritual and physical harmony with nature. In ancient China, the task of the physician was to prevent illness. A first-class physician was one who not only cured an illness but could also prevent disease from occurring. A second-class physician had to wait for his patients to become ill so that he could then treat them. The physician was paid by the patient while he was healthy; when illness occurred, payments stopped. Indeed, the physician not only was not paid for his services when the patient became ill, but he also had to provide and pay for the needed medicine.[2]

In order to understand the Chinese philosophy of health and illness, it is necessary to look back at the age-old philosophies from which more current ideas have evolved. The foundation rests in the religion and philosophy of Taoism. Taoism originated with a man named Lao-Tzu, who is believed to have been born about 604 B.C. The word *Tao* has several meanings: way, path, or discourse. On the spiritual level, it is the way of ultimate reality. It is the way of all nature, the primeval law that regulates all heavenly and earthly matters. In order to live according to the Tao, one must adapt oneself to the order of nature. Chinese medical works revere the ancient sages who knew the way and "led their lives in *Tao.*"[3]

The Chinese view the universe as a vast, indivisible entity; each being has a definite function within it. No one thing can exist without the existence of the others. Each is linked in a chain that consists of concepts related to each other in harmonious balance. Violating this harmony is like hurling chaos, wars, and catastrophies upon humankind—the end result of which is illness. Individuals must adjust themselves wholly within the environment. Five elements—wood, fire, earth, metal, and water—constitute the guiding principles of humankind's surroundings. These elements can both create and destroy each other. For example, "wood creates fire," "two pieces of wood rubbed together produce a spark," "wood destroys earth," "the tree sucks strength from the earth." The guiding principles arise from this "correspondences" theory[4] of the cosmos.

For a person to remain healthy, his actions must conform to the mobile cycle of the correspondences. The exact directions for achieving this were written in such works as the *Lu Chih Ch'un Ch'iu* (Spring and Autumn Annals) written by Lu Pu Wei, who died circa 230 B.C.

Four thousand years before William Harvey described the circulatory system in 1628, *Huang-ti Nei Ching* (Yellow Emperor's Book of Internal Medicine) was written. This is the first known volume that describes the circulation of blood. It described the oxygen-carrying powers of blood and defined the two basic world principles: yin and yang, powers that regulate the universe. Yang represents the male, positive energy that produces light, warmth, and fullness. Yin represents the female, negative energy—the force of darkness, cold, and emptiness. Yin and yang exert power not only over the universe but also over human beings.

The various parts of the human body correspond to the dualistic principles of yin and yang. The inside of the body is yin; the surface of the body is yang. The front part of the body is yin; the back is yang. The five *ts'ang* viscera—liver, heart, spleen, lungs, and kidney—are yin; the six *fu* structures—gallbladder, stomach, large intestine, small intestine, bladder, and "warmer"—are yang. (The "warmer" is now believed to be the lymph system.) The diseases of winter and spring are yin; those of summer and fall are yang. The pulses are controlled by yin and yang. If yin is too strong, the person is nervous and apprehensive and catches colds easily. If the individual does not balance his yin and yang properly, his life will be short. Half of the yin forces will be depleted by age 40; at 40 the body will be sluggish, and at 60 the yin will be totally depleted, at which time the body will deteriorate. Yin stores the vital strength of life. Yang protects the body from outside forces, and it too must be carefully maintained. If yang is not cared for, the viscera will be thrown into disorder and circulation will cease. Yin and yang cannot be injured by evil influences. When yin and yang are sound, the person is living in peaceful interaction with his mind and body in proper order.[5]

Chinese medicine has a long history. The Emperor Shen Nung, who died in 2697 B.C., was known as the patron god of agriculture. He was given this title because of the 70 experiments he performed on himself by swallowing a different plant every day and studying the effects. During this period of self-experimentation, Nung discovered many poisonous herbs and rendered them harmless by the use of antidotes, which he also discovered. His patron element was fire, for which he was also known as the Red Emperor. The Emperor Shen Nung was followed by Huang-ti, whose patron element was earth. Huang-ti was known as the Yellow Emperor and ruled from 2697 B.C. to 2595 B.C. The greater part of his life was devoted to the study of medicine. Many people ascribe to him the recording of the *Nei Ching*, the book that embraces the entire realm of Chinese medical knowledge. The treatments described in the *Nei Ching*—which became characteristic of Chinese medical practice—are almost totally aimed at reestablishing balances that are lost within the body when illness occurs. Disrupted harmonies are regarded as the sole cause of disease. Surgery was rarely resorted to; when it was, it was used primarily to remove malignant tumors. The *Nei Ching* is a dialogue between Huang-ti and his minister, Ch'i Po. It begins with the concept of the Tao and the cosmologic patterns of the universe and goes on to describe the powers of the yin and yang. This learned treatise discusses in great detail the therapy of the pulses and how a diagnosis can be made on the basis of alterations in the pulse beat. It also describes various kinds of fevers and the use of acupuncture.[6]

The Chinese view their bodies as a gift given to them by their parents and forebearers. A person's body is not his personal property. It must be cared for and well maintained. Confucius taught that "only those shall be truly revered who at the end of their lives will return their physical bodies whole and sound."

The body is composed of five solid organs *(ts'ang)*, which collect and store secretions, and five hollow organs *(fu)*, which excrete. The heart and liver are regarded as the noble organs. The head is the storage chamber for knowledge, the back is the home of the chest, the loins store the kidneys, the knees store the muscles, and the bones store the marrow.

The Chinese view the functions of the various organs as comparable to the functions of persons in positions of power and responsibility in the government. For example, the heart is the ruler over all other civil servants, the lungs are the administrators, the liver is the general who initiates all the strategic actions, and the gallbladder is the decision maker.

The organs have a complex relationship that maintains the balance and harmony of the body. Each organ is associated with a color. For example, the heart—which works in accordance with the pulse, controls the kidneys, and harmonizes with bitter flavors—is red. In addition, the organs have what is referred to as an "aura," the meaning of which, in the medical context, is health. The aura is determined by the color of the organ. In the balanced, healthy body, the colors look fresh and shiny.[7]

Disease is caused by an upset in the balance of yin and yang. The weather, too, has an effect on the body's balance and the body's relationship to yin and yang. For example, heat can be injurious to the heart, and cold is injurious to the lungs. Overexertion is also harmful to the body. Prolonged sitting is harmful to the flesh and spine, and prolonged lying in bed can be harmful to the lungs.

Disease is diagnosed by the Chinese physician through inspection and palpation. During inspection, the Chinese physician looks at the tongue (glossoscopy), listens and smells (osphretics), and asks questions (anamnesis); during palpation, the physician feels the pulses (sphygmopalpation).

The Chinese believe there are many different pulse types, which are all grouped together and must be felt with the three middle fingers. The pulse is considered the storehouse of the blood, and a person with a strong, regular pulse is considered to be in good health. By the nature of the pulse, the physician is able to determine various illnesses. For example, if the pulse is weak and skips beats, the person may have a cardiac problem. If the pulse is too strong the person's body is distended.[8]

There are six different pulses, three in each hand. Each pulse is specifically related to various organs, and each pulse has its own characteristics. According to ancient Chinese sources, there are 15 ways of characterizing the pulses. Each of these descriptions accurately determines the diagnosis. There are seven *piao* pulses (superficial) and eight *li* pulses (sunken). An example of an illness that manifests with a *piao* pulse is headache; anxiety manifests with a *li* pulse. The pulses also take on a specific nature with various conditions; for example, specific pulses are associated with epilepsy, pregnancy, and the time just before death.[9]

The Chinese physician is also aided in making a diagnosis by the appearance of the patient's tongue. There are more than 100 conditions that can be determined by glossoscopic examination. The color of the tongue and the part of the tongue that does not appear normal are the essential clues to the diagnosis.[10]

Breast cancer has been known to the Chinese since early times: "The disease begins with a knot in the breast, the size of a bean, and gradually swells to the size of an egg. After seven or eight months it perforates. When it has perforated, it is very difficult to cure.''[11]

TRADITONAL METHODS OF HEALING

Traditional Healers

The physician was the primary healer in Chinese medicine. Physicians who had to treat women encountered numerous difficulties because men were not allowed to touch women directly. Thus a diagnosis might be made through a ribbon that was attached to the woman's wrist. As an alternative to demonstrating areas of pain or discomfort on a woman's body, an alabaster figurine was substituted. The area of pain was then pointed out on the figurine.[12]

Not much is known about women doctors except that they did exist. Women were known to possess a large store of medical talent. There were also midwives and female shamans. The female shamans possessed gifts of prophecy; they danced themselves into ecstatic trances and had a profound effect on the people around them. As the knowledge that these women possessed was neither known nor understood by the general population, they were feared rather than respected. They were said to know all there was to know about life, death, and birth.[13]

Chinese Pediatrics

Babies are breast-fed because neither cows' milk nor goats' milk is acceptable to the Chinese. Sometimes babies are nursed for as long as four or five years.

Since early times the Chinese have known about and practiced immunization against smallpox. A child was inoculated with the live virus from the crust of a pustule from a smallpox victim. The crust was ground into a powder, and this powder was subsequently blown into the nose of the healthy child through the lumen of a small tube. If the child was healthy, he did not generally develop a full-blown case of smallpox but instead acquired immunity to this dreaded disease.[14]

Acupuncture

Acupuncture is an ancient Chinese practice of puncturing the body to cure disease or relieve pain. The body is punctured with special metal needles at points that are precisely predetermined for the treatment of specific symptoms. According to one source, the earliest use of this method was recorded between 106 B.C. and 220 A.D.; however, according to other sources, it was used earlier than this time. This treatment modality stems from diagnostic procedures described earlier. The most important aspect of the practice of acupuncture is the acquired skill and ability to know precisely where to puncture the skin. Nine needles are used in acupuncture, each with a specific purpose. The following is a list of the needles and their purposes:[15]

- Superficial pricking: arrowhead needle
- Massaging: round needle
- Knocking or pressing: blunt needle
- Venous pricking: sharp three-edged needle
- Evacuating pus: swordlike needle
- Rapid pricking: sharp, round needle
- Puncturing thick muscle: sharp, round needle
- Puncturing thick muscle: long needle
- Treating arthritis: large needle
- Most extensively used: filiform needle

The specific points of the body into which the needles are inserted are known as meridians. Acupuncture is based on the concept that certain meridians extend internally throughout the body in a fixed network. There are 365 points on the skin where these lines emerge. As all of the networks merge and have their outlets on the skin, the way to treat internal problems is to puncture the meridians, which are also categorically identified in terms of yin and yang, as are the diseases. The treatment goal is to restore the balance of yin and yang.[16] The practice of this art is far too complex to explain in greater detail in these pages; there is a suggested reading list included in the Bibliography.

Readers may find it interesting to visit acupuncture clinics in their area. After the therapist carefully explains the art and science of acupuncture, one may be able to grasp the fundamental concepts of this ancient treatment. The practice of acupuncture is based in antiquity, yet it took a long time for it to be accepted as a legitimate method of healing by practitioners of the Western medical system. Currently, there are numerous acupuncture clinics that attract a fair number of non-Asians, and acupuncture is being used as a method of anesthesia in some hospitals.

Moxibustion

Moxibustion has been practiced for as long a time as acupuncture. Its purpose, too, is to restore the proper balance of yin and yang. Moxibustion is based on the therapeutic value of heat, whereas acupuncture is a cold treatment. Acupuncture is used mainly in diseases in which there is an excess of yang, and moxibustion is used in diseases in which there is an excess of yin. Moxibustion is performed by heating pulverized wormwood and applying this concoction directly to the skin over certain specific meridians. Great caution must be used in this application because it cannot be applied to all the meridians that are used for acupuncture. Moxibustion is believed to be most useful during the period of labor and delivery, if applied properly.[17]

There are additional ancient forms of treatment, such as local and widespread body massage and special exercises performed to prolong life.

Herbal Remedies

Medicinal herbs were widely used in the practice of ancient Chinese healing. Many of these herbs are available and in use today.

Herbalogy is an interesting subject. The gathering season of an herb was important for its effect. It was believed that some herbs were better if gathered at night and that others were more effective if gathered at dawn. The ancient sages understood quite well the dynamics of growth: it is known today that a plant may not be effective if the dew has been allowed to dry on its leaves.[18] The herbalist believes that the ginseng root must be harvested only at midnight in a full moon if it is to have therapeutic value. Ginseng's therapeutic value is due to its nonspecific action. The herb, which is derived from the root of a plant that resembles a man,* is recommended for use in more than two dozen ailments including anemia, colics, depression, indigestion, impotence, and rheumatism.[19] It has maintained its reputation for centuries and continues to be a highly valued and widely used substance.

To release all the therapeutic properties of ginseng and to prepare it properly are of paramount importance. Ginseng must not be prepared in anything made of metal because it is believed that some of the necessary constituents are leeched out by the action of the metal. It must be stored in crockery. It is boiled in water until only a sediment remains. This sediment is pressed into a crock and stored. Some of the specific uses of ginseng follow.

- *To stimulate digestion*
  Rub ginseng to a powder, mix with the white of an egg, and take three times per day.
- *As a sedative*
  Prepare a light broth of ginseng and bamboo leaves.
- *For faintness after childbirth*
  Administer a strong brew of ginseng several times a day.
- *As a restorative for frail children*
  Give a dash of raw, minced ginseng several times per day.[20]

---

*Early Chinese healers believed that if the name of a plant resembled the disease in question, the plant would be effective in the treatment of the disease.

There are many Chinese medicinal herbs, but none is so famous as ginseng.

I had the opportunity to visit, with one of my Asian-American students, an import-export store in Boston's Chinatown where they sell Chinese herbs—if one has the proper prescriptions. The front of the store is a gift shop that attracts tourists. A room in the back is separated from the rest of the store. We were allowed to enter this room when the student explained to the proprietor, in Chinese, that I was her teacher and that she had brought me to the store to purchase herbs. We stayed there for quite a long time, observing the people who came in with prescriptions. The man carefully weighed different herbs, mixed them together, and dispensed them. We asked to purchase some of the herbs that he took from the drawers lining the entire wall behind him. He refused to sell us anything except some of the preparations that were on the counter because a prescription was necessary to purchase any of the herbal compounds that he prepared. Undaunted, we purchased a wide variety of herbs that could be used for indigestion, in addition to ointments and liniments used for sore muscles and sprains.

In addition to herbs and plants, the Chinese used other products with medicinal and healing properties. Some of these products were also used in ancient Europe and are still used today. For example, in China, boys' urine was used to cure lung diseases, soothe inflamed throats, and dissolve blood clots in pregnant women. In Europe it was used during the two world wars as emergency treatment for open wounds. Urea is still used today as a treatment that promotes the healing of wounds. Other popular Chinese remedies include the following:[21]

- *Deer antlers*
  Used to strengthen bones, increase a man's potency, and dispel nightmares
- *Lime calcium*
  Used to clear excessive mucus
- *Quicksilver*
  Used externally to treat venereal diseases
- *Rhinoceros horns*
  Highly effective when applied to pus boils; an antitoxin for snakebites
- *Turtle shells*
  Used to stimulate weak kidneys and to remove gallstones
- *Snake flesh*
  Eaten as a delicacy to keep eyes healthy and vision clear
- *Seahorses*
  Pulverized and used to treat gout

CURRENT HEALTH PROBLEMS

The residents of Chinatowns today experience all the socioeconomic and other problems faced by groups who are victims of poverty and poor living conditions. The overall death rates for both men and women are higher than those of their white counterparts. Tuberculosis, although eradicated from the majority population, still leaves its mark on the Chinese, whose living conditions continue to be crowded. It has been reported that many ill and disabled Chinese return to China to die; figures may even be low with respect to the overall morbidity and mortality rates.[22]

Poor health is found among the residents of Chinatowns partly because of poor working conditions. Many people work long hours in restaurants and laundries and receive the lowest possible wages for their hard work. Many cannot afford even minimal, let along preventive, health care.[23]

Language difficulties and adherence to native Chinese culture compound problems already associated with poverty, crowding, and poor health. Many people still prefer the traditional forms of Chinese medicine and seek help from Chinatown "physicians" who treat them with traditional herbs and other methods. Often they do not seek help from the Western system at all. Others use Chinese methods in conjunction with Western methods of health care, although the Chinese find many aspects of Western medicine distasteful. For example, they cannot understand why so many diagnostic tests, some of which are painful, are necessary. However, they accept the practice of immunization and the use of x-rays.

They are most upset by the practice of drawing blood. Often, numerous blood tests are done, and the Chinese people cannot understand why they are necessary. Blood is seen as the source of life for the entire body, and they believe that it is not regenerated. The Chinese people also believe that a good physician should be able to make a diagnosis simply be examining a person; consequently, they do not react well to the often-painful procedures used in diagnostic workups. Some people—because of their distaste for this procedure—leave the Western system rather than tolerate the pain. The Chinese have deep respect for their bodies and believe that it is best to die with their bodies intact. For this reason, many people refuse surgery or consent to it only under the most dire circumstances.[24] This reluctance to undergo intrusive surgical procedures has deep implications for those concerned with providing health care to Asian Americans. Even their reluctance to have blood drawn for diagnostic tests may have its roots in the revered teachings of Confucius.

The hospital is an alien place to the Chinese. Not only are the customs and practices strange, but the patients are often isolated from the rest of their people, which enhances the language barrier and feelings of helplessness. Something as basic as food creates another problem. Hospital food is strange and is served in an unfamiliar manner. The typical Chinese patient rarely complains about what bothers him. Often the only indication that there may be a problem is an untouched food tray and the silent withdrawal of the patient. Unfortunately, the silence may be regarded by the nurses as reflecting good, complacent behavior, and the health-care team exerts little energy to go beyond that assumption. The Chinese patient who says little and complies with all treatment is seen as stoic, and there is little awareness that deep problems may underly this "exemplary" behavior. Ignorance on the part of health-care workers may cause the patient a great deal of suffering.

Much action has been taken in recent years to make Western health care more available and appealing to the Chinese. In Boston, for example, there is a health clinic staffed primarily by Chinese-speaking nurses and physicians who work as paid employees and as volunteers. Most of the common health-related pamphlets have been translated into Chinese and are distributed to the patients. Booklets on such topics as breast self-examination and how to quit smoking are available. Since the language spoken in the clinic is Chinese, the problem of interpreters has been eliminated. The care is personal, and the clients are made to feel comfortable. Unnecessary and painful tests are avoided as much as possible. In addition, the clinic, which is open for long hours, provides social services and employment placements and is quite popular with the community. Although it began as a part-time, store-front operation, the clinic is now housed in its own building.[25]

ASIAN-AMERICAN HEALTH MANPOWER

In most areas of health manpower, except nursing, there is a fairly significant number of people representing the Asian-American community: 1.5 percent of physicians, 2.2 percent of dentists, and 3.8 percent of optometrists are Asian-Americans. In the nursing profession, the percentage is quite low, with only a small number of Asian-American nurses.[26] Today, a person who desires to be a physician in China has the option of studying either Chinese or Western medicine. If he selects Western medicine, he is also taught a limited amount of Chinese medicine. As Chinese traditional medicine is becoming better recognized and better understood in the United States, more doors are being opened to those who prefer or understand this mode of treatment.

REFERENCES

1. Frederick P. Li et al., "Health Care for the Chinese Community in Boston," *American Journal of Public Health,* April 1972, pp. 536–37.
2. Felix Mann, *Acupuncture* (New York: Vintage Books, 1972), p. 222.

3. Houston Smith, *The Religions of Man* (New York: Harper and Row, 1958), pp. 175–92.
4. Heinrich Wallnöfer and Anna von Rottauscher, *Chinese Folk Medicine,* trans. Marion Palmedo (New York: American Library, 1972), pp. 12–16; 19–21.
5. Ibid.
6. Ibid., pp. 26–28.
7. Ibid., pp. 79–81.
8. Ibid., pp. 97–109.
9. Ibid., p. 99.
10. Ibid., p. 109.
11. Ibid., p. 115.
12. Josephine Dolan, *Nursing in Society: A Historical Perspective* (Philadelphia: Saunders, 1973), p. 30.
13. Wallnöfer and Von Rottauscher, *Chinese Folk Medicine,* pp. 39–40.
14. Ibid., p. 119.
15. Ibid., p. 126.
16. Ibid., pp. 127–28.
17. Ibid., pp. 135–38.
18. Ibid., p. 43.
19. Ibid., pp. 42–43.
20. Ibid., pp. 44–47.
21. Ibid., p. 71.
22. Li et al., "Health Care" p. 537.
23. Ibid., p. 538.
24. Ibid.
25. Ibid., p. 539.
26. William H. MacBeath et al., "Minority Chart Health Book" (Paper presented at the 102nd Annual Meeting, American Public Health Association, New Orleans, 20–24 October 1974), pp. 86–89.

BIBLIOGRAPHY

Leong, Lucille. *Acupuncture: A Layman's View.* New York: Signet, 1974.
   Acupuncture is, above all, preventive medicine, and the patient is treated as a whole—body, mind, and spirit being inseparable. There is a precept that applies to acupuncture as well as to all Chinese healing. The acupuncturist admonishes: "Curing is not so good as preventing, and preventing is not so good as taking care of oneself." Physicians are paid to keep people healthy; when clients fall ill, they stop payment.
Mann, Felix. *Acupuncture: The Ancient Chinese Art of Healing and How it Works Scientifically.* New York: Vintage Books, 1972.
   This general book discusses the theories of acupuncture, the acupuncture points, the meridians, yin and yang, various diagnostic and therapeutic techniques, and preventive medicine.
Palos, Stephan. *The Chinese Art of Healing.* New York: Herter and Herter, 1971.
   Palos includes a history of the Chinese art of healing; a discussion of man and nature, yin and yang; and a description of the human body in ancient Chinese thought. The traditional methods of treatment discussed are acupuncture, moxibustion, remedial massage, and physiotherapy.

Shih-Chen, Li. *Chinese Medicinal Herbs*. Translated by F. Porter Smith and G. A. Stuart. San Francisco: Georgetown Press, 1973.
   Containing an alphabetical listing of numerous Chinese herbs, this book discusses the history and use of each herb. It also includes a glossary of terms. Excellent reference.

Wei-Kang, Fu. *The Story of Chinese Acupuncture and Moxibustion*. Peking: Foreign Languages Press, 1975.
   A booklet that vividly and precisely describes ancient Chinese medical techniques, this work also describes today's search in China for breakthroughs in medical science.

Wollnöfer, Heinrich, and Von Rottauscher, Anna. *Chinese Folk Medicine*. Translated by Marion Palmedo. New York: American Library, 1972.
   This book discusses many treatments and alleged cures that were used in China for centuries. It describes the fundamentals of Chinese medicine and evaluates its approach to anatomy, physiology, and pathology.

FURTHER SUGGESTED READINGS

BOOKS

Academy of Traditional Chinese Medicine. *An Outline of Chinese Acupuncture*. Peking: Foreign Languages Press, 1975.

Burang, Theodore. *The Tibetan Art of Healing*. London: Watkins, 1974.

Dolan, Josephine. *Nursing in Society: A Historical Perspective*. Philadelphia: Saunders, 1973.

Duke, M. *Acupuncture*. New York: Pyramid, 1972.

Kitano, Harry. *Japanese Americans*. Englewood Cliffs, N.J.: Prentice-Hall, 1969.

Kleinman, Arthur; Kunstader, Peter; Alexander, E. Russel; and Gale, James L., editors. *Medicine in Chinese Cultures*. Washington, D.C.: Fogarty International Center, 1975.

Kroening, R. J., and Bresler, D. E. *Acupuncture for Management of Facial and Dental Pain*. Beverly Hills: Center for Integral Medicine, 1972.

Kung, S. W. *Chinese in American Life*. Seattle: University of Washington Press, 1962.

Leslie, Charles, ed. *Asian Medical Systems*. Los Angeles and Berkeley: University of California Press, 1976.

Lieban, Richard W. *Cebuano Sorcery*. Berkeley: University of California Press, 1967.

Lyman, Stanford M. *Chinese Americans*. New York: Random House, 1974.

Palos, S. *The Chinese Art of Healing*. New York: Herter & Herter, 1971.

Peterson, William. *Japanese Americans*. New York: Random House, 1971.

Porkert, Manfred. *The Theoretical Foundations of Chinese Medicine*. Cambridge: MIT Press, 1974.

Rechung, Rinpoche. *Tibetan Medicine*. Los Angeles and Berkeley: University of California Press, 1973.

Silverstein, Martin Elliot; Chang, I-Lok; and Macon, Nathaniel, trans. *Acupuncture and Moxibustion*. New York: Schocken Books, 1975.

Smith, Houston. *The Religions of Man*. New York: Harper and Row, 1958.

Sue, Stanley, and Wagner, Nathaniel. *Asian Americans: Psychological Perspectives*. Palo Alto, Calif.: Science and Behavioral Books, 1973.

U.S., Department of Commerce, Bureau of the Census. *The Asian Americans.* Washington, D.C.: Government Printing Office, 1973.
Veith, Ilza. *The Yellow Emperor's Classic of Internal Medicine.* Los Angeles and Berkeley: University of California Press, 1972.

Numerous books are available in the area of Chinese medicine. For further information and a complete list of literature, I suggest writing to China Books and Periodicals, 125 Fifth Avenue, New York, New York 10003.

ARTICLES

Armstrong, M. E. "Acupuncture." *American Journal of Nursing* 72 (September 1972): 1582–88.
Bersi, Robert M. "In Search of Identity: Asians in America." Report of Activities, Asian American Research Project, California State College, Dominquez Hills, 1971.
Bourne, Peter G. "Suicide among Chinese in San Francisco." *American Journal of Public Health* 63, no. 8 (August 1973): 744–50.
Campbell, Teresa, and Chang, Betty. "Health Care of the Chinese in America." *Nursing Outlook* 21 (April 1973): 245–49.
Caringer, Beatrice. "Caring for the Institutionalized Filipino." *Journal of Gerontological Nursing* 3, no. 5 (September-October 1977): 33–37.
Chinn, Catherine Natsuko. "How Orientals Deal with Stress." *Washington State Journal of Nursing,* Winter 1977, p. 6.
Chung, Hyo Jin. "Understanding the Oriental Maternity Patient." *Nursing Clinics of North America* 12 (March 1977): 67–75.
Connelly, Dianne. "The Art of Acupuncture." *Social Policy,* May/June 1974, pp. 50–56.
DeGarcia, Rosario T. "Cultural Influences on Filipino Patients." *American Journal of Nursing,* August 1979, pp. 1412–14.
Ellis, Donelda, and Mayeeta S.L. Ho. "Attitudes of Chinese Women Towards Sexuality and Birth Control." *Canadian Nurse,* March 1982, pp. 28–31.
Kim, Bok-Him C. "Asian Americans: No Model Minority." *Social Work,* May 1973, pp. 44–53.
Li, Frederick P.; Schlief, Nyuk Yoong; Chang, Caroline J.; and Gaw, Albert G. "Health Care for the Chinese Community in Boston." *American Journal of Public Health* 62 (April 1972): 536–39.
McKenzie, Joan L., and Noel J. Chrisman. "Healing Herbs, Gods, and Magic." *Nursing Outlook* 25, no. 5 (May 1977): 326–29.
Parreno, Sister Heide. "How Philipinos Deal With Stress." *Washington State Journal of Nursing,* Winter 1977, pp. 3–5.
Tao-Kim-Hai, Andre M. "Orientals Are Stoic." In *Social Interaction and Patient Care,* edited by James K. Skipper, Jr., and Robert C. Leonard. Philadelphia: Lippincott, 1965, pp. 143–53.
Williamson, Deborah, and Foster, Joyce Cameron. "American Childbirth Educators in China: A Transcultural Exchange." *Journal of Nurse-Midwifery* 27, no. 5 (September/October 1982): 15–22.

CHAPTER 8

Health and Illness in the Black-American Community

Members of the black community have their origins in Africa; the majority were brought here as slaves from the west coast of Africa.[1] The largest importation of slaves occurred during the seventeenth century. Today, there are a number of blacks who have immigrated to the United States voluntarily—from African countries, the West Indian islands, the Dominican Republic, Haiti, and Jamaica. The majority of the people in this community, however, are the descendants of slaves.

BACKGROUND

According to some sources the first black people to enter this country arrived a year earlier than the Pilgrims, in 1619; other sources claim that blacks arrived with Columbus in the fifteenth century.[2] In any event, the first blacks who came to the North American continent did not come as slaves. Between 1619 and 1860 more than 4 million people were transported here to be indentured as slaves. One need only read a sampling of the many accounts of slavery to appreciate the tremendous hardships that the captured and enslaved people experienced during that time. Not only was the daily life of the slave very difficult, but the experience of being captured, shackled, and transported in steerage was devastating. Many of those captured in Africa died before they arrived here. According to reliable accounts, the strongest and healthiest people were snatched from their homes by slave dealers

The author especially acknowledges those students who, over several years, have provided much of the data for this chapter.

and transported *en masse* in the holds of ships to the North American continent. In general, the people were not cared for, nor were they recognized as human beings and treated accordingly. Once here, they were sold and placed on plantations and in homes all over the country—it was only later that the practice was confined to the South. Families were separated; children were wrenched from their parents and sold to other buyers. Some slave owners engaged in breeding: men were purchased to serve as breeders, and women were judged as to whether they should be mated with a particular man.[3] Yet, in the midst of all this inhuman and inhumane treatment, the black family grew and survived. Gutman[4] traces the history of the black family from 1750 to 1925. His careful documentation of plantation and family records points out the existence of families and family or kinship ties before and after the Civil War, dispelling many of the myths about the black family and its structure. Despite overwhelming hardships and enforced separations, the people managed in most circumstances to maintain both a family and community awareness.

Ostensibly, the Civil War ended slavery, but in many ways, it did not emancipate blacks. Daily life after the war was fraught with tremendous difficulty, and black people—according to custom—were stripped of their civil rights. In the South the people were overtly segregated, and most lived in conditions of extreme hardship and poverty. Those who migrated to the North over the years were subject to all the problems of fragmented urban life: poverty, racism, and covert segregation.[5]

The historic problems of the black community need to be appreciated by the health-care provider who wants to juxtapose modern practices and traditional health and illness beliefs.

TRADITIONAL DEFINITIONS OF HEALTH AND ILLNESS

The traditional definition of health stems from the African belief about life and the nature of being. To the African, life was a process rather than a state. The nature of a person was viewed in terms of energy force rather than matter. All things, whether living or dead, were believed to influence each other. Therefore, one had the power to influence one's destiny and that of others through the use of *behavior*, whether proper or otherwise, as well as through *knowledge* of the person and the world. When one possessed health, one was in harmony with nature; illness was a state of disharmony. Traditional black belief regarding health did not separate the mind, body, and spirit.[6]

Disharmony—therefore, illness—was attributed to a number of sources, primarily demons and evil spirits. These spirits were generally believed to act on their own accord, and the goal of treatment was to remove them from the body of the ill person. Several methods were employed to attain this result in addition to voodoo, which is discussed in the next section. The traditional healers, usually women, possessed extensive knowledge regarding the use of herbs and roots in the treatment of illness. Apparently, an early form of smallpox immunization was used by slaves. Women practiced inoculation by scraping a piece of cowpox crust into a place on a child's arm. These children appeared to have a far lower incidence of smallpox than those who did not receive the immunization.

The old and the young were cared for by all members of the community. The elderly were held in high esteem, because the people believed that the living of a long life indicated that a person had the opportunity to acquire much wisdom and knowledge. Death was described as the passing from one realm of life to another[7]—or as a passage from the evils of this world to another state. The funeral was often celebrated as a joyous occasion, with a party after the burial. Children were passed over the body of the deceased so that the dead person could carry any potential illness of the child away with him.

Many of the preventive and treatment practices have their roots in Africa, but have been merged with the approaches of Native Americans to whom the blacks were exposed and of the whites among whom they lived and served. Then as today, illness was treated in a combination of ways. Methods found to be most useful were handed down through the generations.

TRADITIONAL METHODS OF HEALING

Voodoo

Voodoo involves a belief system often alluded to but rarely described in any detail. At various times, patients may mention terms such as "fix," "hex," or "spell." It is not clear whether voodoo is *fully* practiced today, but there is some evidence in the literature that there are people who still believe and practice it to some extent.[8] It has also been reported that many people continue to fear voodoo and believe that when they become ill they have been "fixed." There are two forms of magic involved: white magic is described as harmless, whereas black magic is quite dangerous. Belief in magic is, of course, ancient.[9]

Voodoo came to this country well over 200 years ago—about 1724, with the arrival of slaves from the West African coast. The people who brought it with them were "snake worshippers." They were initially sold in the West Indies. *Vodu,* the name of their god, became with the passage of time voodoo (also *hoodoo*), an all-embracing term that included the god, the sect, the members of the sect, the priests and priestesses, the rites and practices, and the teaching.[10]

The sect spread rapidly from the West Indies. In 1782, the governor of Louisiana prohibited the importation of slaves from Martinique because of their practice in voodooism. (Despite the fact that gatherings of slaves were forbidden in Louisiana, small groups practiced voodoo). In 1803, blacks were finally allowed to come to Louisiana from the West Indies, and with them came a strong influence of voodoo.[11] The practice entailed a large number of rituals and procedures. The ceremonies were held with large numbers of people, usually at night and in the open country. "Sacrifice and the drinking of blood were integral parts of all the voodoo ceremonies."[12] There were those who believed that this blood was from children; however, it was most commonly thought to be the blood of a cat or young goat. Such behavior evolved from primitive African rites, to which Christian rituals[13] were added to form the ceremonies that exist today. Leaders of the voodoo sect tended to be women, and stories abound in New Orleans about the workings of the sect and the women who ruled it— such as Marie Laveau.

In 1850, the practice of voodoo reached its height in New Orleans.[14] At that time the beliefs and practices of voodoo were closely related to beliefs about health and illness. For example, many illnesses were attributed to a "fix" that was placed on one person out of anger. *Gris-gris,* the symbols of voodoo, were used to prevent illness or to give illness to others. Some examples of commonly used *gris-gris* follow.[15]

1. Good *gris-gris.* Powders and oils that are highly and pleasantly scented. The following are examples of good *gris-gris:* love powder, colored and scented with perfume; love oil, olive oil to which gardenia perfume has been added; luck water, ordinary water that is purchased in many shades (red is for success in love, yellow for success in money matters, blue for protection and friends).
2. Bad *gris-gris.* Oils and powders that have a vile odor. The following are examples of bad *gris-gris:* anger powder, war powder, and moving powder, which are composed of soil, gunpowder, and black pepper, respectively.
3. Flying devil oil is olive oil that has red coloring and cayenne pepper added to it.
4. Black cat oil is machine oil.

In addition to these oils and powders, a variety of colored candles is used, the color of the candle symbolizing the intention. For example, white symbolizes peace; red, victory; pink, love; yellow, driving off enemies; brown, attracting money; and black, doing evil work and bringing bad luck.[16]

There are also a number of Catholic saints or relics to whom or which the practitioners of voodoo attribute special powers. There may be a prominent display of portraits of Saint Michael, who makes possible the conquest of enemies; Saint Anthony de Padua, who brings luck; Saint Mary Magdalene, who is popular with women who are in love; the Virgin Mary, whose presence in the home prevents illness; and the Sacred Heart of Jesus, which cures organic illness.[17] These *gris-gris* are available today and can be purchased in stores in many American cities.

Other Practices

Many blacks believe in the power of some person to heal and help others, and there are many reports of numerous healers among the communities. This reliance on healers reflects the deep religious faith of the people. (Maya Angelou vividly describes this phenomenon in her book, *I Know Why the Caged Bird Sings.*[18]) For example, many blacks followed the Pentecostal movement long before its present popularity; similarly, people often went to tent meetings and had an all-consuming belief in the healing powers of religion.

Another practice takes on significance when one appreciates its historical background: the eating of Argo starch. "Geophagy," or eating clay and dirt, occurred among the slaves, who brought the practice to this country from Africa. In *Roots,* Haley mentions that pregnant women were given clay because it was believed to be beneficial to both the mother and the unborn child.[19] In fact, this clay was rich in iron. When clay was not available, dirt was substituted. In more modern times, when people were no longer living on farms and no longer had access to clay and dirt, Argo starch became the substitute.[20]

> It was my fortune, or misfortune to be born into a family that practiced geophagy (earth eating) and pica (eating Argo laundry starch). Even before I became pregnant I showed an interest in eating starch. It was sweet and dry, and I could take it or leave it. After I became pregnant, I found I wanted not only starch, but bread, grits, and potatoes. I found I craved starchy substances. I stuck to starchy substances and dropped the Argo because it made me feel sluggish and heavy.*

It is believed that anemia gave rise to this practice and that in all probability the habit was both the cause and the consequence of anemia. Clay was eaten by people who were anemic, and the more of it that was eaten, the greater the anemia and the greater the craving. The practice or the habit of eating Argo starch today is a substitute for clay ingestion in the past.

Black Muslims†

Many members of the black community are practicing Muslims. Religious beliefs are an important part of the Muslim life-style, and health care providers should be familiar with them. Dietary restrictions consist of eating a strictly kosher diet, and a newly admitted patient who

---

*This experience was reported by a student, who consented that her description be included here.

†This material is adapted from a paper prepared by a student who is a practicing Muslim, and who wanted to share her beliefs. She concluded: "I hope this will help a bit in understanding a Muslim who may be a patient."

refuses to eat should be asked if he prefers to observe this diet. "Kosher" means that a practicing Muslim does not eat pork or any pork products (such as nonbeef hamburger and ham), or any "soul foods" (such as black-eyed beans, kidney beans, ham hocks, bacon, and pork chops). Muslims consider such foods to be filthy, and they are taught that a "person is what he eats."

Certain foods affect the way a person thinks and acts; therefore, one's diet should consist of food that has a clean, positive effect. Beans, such as black-eyed, kidney, and lima—are avoided because they are hard to digest and are meant for animal (not human) consumption. Muslims do not drink alcohol because they feel that it dulls the senses and causes illness.

Muslims fast for a 30-day period during September and October, at which time they consume no meat of land animals and eat only one meal per day, in the evening. Nothing is taken by mouth from 5:00 A.M. until sundown, although an ill Muslim is exempt from this rule.

The Muslim life-style is strictly regulated. According to those who have practiced the religion for many generations, this stems in part from the need for self-discipline, which many black people have not had because of living conditions associated with urban decay and family disintegration. Muslims believe in self-help and assist in uplifting each other. The Muslim life-style is not so rigid that the people do not have good times. Good times, however, are tempered with the realization that too much indulgence in sport and play can present problems.

Muslims differ from Seventh-Day Adventists and Jehovah's Witnesses. Seventh-Day Adventists do not eat pork and do not permit smoking and drinking. Jehovah's Witnesses do not believe in using another person's blood—that is, in accepting transfusions. To Muslims, however, life is precious: if they need a transfusion to live, they will accept it. Another fact of hospital life that is important to understand is the refusal of a Muslim who is diabetic to take insulin that has a pork base. If the insulin is manufactured from the pancreas of a pig it is considered unclean and will not be accepted.

Many Muslim subsects differ in practice and philosophy. The members of some sects dress in distinctive clothing—for example, the women wear long skirts and a covering on the head at all times. Other sects are less strict about dress. Some adherents do not follow the kosher diet and are allowed to smoke and drink alcoholic beverages in moderation. In some sects men practice polygamy and have a number of concubines.

CURRENT HEALTH PRACTICES

In the following paragraphs practices employed to prevent illness and then to treat various types of maladies are described. They do not encompass all of the types of care given to and by the members of the black community, but they do present a sample of the richness of the folk medicine that has survived over the years.

Prevention

Essentially, health is maintained with the proper diet—that is, eating three nutritious meals a day including a hot breakfast. Rest and a clean environment are also important. Laxatives were and are used to keep the system "running" or "open."

Asafetida—rotten flesh that looks like a dried-out sponge—is worn around the neck to prevent the contraction of contagious diseases. Cod-liver oil is taken to prevent colds. A sulfur-and-molasses preparation is used in the spring because it is believed that at the start of a new season people are more susceptible to illness. This preparation is rubbed up and down the back; it is not taken internally. A physician is not routinely consulted and he is not generally regarded as the person to whom one goes for the prevention of disease.

Copper or silver bracelets may be worn around the wrist from the time a woman is a baby or young child. These bracelets are believed to protect the wearer as she grows. If for any reason these bracelets are removed, harm will befall the owner. In addition to granting protection, these bracelets indicate when the wearer is about to become ill: the skin around the bracelet turns black, and she can then take precaution against the impending illness. These precautions consist of getting extra rest, praying more frequently, and eating a more nutritious diet.

Treatment of Illness

The most common method of treating illness is prayer. The laying on of hands is described quite frequently. Rooting, a practice derived from voodoo, is also mentioned. In rooting, a person (usually a woman) is consulted as to the source of a given illness, and she then prescribes the appropriate treatment. Magic rituals are often employed.

The following home remedies have been reported by people as being successful in the treatment of disease:

1. Sugar and turpentine are mixed together and taken by mouth to get rid of worms. This combination can be also used to cure a backache when rubbed on the skin from the navel to the back.
2. Numerous types of poultices are employed to fight infection and inflammation. The poultices are placed on the part of the body that is painful or infected, in order to draw out the cause of the affliction.

   One type of poultice is made of potatoes. The potatoes are sliced or grated and placed in a bag, which is placed on the affected area of the body. The potatoes turn black and, as this occurs, the disease goes away. It is not believed that, as these potatoes spoil, they produce a penicillin mold that is able to destroy the infectious organism. Another type of poultice is prepared from cornmeal and peach leaves that are cooked together and placed either in a bag or in a piece of flannel cloth. The cornmeal ferments and combines with an enzyme in the peach leaves. The antiseptic from the fermented cornmeal and the enzyme destroy the bacteria and hasten the healing process. A third poultice, made with onions, is used to heal infections and a flaxseed poultice is used to treat earaches.

3. Herbs from the woods are used in many ways. Herb teas are prepared—for example, from goldenrod root—to treat pain and reduce fevers. Sassafras tea is frequently used to treat colds. Other herbs that are boiled to make a tea include the root or weed of rabbit tobacco.

4. Bluestone, a mineral found in the ground, is used as medicine for open wounds. The stone is crushed into a powder and sprinkled on the affected area. It prevents inflammation and is also used to treat poison ivy.

5. To treat a "crick" in the neck, two pieces of silverware are crossed over the painful area in the form of an X.

6. Nine drops of turpentine nine days after intercourse act as a contraceptive.

7. Cuts and wounds can be treated with sour or spoiled milk that is placed on stale bread, wrapped in a cloth, and placed on the wound.

8. Salt and pork (salt pork) placed on a rag can also be used to treat cuts and wounds.

9. A sprained ankle can be treated by placing clay in a dark leaf and wrapping it around the ankle.

10. A method for treating colds is hot lemon water with honey.

11. When congestion is present in the chest and the person is coughing, he can be wrapped with warm flannel after his chest is rubbed with hot camphorated oil.

12. An expectorant for colds consists of chopped raw garlic, chopped onion, fresh parsley, and a little water, all mixed in a blender.

13. Hot toddies are used to treat colds and congestion. These drinks consist of hot tea with honey, lemon, peppermint, and a dash of brandy or whatever alcoholic beverage the person likes and is available. Vicks Vaporub is also swallowed.

14. A fever can be broken by placing raw onions on the feet and wrapping them in warm blankets.

15. Boils are treated by cracking a raw egg, peeling the white skin off the inside of the shell, and placing it on the boil. This brings the boil to a head.

16. Garlic can be placed on the ill person or in the room to remove the "evil spirits" that have caused the illness.

Folk Medicine

In the black community, folk medicine previously practiced in Africa is still employed. The methods have been tried and tested and they are still relied upon. When the people go to a healer or practice voodoo, no class or status distinctions are made. Whoever receives folk treatment is dealt with fairly and honestly. The people have faith in the practices of the healer and in other methods because they work for them and because they believe in them. In fact, the home remedies that are used by some members of the black community have been employed for many generations. Another reason for their ongoing use is that hospitals are far away from the people who live in rural areas: "By the time you would get to the hospital you would be dead." Yet many of the people who continue to use these remedies live in urban areas in close proximity to hospitals—sometimes world-renowned hospitals. Nonetheless, the use of folk medicine persists, and many people avoid the local hospital except in extreme emergencies.

CURRENT HEALTH-CARE PROBLEMS

Health Differences between Black and White Populations

Mortality. Blacks in the United States, on the average, live 6½ fewer years than whites: the life expectancy for whites is 71.1 years; for blacks, it is 65.3 years.

The black population has an excess of deaths in all age groups until the age of 75 years, with the first year of life having an extremely high death rate.

The leading causes of death for the entire United States population are cardiovascular diseases, malignant neoplasms, accidents, and influenza and pneumonia; the adjusted rates for all these causes are higher among blacks than among whites. For example, the differential for hypertension was 9.5 per 100,000 for blacks and 2.4 per 100,000 for whites. The cancer death rate was 159 per 100,000 for blacks and 127 per 100,000 for whites.

The maternal morality rate is almost four times higher for blacks than whites.[21]

Morbidity. The available data demonstrate a low utilization of health services by black and lower incidences of diseases. This is misleading, however, and can be attributed to such factors as the lack of access to the health services, low income, and a tendency to self-treat illness and to wait until symptoms are so severe that a doctor must be seen. When statistical adjustments are made for age, blacks exceed whites in the average number of days spent in bed disability and the number of days in restricted activity.

Blacks have a greater incidence of tooth decay than whites and have greater periodontial disease.[22] Blacks are twice as likely as whites to have chronic cardiovascular diseases. A disease that is a major killer of blacks is hypertension. Compared with the incidence among whites, it is twice as prevalent and kills 3 to 12 times as many people (depending on the age brackets under consideration). It occurs 7 times more often in women of any age group and 15 times more often in men between the ages of 15 and 40. Only 20 percent of the people afflicted with hypertension receive adequate treatment.[23] Other health problems of the black population include drug and alcohol abuse, mental health difficulties, with a reluctance to seek help, and malnutrition.[24]

Sickle-Cell Anemia. A genetically inherited disorder that occurs only in blacks, sickle-cell anemia causes the normal disclike red blood cell to assume a sickle shape. This causes hemolysis and thrombosis of red blood cells because these deformed cells do not flow properly through the blood vessels. The term *sickle-cell disease* is applicable in the following situations:

1. The presence of two hemoglobin-S genes (Hb SS).
2. The presence of the hemoglobin-S gene with another abnormal hemoglobin gene (Hb SC, Hb SD, etc.).
3. The presence of the hemoglobin-S gene with a different abnormality in hemoglobin synthesis.

There are people who have the sickle-cell trait (HbSS, HbSC, or others) but do not have the disease.

The clinical manifestations of sickle-cell disease include hemolysis, anemia, and states of sickle-cell crises where there is severe pain in the areas of the body where the thrombosed red cells are located. The cells also tend to clump in abdominal organs such as the liver and the spleen. Presently, statistics indicate that 50 percent of children with sickle-cell disease live to adulthood. Some children do die before the age of 20, and some do suffer complications during their lifetime that are chronic and irreversable.

It is possible to detect the sickle-cell trait in healthy adults, and to counsel people as to the risk of bearing children with the disease. However, for many people this is not an option of choice.[25]

Blacks and Health-Care Systems

To the black person, receiving health care is all too often a degrading and humiliating experience. In many settings, he continues to be viewed as someone beneath the white health-care giver. Quite often the insults are subtle and not "seen" but rather are *experienced* by the black person. The insult may be intentional or unintentional. An intentional insult is, of course, an *open* remark or mistreatment. An unintentional insult is more difficult to define. A health-care provider may not *intend* to demean a person, yet his action or his tone of voice may be interpreted as insulting. Or the provider may have some underlying fears or difficulties in relating to blacks that are covert, but the patient quite often senses the difficulty. An unintentional insult may occur because the provider is not fully aware of the client's background and is unable to comprehend many of the client's beliefs and practices. The client, for example, may be afraid of the procedures that he must undergo and the possibility of misdiagnosis or mistreatment. It is not a secret among the people of the black community that those who receive care in public clinics and hospitals—and even in clinics of private institutions—are the "material" on whom students practice and on whom medical research is done.

Some blacks fear or resent health clinics. When they have a clinic appointment they usually lose a day's work because they have to be at the clinic at an early hour and often spend many hours waiting to be seen by a physician. They often receive inadequate care, are told what their problem is in medical jargon that they cannot understand, and are not given an identity—being seen rather as a body segment ("the appendix in treatment room A"). Such people experience a tremendous feeling of powerlessness and feel alienated by the system. In some parts of the country segregation and racism are overt. There continue to be reports of hospitals that refuse admission to black patients. In one case, a black woman in labor was not admitted to a hospital because she had not "paid the bill from the last baby." There was not enough time to get her to another hospital, and she was forced to deliver in an ambulance. In light of this type of treatment, it is small wonder that people prefer to use time-tested home remedies rather than be exposed to the humiliating experiences of hospitalization.

Another reason for the ongoing use of home remedies is poverty. Indigent people cannot afford the high costs of American health care. Quite often—even with the help of Medicaid and Medicare—the "hidden costs" of acquiring health services, such as transportation and child care, are a heavy burden. As a result, blacks may stay away from clinics or out-patient departments, or receive their care with passivity while appearing to be evasive. Some black patients believe that they are being talked down to by health-care providers and that the providers fail to listen to them. They choose, consequently, to "suffer in silence." Many of the problems that blacks relate in terms of dealing with the health-care system can apply to anyone, but the inherent racism within the health system cannot be denied. Currently, efforts are being made to overcome these barriers.

Since the 1960s, the health-care services available to blacks and other people of color have improved. A growing number of community health centers have emphasized health maintenance and promotion. Community residents serve on the boards.

Many services are provided. For example, efforts are made to discover children with high blood levels of lead in order to provide early diagnosis of and treatment for lead poisoning. Once a child is found to have lead poisoning, the law requires that the source of the lead be found and eradicated. Today, only apartments free of lead paint can be rented to families with young children. Apartments that are found to have lead paint must be stripped and repainted with nonlead paint. Another ongoing effort by the community health centers is to inform blacks who are at risk of producing children with sickle-cell anemia that they are carriers of this genetic disease. This program is fraught with conflict because many people prefer not to be screened for the sickle-cell trait, fearing they may become labeled once the tendency is discovered.

Birth control is another problem that is recognized with mixed emotions. To some, especially women who want to space children or do not want to have numerous children, birth control is a welcome development. People who believe in birth control prefer selecting the time when they will have children, how many children they will have, and when they will stop having children. To many other people, birth control is considered a form of "black genocide" and a way of limiting the growth of the community. Health workers in the black community must be aware of both sides and, if asked to make a decision, remain neutral. The decision must be made by the clients themselves.

Special Considerations for Black Health Care

White health-care providers know far too little about how to care for a black person's skin, how to care for his hair, or how to understand both his nonverbal and verbal behavior.

Physiologic Assessment. Examples of possible physiologic problems include (in observing skin problems it is important to note that skin assessment is best done in indirect sunlight):

1. Pallor. There is an absence of underlying red tones; the brown-skinned person appears yellow brown and the black-skinned person appears ashen gray. Mucus membranes appear ashen, and the lips and nails beds, can be similarly observed.
2. Erythema. Inflamation must be detected by palpation; the skin is warmer in the area, tight, edematous, and the deeper tissues are hard. Fingertips must be used for this assessment, as with rashes, as they are sensitive to the feeling of different textures of skin.
3. Cyanosis. Cyanosis is difficult to observe, but it can be seen by close inspection of the lips, tongue, conjunctiva, palms of the hands, and the soles of the feet. If the palms are pressed and the blood return is slow and the color does not return to normal in a second, this is one sign. Another sign is that the lips and tongue become ashen gray.
4. Ecchymosis. History of trauma to a given area can be detected from a swelling of the skin surface.
5. Jaundice. The sclera are observed for yellow discoloration to reveal jaundice. This is not always a valid indication as caro-tene deposits in the sclera of the eye can also cause the sclera

to appear yellow. The buccal mucosa and the palms of the hands and soles of the feet may appear yellow.[26]

Skin Problems.   There are several skin conditions to be aware of, such as:

1. Keloids. Keloids are scars that form at the site of a wound and grow beyond the normal boundaries of the wound. They are sharply elevated and irregular and continue to enlarge.
2. Pigmentary Disorders. Pigmentary disorders can be postinflamatory hypopigmentation or hyperpigmentation areas that appear as dark or light spots.
3. Pseudofolliculitis. "Razor bumbs" and "ingrown hairs" are caused by shaving too closely with an electric razor or straight razor. The sharp point of the hair, if shaved too close, enters the skin and induces a foreign-body reaction. The symptoms include papules, pustules, and sometimes even keloids.
4. Melasma. The "mask of pregnancy," melasma is a patchy tan to dark brown discoloration of the face more prevalent in dark people and exclusive in pregnant women.[27]

Hair-Care Needs.   The care of the hair of blacks is not complicated, but special consideration must be given to help maintain it at its optimum.

1. The hair must be assessed as to whether it is oily, dry, or normal; whether the texture is straight or extra curly; and what is the hairstyle preference.
2. The hair must be shampooed as needed and groomed according to the person's preference.
3. Hair must be combed well, with the appropriate tools, such as a "pic" or comb with big teeth, before drying to prevent tangles.
4. If the hair is dry and needs oiling, the preparations that the person generally uses for this purpose ought to be on hand.
5. Once dry, the hair is ready to be styled (curled, braided, or rolled) as the person desires.[28]

CONSIDERATIONS FOR HEALTH-CARE PROVIDERS

The majority of the members of the health-care profession are, when they enter the profession, steeped in a middle-class value system. In clinical settings these people are being helped to become familiar with and to understand the value systems of other ethnic groups. They are being taught to recognize the symptoms of illness in blacks and to provide proper skin and hair care. The following are guidelines that a health-care provider can follow in caring for members of the black community.

1. The education of an ever-increasing number of blacks in the health professions must continue to be encouraged. Many black men and women are currently students in schools of nursing as well as in medical schools, social-work programs, dentistry, and other allied health fields.
2. The needs of the patient must be realistically assessed.
3. When a treatment or special diet is prescribed, every attempt must be made to ascertain whether it is consistent with the patient's physical needs, cultural background, income, and religious practices.
4. The patient's belief in and practice of folk medicine must be respected; the patient must not be criticized for these beliefs. Every effort should be made to assist the patient to combine folk treatment with standard Western treatment as long as the two are not antagonistic. Most people who have a strong belief in folk remedies will continue to use them with or without medical sanctions.
5. Providers should be familiar with formal and informal sources of help in the black community. The former sources consist of churches, social clubs, and community groups. The latter includes those women who provide care for members of their community in an informal way.
6. The beliefs and values of the health-care provider should not be forced upon the client.
7. The treatment plan and the reasons for a given treatment must be shared with the patient.

REFERENCES

1. Bonnie Bullough and Vern L. Bullough, *Poverty, Ethnic Identity and Health Care* (New York: Appleton-Century-Crofts, 1972), pp. 39–41.
2. Ibid.
3. Alex Haley, *Roots* (New York: Doubleday, 1976).
4. Herbert G. Gutman, *The Black Family in Slavery and Freedom, 1750–1925* (New York: Pantheon, 1976).
5. Bullough and Bullough, *Poverty*, p. 43; John F. Kain, ed., *Race and Poverty* (Englewood Cliffs, N.J.: Prentice-Hall, 1969), pp. 1–30.
6. Gladys Jacques, "Cultural Health Traditions: A Black Perspective," in *Providing Safe Nursing Care for Ethnic People of Color*, ed. Marie Branch and Phyllis Perry Paxton (New York: Appleton-Century-Crofts, 1976), p. 116.
7. Ibid., p. 117.
8. Ronald Wintrob, "Hexes, Roots, Snake Eggs? M.D. vs. Occults," *Medical Opinion* 1, no. 7 (1972): 54–61.
9. Langston Hughes and Arna Bontemps, eds., *The Book of Negro Folklore* (New York: Dodd, Mead, 1958), pp. 184–185.
10. Robert Tallant, *Voodoo in New Orleans*, 7th printing (New York: Collier, 1946), p. 19.

11. Ibid., p. 21.
12. Ibid., p. 25.
13. Ibid., p. 38.
14. Ibid., p. 73.
15. Ibid., p. 226.
16. Ibid.
17. Ibid., p. 228.
18. Maya Angelou, *I Know Why the Caged Bird Sings* (New York: Random House, 1970).
19. Haley, *Roots*, p. 32.
20. Beverly Dunstin, "Pica during Pregnancy," in *Current Concepts in Clinical Nursing* (St. Louis: Mosby, 1969), chap. 26.
21. M. Alfred Haynes, "The Gap in Health Status Between Black and White Americans," in *Textbook of Black-Related Diseases*, ed. Richard Allen Williams (New York: McGraw-Hill, 1975), pp. 2–11.
22. Ibid., pp. 11–30.
23. Lauranne Sams, "Blacks and Health Care: Spanning the Life Cycle" (Paper presented at the New England Regional Black Nurses Association Meeting, Statler Hilton Hotel, Boston, Mass., 20 May 1977).
24. Ibid.
25. William H. Bullock and Pongrac N. Jilly, "Hematology," in *Textbook of Black-Related Diseases*, ed. Richard Allen Williams (New York: McGraw-Hill, 1975), pp. 234–72.
26. Bobbie Bloch and Mary L. Hunter, "Teaching Physiological Assessment of Black Persons," *Nurse Educator*, January/February 1981, p. 26; and Lora B. Roach, "Color Changes in Dark Skin," *Nursing* 77 (January 1977): 48–51.
27. Julie Sykes and A. Paul Kelly, "Black Skin Problems," *American Journal of Nursing*, June 1979, pp. 1092–94.
28. Sarah Fisher Giles, "Hair: The Nursing Process and the Black Patient," *Nursing Forum* 11, no. 1 (January 1972): 86.

BIBLIOGRAPHY

Angelou, Maya. *I Know Why the Caged Bird Sings*. New York: Random House, 1970.
   Maya Angelou confronts her life with wonder and dignity. She tells of her childhood and growth, describes her friends and neighbors, and shows how life flourishes even in the midst of death.
Bennett, John. *The Doctor to the Dead: Grotesque Legends and Folk Tales of Old Charleston*. Westport, Conn.: Negro University Press, 1943.
   Contents are folk stories that have been compiled after many years of searching for the various parts of each story.
Grier, William H., and Cobbs, Price M. *Black Rage*. New York: Bantam Books, 1968.
   Two black psychiatrists tell what it is like to be black in white America. They display the anger, pain, and frustration that is so much a part of a black person's life.
Griffin, John Howard. *Black Like Me*. Boston: Houghton Mifflin, 1960.
   This popular book answers the question: What is it like to be black? It

is the story of men who destroy other men for reasons that they do not understand.

Gutman, Herbert G. *The Black Family in Slavery and Freedom, 1750–1925.* New York: Pantheon Books, 1976.

This work is a study of the Afro-American family between 1750 and 1925. It also discusses the origins and early development of Afro-American culture.

Haley, Alex. *Roots.* Garden City, N.Y.: Doubleday, 1976.

Haley traces his family back to its believed origins in Africa. It is an intriguing study of the capture of the black person, slavery, and emancipation.

Hughes, Langston, and Bontemps, Arna, eds. *The Book of Negro Folklore.* New York: Dodd, Mead, 1958.

In this book the reader will encounter numerous short folk tales relating to animals; memories of slavery; God, human beings, and the devil; black magic and chance; ghosts; and spirituals.

Osofsky, Gilbert. *Harlem: The Making of a Ghetto.* New York: Harper and Row, 1963.

Osofsky explores the history of the black community in New York City. The book describes black life in New York before Harlem, and the changes that have occurred in that community.

Parsons, Elsie Clews. *Folk-Lore of the Sea Islands, South Carolina.* Chicago: Afro-American Press, 1969.

This book is composed of tales, riddles, beliefs, and odds and ends of Sea Island folk lore. The Sea Islands stretch out along the coast of South Carolina from Savannah to Charleston, and the inhabitants are predominantly black. Many of these folk-lore tales and riddles come from the Bahamas. They are written in dialect and convey much spirit.

Smith, Lillian. *Killers of the Dream.* Garden City, N.Y.: Doubleday, 1963.

Smith describes the changes of life in the South. She recreates the texture of the Southern experience and what it is like to grow up there from infancy to adulthood. She attempts to show how during this period negative feelings toward blacks are allowed to grow.

Tallant, Robert. *Voodoo in New Orleans.* New York: Collier, 1946.

Tallant traces the history of voodoo from its origins in Africa to its time of greatest popularity in New Orleans. He reports the legends as they have been passed on through generations, and describes the dances and *gris-gris* of voodoo.

FURTHER SUGGESTED READINGS

BOOKS

Achebe, Chinua. *Things Fall Apart.* Greenwich, Conn.: Fawcett Crest, 1959.

Banks, James A., and Crambs, D. Leah. *Black Self-Concept.* New York: McGraw-Hill, 1972.

Clift, Virgil A., ed. *Negro Education in America.* New York: Harper and Row, 1962.

Comer, James P., and Poussaint, Alvin F. *Black Child Care: How to Bring Up a Healthy Black Child in America.* New York: Simon and Schuster, 1975.

Genovese, Eugene D. *Roll, Jordan, Roll.* New York: Vintage Books, 1972.
Hill, R. *The Strengths of Black Families.* New York: Emerson Hall, 1971.
Hughes, Langston, and Arna Bontemps, eds. *The Book of Negro Folklore.* New York: Dodd, Mead, 1958.
Luckcraft, Dorothy. *Black Awareness: Implications for Black Patient Care.* New York: American Journal of Nursing Company, 1976.
Malcolm X. *The Autobiography of Malcolm X.* New York: Grove Press, 1964.
Metraux, Alfred. *Voodoo in Haiti.* New York: Schocken Books, 1972.
Milio, Nancy. *The Care of Health in Communities: Access for Outcasts.* New York: Macmillan, 1975.
Parsons, Talcott, and Clark, Kenneth B. *The Negro American.* Boston: Beacon Press, 1965.
Scanzoni, J. *The Black Family in Modern Society.* Boston: Allyn and Bacon, 1971.
Stack, Carol B. *All Our Kin.* New York: Harper and Row, 1974.
Styron, William. *The Confessions of Nat Turner.* New York: Random House, 1966.
Walker, Alice. *The Color Purple.* New York: Simon and Schuster, 1982.
Williams, Richard, ed. *The Textbook of Black-Related Diseases.* New York: McGraw-Hill, 1975.
Willams, Robert. *Ebonics: The True Language of Black Folks.* St. Louis: Institute of Black Studies, 1975.
Wright, Richard. *Black Boy.* New York: Harper and Brothers, 1937.
————. *Native Son.* New York: Grosset & Dunlop, 1940.

ARTICLES

Ashmore, Richard D., ed. "Black and White in the 1970's." Journal of Social Issues 32, no. 2 (1976).
Bloch, Bobbie and Hunter, Mary L. "Teaching Physiological Assessment of Black Persons." *Nurse Educator,* January–February 1981, pp. 24–27.
Brims, Hamilton. "The Black Family: A Proud Reappraisal." *Ebony,* March 1974, pp. 118–27.
Brunswick, Ann F. "What Generation Gap? A Comparison of Some Generational Differences among Blacks and Whites." *Social Problems* 17 (1969–1970): 358–70.
Brunswick, Ann F., and Josephson, Eric. "Adolescent Health in Harlem." *American Journal of Public Health* 62, no. 10, pt. 2 (a separate supplement to October 1972 issue).
Bucher, K. A., Patterson, A. M., Jr.; Elston, R. C.; Jones, C. A.; and Kirkman, H., Jr. "Racial Differences in Incidence of ABO Hemolytic Disease." *American Journal of Public Health* 66 (1976): 854–58.
Cappannari, Stephen C.; Garn, Stanley M.; and Clark, Dave C. "Voodoo in the General Hospital: A Case of Regional Enteritis." *Journal of the American Medical Association* 232 (2 June 1975): 938–40.
Carter, H. James. "Recognizing Psychiatric Symptoms in Black Americans." *Geriatrics,* November 1974, pp. 95–99.
Clark, Cedric, ed. "The White Researcher in Black Society." *Journal of Social Issues* 21, no. 1 (1973).
Davis, Donald. "Growing Old Black." *Employment Prospects of Aged Blacks, Chicanos and Indians.* Washington, D.C.: National Council on the Aging, 1971, pp. 27–53.

Del Giudice, Marguerite. "Voodoo, USA." *Boston Globe Magazine* 10 February, 1980, pp. 17–38.

Garn, Stanley M. "Problems in the Nutritional Assessment of Black Individuals." *American Journal of Public Health* 66 (March 1976): 262–67.

Giles, Sarah Fisher. "Hair: The Nursing Process and the Black Patient." *Nursing Forum* 11, no. 1 (January 1972): 79–89.

Grier, Marian. "Hair Care for the Black Patient." *American Journal of Nursing* 76 (November 1976): 1781.

Harburg, Ernest et al. "Skin Color, Ethnicity, and Blood Pressure 1: Detroit Blacks." *American Journal of Public Health* 68, no. 12 (December 1978): 1177–83.

Hess, Gertrude. "Racial Tensions: Barriers in Delivery of Nursing Care." *Journal of Nursing Administration* 5 (May-June 1972): 47–49.

"Higher Education of Minority Groups in the U.S." *Journal of Negro Education* 37 (Summer 1969): 291–303.

Houston, Susan. "Black English." *Psychology Today,* March 1973, pp. 45–48.

Jackson, J. "Aged Negroes: Their Cultural Departures from Statistical Stereotypes and Rural-Urban Differences." *Gerontologist,* Summer 1970, pp. 140–45.

————, "Kinship Relations among Negro Americans." *Journal of Social and Behavioral Sciences* 16 (1970): 5–17.

Jekel, James F. et al. "Factors Association with Rapid Subsequent Pregnancies among School-Age Mothers." *American Journal of Public Health* 63, no. 9 (September 1973): 769–73.

Keil, Julian E. et al. "Hypertension: Effects of Social Class and Racial Admixture." *American Journal of Public Health* 67, no. 7 (July 1977): 634–39.

Kelly, Cynthia. "Health Care in the Mississippi Delta." *American Journal of Nursing,* April 1969, pp. 759–63.

Koenig, R.; Goldner, N. S.; Kresojevich, R.; and Lockwood, G. "Ideas about Illness of Elderly Black and White in an Urban Hospital." *Aging and Human Development* 2 (1971): 217–25.

Lackler, C. "Aged Black and Poor: Three Case Studies." *Aging and Human Development* 2 (1971): 202–7.

Lynds, Barbara Gentry; Seyler, Suzanne Kiopp; and Morgan, Brenda Martin. "The Relationship between Elevated Blood Pressure and Obesity in Black Children." *American Journal of Public Health* 70, no. 2 (February 1980): 171–73.

McFarlane, Judith Medlin. "The Child with Sickle Cell Anemia—What His Parents Need to Know." *Nursing 75* (May 1975): 29, 32.

Malina, R. M. "Skinfolds in American Negro and White Children." *Journal of American Dietetic Association* 59 (1971): 34–40.

Roach, Lora B. "Assessing Skin Changes: The Subtle and the Obvious." *Nursing 74,* no. 3 (March 1974): 64–67.

————"Assessment: Color Changes in Dark Skin." *Nursing 77* (January 1977): 48–51.

Roark, Anne C. "Witchcraft on the Rise in Africa; Modern Medicine Men Find Out Why." *Chronicle of Higher Education,* 5 November 1979, p. 14.

Snow, Londell F. "Folk Medical Beliefs and Their Implications for Care of Patients." *Annals of Internal Medicine* 81 (July 1974): 82–96.

Staples, Robert. "Towards a Sociology of the Black Family: A Theoretical and

Methodological Assessment." *Journal of Marriage and the Family,* February 1971: pp. 119–38.

Suchman, Edward A., and Rothman, Allen. "The Utilization of Dental Services." *Milbank Memorial Fund Quarterly* 47 (1970): 56–63.

Sykes, Julie; Kelly, A. Paul; and Kenney, John A., Jr. "Black Skin Problems." *American Journal of Nursing,* June 1979, pp. 1092–94.

Tivnan, Edward. "The Voodoo that New Yorkers Do." *New York Times Magazine,* 2 December, 1979, pp. 182–91.

Ware, Donald R. "Task Force Seeks Multi-disciplinary Approach to Hypertension in Blacks. *Urban Health,* June 1979, pp. 24, 29.

Watts, Wilma. "Social Class, Ethnic Background, and Patient Care." *Nursing Forum* 17, no. 2 (February 1967): 155–62.

White, Ernestine Huffman. "Giving Health Care to Minority Patients." *Nursing Clinics of North America* 12, no. 1 (March 1977): 27–40.

Yankauer, Alfred, ed. "Blood Pressure and Skin Color." *American Journal of Public Health* 68, no. 12 (December 1978): 1170–72.

CHAPTER 9

Health and Illness in the Hispanic-American Community

Members of the Hispanic-American community have their origins in Spain, Cuba, Central and South America, Mexico, Puerto Rico, and other Spanish-speaking countries. This chapter focuses on the health and illness beliefs and practices of the Chicanos and the Puerto Ricans.

THE CHICANOS

Who are the Chicanos? In answering this question, one will surely discover who the Mexican-Americans are. What should these people be called? Depending on his socioeconomic status, his age, and the area in which he lives, a member of this large minority group will refer to himself as either Mexican-American, Spanish American, Latin American, Latin, or Mexican.[1] The term *Chicano* is used as an "identifying umbrella that identifies all Americans of Mexican descent,"[2] hence the term is used here to refer to this particular cultural and ethnic group.

Chicanos, according to the 1980 census, number at least 7,693,000 people.[3] This figure is known to be an underenumeration, for in 1978 there were well over 12 million Chicanos in the United States.[4] This population is rapidly increasing because of a high birthrate and both legal and illegal immigration.[5]

> We came to California long before the Pilgrims landed at Plymouth Rock. We settled California, and all the Southwestern part of the United States, including the States of Arizona, New Mexico, Colorado, and Texas. We built the missions and cultivated the ranches.[6]

The Chicanos have been in the United States for a long time, moving from Mexico and later intermarrying with Indians and Spanish people in the southwestern parts of what is now the United States. Santa Fe, New Mexico, was settled in 1609. Most of the descendants of these early settlers now live in Arizona, California, Colorado, New Mexico, and Texas. A large number of Chicanos also live in Illinois, Indiana, Kansas, Michigan, Missouri, Nebraska, New York, Ohio, Utah, Washington, and Wisconsin. Most Chicanos arrived in the latter states as migrant farm workers. While located there as temporary farm workers, they found permanent jobs and stayed.[7] Contrary to the popular views that Chicanos live in rural areas, most live in urban areas.[8] According to 1976 federal government estimates, California and Texas comprised the largest population centers.[9] Chicanos are employed in all types of jobs; however, few have high-paying or high-status jobs in labor or management. The majority work in factories, mines, and construction; others are employed in farm work and service areas. Presently, only a small—although growing—number of the people are employed in clerical and professional areas. The number of unemployed is high (estimated to be between 25 and 30 percent), and the earnings of those employed are well below the national average. The education of Chicanos, like that of most minorities in the United States, lags behind that of most of the population. Many Chicanos fail to complete high school. In the past few years this situation has changed, and Chicano children are being encouraged to stay in school, go on to college, and enter the professions.[10]

Traditional Definitions of Health and Illness
There are conflicting reports with reference to the traditional meaning of health. Some sources maintain that health is considered to be purely the result of "good luck" and that a person will lose his good health if his luck changes.[11] Some Chicanos describe health as a reward for good behavior; seen in this context, health is a gift from God and should not be taken for granted. People are expected to maintain their own equilibrium in the universe by performing in the proper way, eating the proper foods, and working the proper amount of time. The prevention of illness is an accepted practice that is accomplished with prayer, the wearing of religious medals or amulets, and keeping relics in the home. Herbs and spices can also be used to enhance this form of prevention, as can exemplary behavior.[12] Illness is seen as an imbalance in an individual's body or as punishment meted out for some wrongdoing. The causes of illness can be grouped into five major categories.

The Body's Imbalance.   Imbalance may exist between "hot" and "cold" or "wet" and "dry." The theory of hot and cold was brought to Mexico by Spanish priests and was fused with Aztec beliefs.[13] The concept actually dates back to the early Hippocratic theory of disease and the four body "humors." The disrupted relationship between these humors is often mentioned by Chicanos as the cause of disease.

There are four body fluids or humors: (a) *blood,* hot and wet; (b) *yellow bile,* hot and dry; (c) *phlegm,* cold and wet; and (d) *black bile,* cold and dry. When all four humors are balanced, the body is healthy. When any imbalance occurs, an illness is manifested.[14] These concepts, of course, provide one way of determining the remedy for a particular illness. For example, if an illness is classified as hot, it is treated with a cold substance. A cold disease, in turn, must be treated with a hot substance. Food, beverages, animals, and people possess the characteristics of hot and cold to various degrees. Hot foods cannot be combined; they are to be eaten with cold foods. There is no general agreement as to what is a hot disease or food and what is a cold disease or food. The classification varies from person to person, and what is hot to one person may be cold to another.[15] Therefore, if a Chicano patient refuses to eat the meals offered to him in the hospital, it is wise to ask precisely what he can eat and what combinations of foods he thinks would be helpful for the existing condition. It is important to note that *hot* and *cold* do not refer to temperature, but are descriptive of a particular substance itself.

For example, after a woman delivers a baby, a hot experience, she cannot eat pork, which is considered a hot food. She must eat something cold to restore her balance. Penicillin is a hot medication; therefore, it cannot be used to treat a hot disease.[16] The major problem for the health-care provider is to *know* that the rules, so to speak, of hot and cold vary from person to person. If health-care providers understand the general nature of the hot and cold imbalance, they will be able to help the patient reveal the nature of the problem from the perspective of the patient.

Dislocation of Parts of the Body.   Two examples of "dislocation" are *empacho* and *caida de la mollera.*[17]

Empacho is believed to be caused by a ball of food clinging to the wall of the stomach. Common symptoms of this illness are stomach pains and cramps. This ailment is treated by rubbing and gently pinching the spine. Prayers are recited throughout the treatment. Another, more common, cause of such illness is thought to be lying about the amount of food consumed.[18]

A 20-year-old Hispanic woman experienced the acute onset of sharp abdominal pain. She complained to her friend and together they diagnosed the problem as *empacho* and treated it by massaging her stomach and waiting for the pain to dissipate. It did not, and they continued folk treatment for 48 hours. When the pain did not diminish, they sought help in a nearby hospital. The diagnosis was "acute appendicitis." The young woman nearly died and was quite embarrassed when she was scolded by the physician for not seeking help sooner.

Caida de la mollera is a more serious illness. It occurs in infants and young children aged under one year who are dehydrated for some reason (usually because of diarrhea or severe vomiting) and whose anterios fontanelle is depressed below the contour of the skull.[19] There is much superstition and mystery surrounding this problem. Some of the poorly educated and rural people, in particular, believe that it is caused by a nurse's or physician's having touched the head of the baby. This can be understood if we take into account that (a) the fontanelle of an infant does become depressed if the infant is dehydrated and (b) when physicians or nurses measure an infant's head they do touch this area. If a mother brings her baby to a physician for an examination and sees the physician touch the child's head, and if the baby gets sick thereafter with *caida de la mollera*, it might be very easy for this woman to believe it is the fault of the physician's or nurse's touch. Unfortunately, epidemics of diarrhea are common in the rural and urban areas of the Southwest, and a number of children tend to be affected. One case of severe dehydration that leads to *caida de la mollera* may create quite a stir among the people. The folk treatment of this illness has not been found to be effective. Unfortunately, babies are rarely brought to the hospital in time, and the mortality rate for this illness is high.[20]

Magic or Supernatural Causes Outside the Body.   Witchcraft or possession is considered to be culturally patterned role-playing: a safe vehicle for restoring oneself. Witchcraft or possession legitimizes acting out bizarre behavior or engaging in incoherent speech.[21]

A lesser disease that is caused from outside the body is *mal ojo*. *Mal ojo* means "bad eye," and it is believed to result from excessive admiration on the part of another. General malaise, sleepiness, fatigue, and severe headache are the symptoms of this condition. The folk treatment is to find the person who has caused the illness by casting the "bad eye" and have him care for the afflicted person.[22]

Strong Emotional States.   *Susto* is described as an illness arising from fright. It afflicts many people—males and females, rich and poor, rural dwellers and urbanites. It involves *soul loss:* the soul is able to leave the body and wander freely. This can occur while a person is dreaming, or when a person experiences a particularly traumatic event. The symptoms of the disease are as follows: (a) the person is restless while sleeping; (b) when awake, the person is listless, anorexic, and disinterested in personal appearance, which includes both clothing and personal hygiene; (c) the person experiences a loss of strength, is depressed, and becomes introverted. The person is treated by a *curandero* (a folk healer, discussed in the section on curanderismo) who coaxes the soal back into the person's body. During the healing rites the person is massaged and made to relax.[23]

Envidia. *Envidia,* or envy, is also considered to be a cause of illness and bad luck. Many people believe that to succeed is to fail. That is, when one's success provokes the envy of friends and neighbors, misfortune can befall him and his family. For example, a successful farmer, just when he is able to purchase extra clothing and equipment, is stricken with a fatal illness. He may well attribute the cause of this illness to the envy of his peers. There are a number of social scientists who, after much research, conclude that the "low" economic and success rates of the Chicano can ostensibly be attributed to belief in *envidia.* [24]

Religious Rituals

Magico-religious practices are quite common among the Chicano population. The more severe an illness, the more likely that these practices will be observed. There are four types of practices: (1) making promises, (2) visiting shrines, (3) offering medals and candles, and (4) offering prayers. [25] It is not unusual for the people residing near the southern border of the continental United States to return home to Mexico on religious pilgrimages. The film mentioned in Chapter 6, "We Believe in Nino Fedencio," demonstrates how these pilgrimages are conducted. The lighting of candles is also a frequently observed practice. These beautiful candles made of beeswax and tallow can be purchased in many stores, particularly grocery stores and pharmacies that are located in Chicano neighborhoods. Many homes have shrines with statues and pictures of saints. The candles are lit here and prayers are recited. Some homes have altars with statues and pictures on them and are the focal point of the home.

Curanderismo

There are no specific rules for knowing who in the community uses the services of the folk healers. Not all Chicanos do, and not all Chicanos believe in their precepts. Initially, it was thought that only the poor used a folk healer or *curandero* because they were unable to get treatment from the larger, institutionalized health-care establishment. However, it now appears that the use of healers occurs widely throughout the Chicano population. Some people try to use healers exclusively, whereas others use them along with institutionalized care. The healers do not "advertise," but they are well known throughout the population because of informal community and kinship networks.

Curanderismo is defined as a medical system. [26] It is a coherent view with historical roots that combine Aztec, Spanish, spiritualistic, homeopathic, and scientific elements.

The *curandero* is a holistic healer; the people who seek help from him do so for social, physical, and psychological purposes. The *curandero(a)* can be either a male or female, a "specialist" or a "generalist," a full-time or part-time practitioner. Chicanos who believe in *curanderos* consider them to be religious figures.

A *curandero* may receive the "gift of healing" through three means. (1) He may be "born" to heal. In this case it is known from the moment of a *curandero's* birth that there is something unique about him and that he is destined to be a healer. (2) He may learn by apprenticeship—that is, a person is taught the ways of healing, especially the use of herbs. (3) He may receive a "calling"—through a dream, trance, or vision by which he makes contact with the supernatural by means of a "patron" (or "caller") who may be a saint. The "call" comes either during adolescence or during the midlife crises. This "call" is resisted at first. Later the person resigns himself to his fate and gives in to the demands of the "calling."

Treatment

The most popular form of treatment used by folk healers involves herbs, especially when used as teas. The *curandero* knows what specific herbs to use for a problem; this information is revealed in dreams in which the "patron" gives suggestions.

Because the *curandero* has a religious orientation, much of the treatment includes elements of both the Catholic and Pentecostal rituals and artifacts: offerings of money, penance, confession, lighting candles, wooden or metal offerings in the shape of the afflicted anatomic parts (*milagros*), and laying on of hands.

Massage is used in illnesses such as *empacho* (discussed in the section on body imbalance), which is believed to be caused by a ball of food's clinging to the wall of the stomach. The symptoms are stomach pains and cramps, and for treatment the spine is gently pinched and massaged by the healer.

Cleanings, or *limpias,* are done in two ways. The first is to pass an unbroken egg over the body of the ill person. The second method entails passing herbs tied in a bunch over the body. The back of the neck, which is considered a vulnerable spot, is given particular attention.

In contrast to the depersonalized care a Chicano expects to receive in medical institutions, his relationship with and care by the *curandero* are uniquely personal, as demonstrated in Table 9–1. This special relationship between the Chicano and the *curandero* may well account for this folk healer's popularity. In addition to the close, personal relationship between patient and healer, other factors may explain the continuing belief in *curanderismo:*

1. The mind and body are inseparable.
2. The central problem of life is to maintain harmony. This includes the social as well as the physical and psychological aspects of the person.

TABLE 9–1. COMPARISONS: CURANDERO VERSUS PHYSICIAN

Curandero	Physician
1. Maintains informal, friendly, affective relationship with entire family	1. Businesslike, formal relationship; deals only with the patient
2. Comes to house day or night	2. Patient must go to physician's office or clinic, and only during the day; may have to wait for hours to be seen; home visits are rarely made
3. For diagnosis, consults with head of house, creates a mood of awe, talks to all family members, is not authoritarian, has social rapport, builds expectation of cure	3. Rest of family is usually ignored; deals solely with the ill person, and may deal only with the sick part of the patient; authoritarian manner creates fear
4. Is generally less expensive than physicians	4. More expensive than *curanderos*
5. Has ties to the "world of the sacred"; has rapport with the symbolic, spiritual, creative, or holy force	5. Secular; pays little attention to the religious beliefs or meaning of a given illness
6. Shares the world view of the patient— that is, speaks the same language, lives in the same neighborhood or in some similar socioeconomic conditions, may know the same people, understands the life-style of the patient	6. Generally does not share the world view of the patient—that is, may not speak the same language, does not live in the same neighborhood, does not understand the socioeconomic conditions, does not understand the life-style of the patient

3. There must be harmony between the hot and cold, wet and dry. The treatment of illness should restore the body's harmony, which has been lost.

4. The patient is the passive recipient of disease when the disease is caused by an external force. This external force disrupts the natural order of the internal person, and the treatment must be designed to restore this order. The causes of disharmony are evil and witches.

5. A person is related to the spirit world; when the body and soul are separated, there can be "soul loss." This loss is sometimes caused by *susto,* a disease or illness resulting from fright, which may afflict individuals from all socioeconomic levels and life-styles.

6. The responsibility for recovery is shared by the ill person, the family, and the *curandero.*

7. The natural world is not clearly distinguished from the supernatural world; thus the *curandero* can coerce, curse, and appease the spirits. The *curandero* places more emphasis on his connections with the sacred and his gift of healing than on personal properties. (Such personal properties might include, for example, social status, a large home, and expensive material goods.)

PUERTO RICANS

Puerto Rican migrants to the United States mainland are American citizens, albeit with a different language and culture. They are neither immigrants nor aliens. According to the 1980 census, there are at least 1,444,000 Puerto Ricans living on the mainland. They live mostly on the East Coast, with the greatest number living in New York City and Metropolitan New Jersey. Most Puerto Ricans migrate to search for a better life or because relatives, particularly spouses and parents, have previously migrated. Life on the island of Puerto Rico is difficult because there is a high level of unemployment. Puerto Ricans are not well known or understood by the majority of people in the continental United States; little is known about their cultural identity. Mainlanders tend to forget that Puerto Rico is, for the most part, a poor island and that there are many problems for the people who live there. When many Puerto Ricans migrate to the mainland they bring many of their problems—especially those of poor health and social circumstance.[27]

Puerto Ricans, along with Cubans, comprise the most recent major immigration to these shores. They cover the spectrum of racial differences and have practiced racial intermarriage. Many are Catholic, but some belong to Protestant sects.

There are similarities in the ways in which Puerto Ricans and Chicanos perceive health and illness and in the use of folk healers and remedies. There are also differences. Most studies on health and illness beliefs and healing have been done on Chicanos. It is not easy to find information about the beliefs of Puerto Ricans. Much of the information presented here was gleaned from students and patients. Both groups feel that their beliefs should be known by health-care deliverers. One student, whose mother is a healer and is teaching her daughter the art, corroborated much of the following material.

Common Folk Diseases and Their Treatment

Table 9–2 lists a number of folk diseases and the usual source and type of treatment.* Many of these diseases or disharmonies have been mentioned in the section on Chicano approaches. Nonetheless, there are subtle differences in the ways folk diseases are perceived by Chicanos and Puerto Ricans. For example, while diseases are classified as hot and cold, treatments—that is, food and medications—are categorized as hot (caliente), cold (frio), and cool (fresco). Cold illnesses are treated with hot remedies; hot diseases are treated with cold or cool remedies. Table 9–3 lists the major illnesses, foods, and medicines and herbs

---

*The data contained in Table 9–2 were provided by Puerto Rican students and patients who were carefully interviewed several times.

TABLE 9–2. FOLK DISEASES

Name	Description	Treatment	Source of Treatment
Susto	Sudden fright, causing shock	Relaxation	Relative or friend
Fatique	Asthmalike symptoms	Oxygen; medications	"Western" health-care system
Pasmo	Paralysislike symptoms, face or limbs	Prevention; massage	Folk
Empacho	Food forms into a ball and clings to the stomach, causing pain and cramps	Strong massage over the stomach; medication; gently pinching and rubbing the spine	Folk
Mal ojo	Sudden, unexplained illness in a usually well child or person	Prevention; babies wear a special charm	Depends on the severity of the symptoms; usually home or folk
Ataque	Screaming, falling to ground, wildly moving arms and legs	None—ends spontaneously	

associated with the hot-cold system as it is applied among Puerto Ricans in New York City.

A number of activities are carried out to maintain the proper hot-cold balance in the body. The following list was prepared by a patient:

1. *Pasmo,* a form of paralysis, is usually caused by an upset in the hot-cold balance. For example, if a woman is ironing (hot) and then steps out into the rain (cold), she may get facial or other paralyses.
2. A person who is hot cannot sit under a mango tree (cold) because he can get a kidney infection or "back problems."
3. A baby should not be fed a formula (hot) as it may cause rashes; whole milk (cold) is acceptable.
4. A person who has been working (hot) must not go into the coffee fields (cold) or he can contact a respiratory illness.
5. A hot person must not drink cold water as it could cause colic.

There is often a considerable time lag between disregarding these precautions and the occurrence of illness. A patient who had injured himself while lifting heavy cartons in a factory revealed that the "true" reason he was now experiencing prolonged back problems was because as a child he often sat under a mango tree when he was "hot" after running. This childhood habit had significantly damaged his back so that, as an adult, he was unable to lift heavy objects without causing injury.

TABLE 9–3. HOT-COLD CLASSIFICATION AMONG PUERTO RICANS

	Frio (Cold)	Fresco (Cool)	Caliente (Hot)
Illnesses or bodily conditions	Arthritis Colds Friaidad del estó- mago* Menstrual period Pain in the joints Pasmo		Constipation Diarrhea Rashes Tenesmus (pulo) Ulcers

Medicines and herbs		Bicarbonate of soda
		Linden flowers (flor
		  de tilo)
		Mannitol (maná de
		  manito)
		Mastic bark (almá-
		  cigo)
		MgCO₃ (magnesia
		  boba)
		Milk of magnesia
		Nightshade (yerba
		  mora)
		Orange flower
		  water (agua de
		  azahar)
		Sage
			Anise
			Aspirin
			Castor oil
			Cinnamon
			Cod-liver oil
			Iron tablets
			Penicillin
			Rue (ruda)
			Vitamins

Foods	Avocado Bananas Coconut Lima beans Sugarcane White beans	Barley water Bottled milk Chicken Fruits Honey Raisins Salt cod (bacalao) Watercress	Alcoholic beverages Chili peppers Chocolate Coffee Cornmeal Evaporated milk Garlic Kidney beans Onions Peas Tobacco

*This describes a condition known as "cold stomach" and is caused by eating too many foods classified as "cold."

Source: A. Harwood, "The Hot-Cold Theory of Disease: Implications for Treatment of Puerto Rican Patients," Journal of the American Medical Association 216 (1971): 1154–55, copyright 1971, American Medical Association.

Table 9–4 summarizes some of the behaviors a patient may manifest with certain illnesses that are caused by the hot and cold imbalance.

Puerto Ricans also share with others of Hispanic origin a number of beliefs in spirits and spiritualism. They believe that mental illness is caused primarily by evil spirits and forces. People with such disorders are preferably treated by a "spiritualist medium":[28] the psychiatric clinic is known as the place where *locos* go. This attitude is exemplified in the Puerto Rican approach to visions and the like. The

**TABLE 9-4. EXPECTABLE BEHAVIOR OF PATIENTS WHO ADHERE
TO THE HOT-COLD THEORY**

Patient's Condition	Expectable Behavior
Common cold, arthritis, joint pains	Patient will not take cold-classified foods or medications but will accept those classed as hot
Diarrhea, rash, ulcers	Patient will not take hot-classified medications and uses cool substances as therapy
Requires a diuretic as part of a treatment regimen and has been told to supplement his potassium intake by eating bananas, oranges, raisins, or dried fruit	Patient will not eat these cold-classified foods while he has a cold or other cold-classified condition (for female patients this includes the menses)
Requires penicillin or any other hot medication, particularly on an ongoing basis	Patient will stop taking hot medicine when he suffers any hot-classified symptom (e.g., diarrhea, constipation, rash)
Infant requires formula, which contains hot-classified evaporated milk	Mother will put baby on cold-classified whole milk or will, after feeding formula, "refresh" the baby's stomach with various cool substances, some of which are diuretic
Pregnant	Will avoid hot medicine and hot foods and take cool medicine frequently
Postpartum and during menstruation	Will avoid cool foods and medicines, particularly those that are acidic

Source: A. Harwood, "The Hot-Cold Theory of Disease: Implications for Treatment of Puerto Rican Patients," Journal of the American Medical Association 216 (1971): 1154-55, copyright 1971, American Medical Association.

social and cultural environment encourages the acceptance of having visions and hearing voices. In the dominant culture of the continental United States, when one has visions or hears voices one is encouraged to see a psychiatrist. When a Puerto Rican regards this experience as a problem, he may seek help through *santeria*.[29] *Santeria* is a structured system consisting of *espiritismo*, which is practiced by gypsies and mediums who claim to have *facultades*. These special *facultades* provide them with the "license" to practice. The positions of the practitioners form a hierarchy: the head is the *babalow*, a male; second is the *presidente*, the head medium; third are the *santeros*. Novices are the "believers."

The *facultades* are given to the healer from protective Catholic saints, who have African names and are known as *protecciones*. *Santeria* can be practiced in storefronts, basements, homes, and even college dormitories. *Santeros* dress in white robes for ceremonies and wear special beaded bracelets as a sign of their identity.[30]

Puerto Ricans are able to accept much of what Anglos may judge to be idiosyncratic behavior. In fact, behavioral disturbances are seen as symptoms of illness that are to be treated, not judged. There is a sharp distinction between "nervous" behavior and being *loco*. To be *loco* is to be bad, dangerous, evil. It also means losing all of one's social status. Puerto Ricans who seek standard American treatment for mental illness are castigated by the community; they understandably prefer to get help for the symptoms of mental illness from the *santero*, who accepts the symptoms and attributes the cause of the illness to spirits outside the body. Puerto Ricans have great faith in this system of care and maintain a high level of hope for recovery.[31]

The *santero* is an important person: he respects the individual and does not gossip about either the person or his problems. Anyone can "pour his heart out" with no worry of being labeled or judged. The *santero* is able to tell a person what the problem is, prescribe the proper treatment, and tell the person what to do, how to do it, and when to do it. A study in New York found that 73 percent of the Puerto Rican patients in an outpatient mental health clinic reported having visited a *santero*.[32] Often a sick person is taken to a psychiatrist by his family to be "calmed down" and prepared for treatment by a *santero*. Families may become angry if the psychiatrist does not encourage belief in God and prayer during the time that he works with the patient.[33] Because of cultural differences and beliefs, a psychiatrist may often diagnose as illness what Puerto Ricans may define as health. Frequently, a spiritualist will treat the "mental illness" of a patient as *facultades*, which makes the patient a "special person": thus esteem is granted to the patient as a form of treatment.[34]

Entry into Mainland Health Systems
Puerto Ricans living in New York City and other parts of the northern United States experience a high rate of illness and hospitalization during their first year on the mainland,[35] as do other people of Hispanic origin. It is worthwhile considering the vast differences between living in New York and living in Puerto Rico. In Puerto Rico winter weather is unheard of. The winters in the north can be bitter cold, and adjustment to climate change in itself is extremely difficult. Migrant people may also be forced to live in crowded living quarters with poor sanitation.

When a Puerto Rican seeks health care, he may go to a physician or to a folk practitioner or to both. The general progression of seeking care is as follows:

1. The person seeks advice from a daughter, mother, grandmother, or neighbor woman. These sources are consulted because the women of this culture are the primary healers and dispensers of medicine on the family level.
2. If the advice is not sufficient, the person may seek help from a *senoria* (a woman who is especially knowledgeable about the causes and treatment of illness).
3. If the *senoria* is unable to help, the person goes to a more sophisticated folk practitioner, an *espiritista* or a *curandera*. If

the problem is "psychiatric," a *santero* may be consulted. These names describe similar people—those who obtain their knowledge from spirits and treat illness according to the instructions of the spirits. Herbs, lotions, creams, and massage are often used.

4. If the person is still not satisfied, he may go to a physician.
5. If the results are not satisfactory, the person may return to a folk practitioner. He may seek medical help sooner than Step 4, or he may go back and forth between the two systems.

Not all Puerto Ricans use the folk system. Health-care providers should remember that people who appear to have delayed seeking health care have most likely counted on curing their illness through the culturally known and well-understood folk process. Often when people disappear—or "elope" from the established health system—they may have elected to return to the folk system. Those who elope from the larger, institutionalized medical system may visit *botanica*. There are 24 *botanicas* located in one small area of New York City. In these small *botanicas*, one can purchase herbs, potents, Florida water, ointments, and incense prescribed by the spiritualists. Some of these *botanicas* are so busy that each customer is given a number and is assisted only after his number is called.[36] A Spanish-speaking colleague and I visited a *botanica* in Boston that was similar to a pharmacy. The door was locked, but the proprietor admitted us when we revealed our identity. He explained the various remedies that were for sale. We were allowed to purchase only a few items because we did not have a spiritualist's prescription for herbs. The store also sold candles, religious statues, cards, medals, and relics.

A limited number of *santerias* place advertisements in local Spanish daily newspapers. Some of the more industrious ones distribute flyers in the New York City subways. Others maintain a low profile, and patients visit them because of their well-established reputations. I attempted to visit a *santera* in the Boston area but was unable to locate her; she had recently vacated her apartment and no one in the building would or could tell me where she had relocated.

Current Health Problems

There are a number of health problems that Hispanic people have in common. They experience a number of barriers when they seek health care. The most evident one is that of language. In spite of the fact that Spanish-speaking people comprise one of the largest minority groups in this country, there are very few Spanish-speaking health-care deliverers. This is especially true in communities in which there is a limited number of Spanish-speaking people; Hispanics who live in these areas experience tremendous frustration because of the language barrier. Even in large cities there are far too many occasions when a sick person has to rely on a young child to act not only as a translator but also as interpreter. One way of sensitizing young students to the pain of this situation is to ask them to present a health problem to a person who does not speak or understand a word of English. Needless to say, this is extremely difficult; it is also embarrassing. People who try this rapidly comprehend and appreciate the feelings that are experienced by patients who are unable to speak or understand English. (After this experience two of my students decided to take a foreign-language elective: that amounts to two more concerned student nurses!) Language will continue to be a problem until (1) there are more physicians, nurses, and social workers from the Spanish-speaking communities and (2) more of the present deliverers of health care learn to speak Spanish.

A second barrier that Hispanic people encounter is poverty: it is a crucial problem among people of Spanish origin. The diseases of the poor—for example, tuberculosis, malnutrition, and lead poisoning—all have high incidences among Spanish-speaking populations.

A final barrier to adequate health care is the time orientation of Hispanic Americans. To Hispanics, time is a relative phenomenon. Little attention is given to the *exact* time of day. The frame of reference is wider, and the issue is whether it is day or night.[37] The American health-care system, on the other hand, places great emphasis on promptness. Health-care providers demand that clients arrive at the exact time of the appointment—despite the fact that clients are often kept waiting. Health-system workers stress the client's promptness rather than their own. In fact, they tend to deny responsibility for the waiting periods by blaming them on the "system." Many facilities commonly schedule all appointments for 9:00 A.M. when it is clearly known and understood by the staff members that the doctor will not even arrive until 11:00 A.M. or later. The Hispanic person frequently responds to this practice by coming late for appointments or failing to come at all. They prefer to attend walk-in clinics, where the waits are shorter, and they much prefer going to the healer.

Hispanic-American Health-Care Manpower

The number of Hispanic-origin Americans enrolled in health programs is low—for example, 1 percent of the 0.3 percent minority students in medical schools, 0.8 percent of the 7.5 percent minority students in dentistry, and 1 percent of the 5.9 percent minority students in optometry. In nursing programs, too, there is a limited representation of Spanish-speaking people among applicants, whether the program is diploma, baccalaureate, or associate degree.

The number of practicing professionals is limited. For example, 1.1 percent of dentists, 1.6 percent of optometrists, 3.7 percent of pharmacists, and 3.7 percent of physicians (medical and osteopathic) are people of Hispanic origin. In other words, there are 11.3 dentists, 23.1 pharmacists, and 113.9 physicians of Spanish origin per 100,000 people.[38]

REFERENCES

1. Edward Simmen, ed., *Pain and Promise: The Chicano Today* (New York: New American Library, 1972), p. 35.
2. Ibid., p. 36.
3. U.S. Department of Commerce, Bureau of the Census, 1980 Census of the Population: Ancestry of the Population by State, 1980 (Washington, D.C.: Government Printing Office, 1983), p. 3.
4. William H. McBeath et al., "It's Your Turn in the Sun," *Time,* 16 Oct. 1978, p. 48.
5. Ibid.
6. Edward Simmen, "Anonymous, Who Am I?" in *Educating the Mexican American,* ed. Henry Sioux Johnson and William J. Hernandez-M. (Valley Forge, Pa.: Judson Press, 1970), p. 38.
7. Simmen and Bureau of the Census, "We Mexican Americans," pp. 45–47.
8. Ibid., p. 47.
9. McBeath et al., "It's Your Turn in the Sun," p. 51.
10. Ibid., pp. 49–52.
11. Susan Welch; John Comer; and Michael Steinman, "Some Social and Attitudinal Correlates of Health Care among Mexican Americans," *Journal of Health and Social Behavior* 14 (September 1973): 205.
12. Gilberto Lucero, "Health and Illness in the Chicano Community" (lecture given at Boston College School of Nursing, March 1975).
13. Ibid.
14. Richard L. Currier, "The Hot-Cold Syndrome and Symbolic Balance in Mexican and Spanish-American Folk Medicine," *Ethnology* 5 (1966): 251–63.
15. Lyle Saunders, "Healing Ways in the Spanish Southwest" in *Patients, Physicians, and Illness,* ed. E. Gartley Jaco (Glencoe, Ill.: Free Press, 1958), p. 193.
16. Ibid.
17. Frank C. Nall, II, and Joseph Speilberg, "Social and Cultural Factors in the Responses of Mexican-Americans to Medical Treatment," *Journal of Health and Social Behavior* 8 (1967): 302.
18. Ibid.
19. Pauline Rodriquez Dorsey and Herlinda Quinterg Jackson, "Cultural Health Traditions: The Latino/Chicano Perspective" in *Providing Safe Nursing Care for Ethnic People of Color,* ed. Marie Foster Branch and Phyllis Perry Paxton (New York: Appleton-Century-Crofts, 1976), p. 56.
20. Lucero, "Health and Illness."
21. Ibid.
22. Nall and Speilberg, "Responses of Mexican-Americans," p. 302.
23. Arthur J. Rubel, "The Epidemiology of a Folk Illness: Gusto in Hispanic America," *Ethnology* 3, no. 3 (July 1964): 270–71.
24. Lucero, "Health and Illness."
25. Nall and Speilberg, "Responses of Mexican-Americans," p. 303.
26. Renoldo J. Maduro, "Curanderismo: Latin American Folk Healing" (Conference, "Ways of Healing, Ancient and Modern," San Francisco, January 1976); Ari Kiev, *Curanderismo: Mexican-American Folk Psychiatry* (New York: Free Press, 1968); Lucero, "Health and Illness."
27. Raquel E. Cohen, "Principles of Preventive Mental Health Programs for Ethnic Minority Populations: The Acculturation of Puerto Ricans to the

United States," *American Journal of Psychiatry* 128, no. 12 (June 1972): 79.

28. Ibid.
29. Emily Mumford, "Puerto Rican Perspectives on Mental Illness," *Mount Sinai Journal of Medicine* 40, no. 6 (November-December 1973): 771.
30. Ibid.
31. Ibid.
32. Ibid., p. 772.
33. Ibid., p. 773.
34. Ibid., p. 771.
35. Ibid.
36. Ibid., p. 772.
37. Lucero, "Health and Illness."
38. McBeath et al., "Minority Health Chart Book."

BIBLIOGRAPHY

Butler, Helen. *Doctor Gringo.* New York: Rand McNally, 1967.
    This is the story of a young physician who practices modern medicine in a remote village in Mexico. It aptly describes the differences between the cultural beliefs of the people and standard American medicine.

Kiev, Ari. *Curanderismo: Mexican-American Folk Psychiatry.* New York: Free Press, 1968.
    Kiev presents an in-depth study of Mexican-American folk psychiatry in San Antonio, Texas. In this study, the folk healer's sensitivity to the nuances and subtleties of psychopathology among members of his group are examined.

Lewis, Oscar. *The Children of Sanchez: Autobiography of a Mexican Family.* New York: New American Library, 1961.

———. *A Death in the Sanchez Family.* New York: Random House, 1966.

———. *Five Families: Mexican Case Studies in the Culture of Poverty.* New York: New American Library, 1959.

———. *La Vida: A Puerto Rican Family in the Culture of Poverty.* New York: Random House, 1966.
    The works of Oscar Lewis, each in its own way, portray a "slice of life" of the people he observed. The books are very relevant and helpful in the context of cultural diversity in health care.

Padilla, Elena. *Up from Puerto Rico.* New York: Columbia University Press, 1958.
    This book describes the Puerto Rican migration to New York City and explores the issues inherent in a large migration of people.

Rand, Christopher. *The Puerto Ricans.* New York: Oxford University Press, 1958.
    The contrasts between living in New York City and living in Puerto Rico are explored in this book.

Rogler, Lloyd H. *Migrant in the City.* New York: Basic Books, 1972.
    Rogler relates the story of a Puerto Rican action group and how it involved people who came from Puerto Rican slums to New York.

Simmen, Edward, ed. *Pain and Promise: The Chicano Today.* New York: New American Library, 1972.
    Vivid, sensitive accounts of the reawakening of a proud and oppressed

people are presented. The book consists of numerous essays—written mainly by Chicanos—that explore the identity and life problems of the people.

Steiner, Stan. *Al Raza: The Mexican Americans.* New York: Harper and Row, 1969.

This book consists of essays, short stories, and poetry illustrating the life and beliefs of the Chicano people.

Thomas, Piri. *Down These Mean Streets.* New York: Signet, 1958.

————. *Savior, Savior, Hold my Hand.* Garden City, N.Y.: Doubleday, 1972.

Both these books depict life in the streets of Harlem as experienced by the writer.

FURTHER SUGGESTED READINGS

BOOKS

Aiken, R. *Mexican Folk Tales from the Borderland.* Dallas: Southern Methodist University Press, 1980.

Alvarez, H. R. *Health without Boundaries: United States-Mexico Border Public Health Association.* Mexico: 1975.

Andrade, Sally Jones. *Chicano Mental Health: The Case of Cristal.* Austin: Hogg Foundation for Mental Health, 1978.

Chavira, L. *Curanderismo: An Optional Health Care System.* Edinburg, Tex.: Pan American University, 1975.

Chenault, Lawrence R. *The Puerto Rican Migrant in New York City.* New York: Columbia University Press, 1938.

Clark, Margaret. *Health in the Mexican-American Culture: A Community Study.* Berkeley and Los Angeles: University of California Press, 1959.

Coles, Robert. *Uprooted Children: The Early Life of Migrant Farm Workers.* Pittsburgh: University of Pittsburgh Press, 1970.

Farge, Emile J. *La Vida Chicana: Health Care Attitudes and Behaviors of Houston Chicanos.* San Francisco: Robert D. Reed, 1975.

Harwood, Alan. *Rx: Spiritist as Needed: A Study of a Puerto Rican Community Mental Health Resource.* New York: Wiley, 1977.

Kelly, Isabel. *Folk Practice in North Mexico: Birth Customs, Folk Medicine and Spiritualism in the Laguna Zone.* Austin: University of Texas Press, 1965.

Martinez, R. A., ed. *Hispanic Culture and Health Care.* St. Louis: C. V. Mosby, 1978.

Moquin, Wayne. *A Documentary History of the Mexican Americans.* New York: Praeger, 1972.

O'Berennan, Junius and Smith, Nopal. *The Crystal Icon.* Austin: Galagad Press, 1981.

Saunders, Lyle. *Cultural Differences and Medical Care: The Case of the Spanish-Speaking People of the Southwest.* New York: Russell Sage Foundation, 1954.

Senior, Clarence. *The Puerto Ricans: Strangers—Then Neighbors.* Chicago: Quadrangle Books, 1961.

Sexton, Patricia Cayo. *Spanish Harlem.* New York: Harper and Row, 1965.

Spicer, Edward, ed. *Ethnic Medicine in the Southwest.* New York: Russell Sage Foundation, 1977.

Trotter, Robert, II, and Chavira, Juan Antono. *Curanderismo—Mexican American Folk Healing*. Athens: University of Georgia Press, 1981.
Warner, David. *The Health of Mexican Americans in South Texas*. Austin: The LBJ School of Public Affairs, University of Texas at Austin, 1979.
Zavaleta, Anthony N., ed. "Mexican American Health Status: Selected Topics from the Borderlands." *Borderlands Journal—Special Issue* 4, no. 1 (Fall 1980).

ARTICLES

Abril, I. "Mexican American Folk Beliefs That Affect Health Care." *Arizona Nurse* 28 (May-June 1975): 14-20.
Aguirre, Lydia R. "The Meaning of the Chicano Movement." In *We Are Chicanos*, edited by P. D. Orrego. New York: Washington Square, 1973.
Anderson, Ronald, et al. "Access to Medical Care among the Hispanic Population of the Southwestern United States." *Journal of Health and Social Behavior* 22 (March 1981): 78-89.
Baca, Josephine. "Some Health Beliefs of the Spanish-speaking." *American Journal of Nursing*, October 1969, pp. 2172-76.
Bace, J. E. "Some Health Beliefs of the Spanish-speaking." *American Journal of Nursing*, October 1972, pp. 1852-54.
Calhoun, George, Jr., et al. "An Ethnic Comparison of Self-Esteem in Portuguese-, Mexican-, and Anglo-American Pupils." *Journal of Psychology*, 1978, pp. 11-14.
Chesney, Alan P., et al. "Mexican-American Folk Medicine: Implications for the Family Physician." *Journal of Family Practice* 11, no. 4 (April 1980): 567-74.
Cohen, Raquel. "Principles of Preventive Mental Health Programs for Ethnic Minority Populations: The Acculturation of Puerto Ricans to the United States." *American Journal of Psychiatry* 128 (June 1972): 79-83.
Currier, Richard. "The Hot-Cold Syndrome and Symbolic Balance in Mexican and Spanish-American Folk Medicine." Ethonology 5 (1966): 251-53.
Delgado, Melvin, and Montalvo, Susanne. "Preventive Mental Health Services for Hispanic Preschool Children." *Children Today*, January/February 1979, pp. 6-8, 34.
Fabrega, Horacio, Jr. "On the Specificity of Folk Illness." *Southwestern Journal of Anthropology* 29 (1970): 305-14.
Fernandez-Marina, Ramon; Maldonado-Sierra, Eduardo; and Trent, Richard D. "Three Basic Themes in Mexican and Puerto Rican Family Values." *Journal of Social Psychology* 48 (1958): 167-81.
Garrison, Vivian. "Doctor, *Espiritista*, or Psychiatrist? Health-Seeking Behavior in a Puerto Rican Neighborhood in New York City." *Medical Anthropology* 1 (1977): 65-180.
———. "The 'Puerto Rican Syndrome' in Psychiatry and *Espiritismo*." In *Case Studies in Spirit Possession*, edited by Vincent Crapanzano and Vivian Garrison. New York: Wiley, 1977.
Harwood, Alan, "The Hot-Cold Theory of Disease." *Journal of the American Medical Association* 216 (17 May 1971): 1153-58.
Hayes-Bautista, David E. "Identifying Hispanic Populations: The Influence of Research Methodology upon Public Policy." *American Journal of Public Health* 70, no. 4 (April 1980): 353-58.

Hoppe, Sue Keir, and Heller, Peter L. "Alienation, Familism, and the Utilization of Health Services by Mexican Americans." *Journal of Health and Social Behavior* 16 (September 1975): 304–14.

Johnson, Carmen Acosta. "Mexican-American Women in the Labor Force and Lowered Fertility." *American Journal of Public Health* 66, no. 12 (December 1976): 1186–88.

Koss, Joan. "Social Process, Healing and Self-Defeat among Puerto Rican Spiritists." *American Ethnologist* 4 (1977): 453–69.

————. "Therapeutic Aspects of Puerto Rican Cult Practices." *Psychiatry* 38 (1975): 160–71.

Lauria, Anthony, Jr. " 'Respeto,' 'Rela Jo' and Interpersonal Relations in Puerto Rico." *Anthropological Quarterly* 5 (April 1964): 53–67.

Lawrence, T. F. L.; Bozzetti, L.; and Kane, T. J. "Curanderas: A Unique Role for Mexican Women." *Psychiatric Annals* 2 (February 1976): 65–73.

Martinez, C., and Martin, Harry. "Folk Diseases among Urban Mexican Americans." *Journal of the American Medical Association* 196 (11 April 1966): 147–50.

Mumford, Emily. "Puerto Rican Perspectives on Mental Health." *Mount Sinai Journal of Medicine* 40 (November-December 1973): 768–79.

Nall, Frank C., II, and Speilberg, Joseph. "Social and Cultural Factors in the Responses of Mexican-Americans to Medical Treatment." *Journal of Health and Social Behavior* 8 (1967): 299–308.

O'Brien, Mary Elizabeth. "Pragmatic Survivalism: Behavior Patterns Affecting Low-Level Wellness Among Minority Group Members." *Advances in Nursing Science*, April 1982, pp. 13–26.

Olesen, Virginia, and Hayes-Bautista, David E. "A Myth Destroyed: Chicanos Care about Health." *New Physician*, February 1973, pp. 81–85.

Ortiz, Jesse S. "The Prevalence of Intestinal Parasites in Puerto Rican Farm Workers in Western Massachusetts." *American Journal of Public Health* 70, no. 10 (October 1980): 1103–5.

Phillipos, M. J. "Successful and Unsuccessful Approaches to Mental Health Services for an Urban Hispano American Population." *American Journal of Public Health* 61 (April 1971): 820–30.

Roberts, Angela. "Child-Care Customs in Colombia." *Nursing Mirror*, April 1975, pp. 64–66.

Roberts, Robert E. "The Health of Mexican-Americans: Evidence from the Human Population Laboratory Studies." *American Journal of Public Health* 70, no. 4 (April 1980): 375–84.

Rogler, Lloyd H., and Hollingshead, August B. "The Puerto Rican Spiritualist as a Psychiatrist." *American Journal of Sociology* 5 (July 1961): 17–21.

Rubel, Arthur J. "Concepts of Disease in Mexican-American Culture." *American Anthropologist* 62 (October 1960): 795–814.

————. "The Epidemiology of a Folk Illness: Susto in Hispanic America." *Ethnology* 6 (July 1964): 268–82.

Russell, George. "It's your Turn in the Sun." *Time* 112, no. 16 (16 October 1978): 48–61.

Sabagh, Georges. "Fertility Planning Status of Chicano Couples in Los Angeles." *American Journal of Public Health* 70, no. 1 (January 1980): 56–61.

Saunders, Lyle. "Healing Ways in the Spanish Southwest." In *Patients, Phy-*

sicians, and Illness, edited by E. Gartley Jaco. Glencoe, Ill.: Free Press, 1958.

Simmons, Leo W. "Cultural Patterns in Childbirth." *American Journal of Nursing* 52, no. 8 (August 1952): 989–91.

Staton, Ross D. "A Comparison of Mexican and Mexican-American Families." *Family Coordinator* 21 (July 1972): 325–29.

Trotter, Robert T. and Chavira, Juan Antonio. *"Curanderismo:* An Emic Theoretical Perspective of Mexican-American Folk Medicine." *Medical Anthropology,* Fall 1980, pp. 423–87.

Weaver, Jerry L. "Mexican American Health Care Behavior: A Critical Review of the Literature." *Social Science Quarterly* 54, (June 1973): 85–102.

Weaver, Thomas. "Use of Hypothetical Situations in a Study of Spanish-American Illness Referral Systems." *Human Organization,* Summer 1970, pp. 140–54.

Welch, Susan; Comer, John; and Steinman, Michael. "Some Social and Attitudinal Correlates of Health Care among Mexican Americans." *Journal of Health and Social Behavior* 14 (September 1975): 205–13.

Wolf, Eric R. "The Virgin of Guadalupe: A Mexican National Symbol." In *Introduction to Chicano Studies,* edited by L. Isauro Duran and H. Russell Bernard. pp. 246–52. New York: Macmillan, 1973.

Zepeda, Marlene. "Selected Maternal–Infant Care Practices of Spanish Speaking Women." *JOGN Nursing,* November/December 1982, pp. 371–74.

CHAPTER 10

Health and Illness in the Native-American Community

To be an Indian in modern American society is in a very real sense to be unreal and antihistorical.

—**Vine Deloria**

To realize the plight of today's American Indian, it is necessary to journey back in time to the years when whites settled in this land. Before the arrival of Europeans, this country had no name but was owned and inhabited by groups of people who called themselves nations. The people were strong both in their knowledge of the land and in their might as warriors. The Vikings reached the shores of this country about 1010 A.D. They were unable to settle on the land and left after a decade of frustration. Much later, another group of settlers were repulsed and have since been termed the "Lost Colonies." More people came to these shores, however, and the land was taken over by Europeans. As the settlers expanded westward, they signed "treaties of peace" or "treaties of land cession" with the Indians. These treaties were similar to those struck between nations, although in this case it was "big" nation versus "small" nation. One reason for treaties was to legitimize the takeover of the land that the Europeans had "discovered." Once the land was "discovered" it was divided among the Europeans, who set out to create a "legal" claim to it. The Indians signed the resultant treaties, ceding small amounts of their land to the settlers and keeping the rest for themselves. As time passed, the number of whites rapidly grew and the number of Indians diminished because of wars and disease. As these events occurred, the treaties began to lose their meaning; the Europeans came to consider them as nothing but a joke. They decided that these "natives" had no real claim to the land and shifted them around like cargo from one reservation to another. Although the Indians tried to seek just settlements through court litigation, they failed to win back the land that had been taken from them through misrepresentation. For example, by 1831 the Cherokees were fighting in the court system to keep their nation in Georgia. However, they lost, and, like other Indian nations since the time of the early European settlers, were forced to move westward. During this forced westward movement many Indians died and all suffered. Today, many tribes are seeking to reclaim their land through the courts.[1] Several claims, such as those of the Penebscot and Passamaquody tribes in Maine have been successful.

As the Indians migrated westward, they carried with them the fragments of their culture. Their lives were disrupted, their land was lost, and many of their leaders and teachers had perished. Yet much of their history and culture somehow remain. Today, more and more Indians are seeking to know their history. The story of the colonization and settlement of the United States is being retold with a different emphasis.

There are approximately 200 Indian tribes in the United States. Native Americans live predominantly in 26 states, with most residing in the western part of the country as a result of the forced westward migration. Although many Indians remain on reservations and in rural areas, just as many of them live in cities, especially those on the West Coast. Oklahoma, Arizona, California, New Mexico, and Alaska have the largest numbers of Native Americans.[2]

TRADITIONAL DEFINITIONS OF HEALTH AND ILLNESS

Each Native-American nation or tribe had its own history and belief system regarding health and illness and the traditional treatment of illness. Yet some general beliefs and practices underlie the more specific tribal ideas. Certain specifics are noted, either in the text or in footnotes. The data—collected through a review of the literature and from interviews granted by members of the groups—come from the Navaho nation, the Hopis, the Cherokees, and Shoshones, and New England Indians with whom I have worked closely.

The traditional Native-American belief about health is that it reflects living in total harmony with nature and having the ability to survive under exceedingly difficult circumstances.[3] Humankind has an intimate relationship with nature.[4]* The earth is considered to be a living organism—the body of a higher individual, with a will and a desire to be well. The earth is periodically healthy and less healthy,

---

*This philosophy was reiterated in a lecture at Boston College School of Nursing in April 1975 by Will Basque, a Micmac Indian and former president of the Boston Indian Council.

just as human beings are. According to the Native-American belief system, a person should treat his body with respect, just as he should treat the earth with respect. When he harms the earth he harms himself and, conversely, when he harms himself he harms the earth.[5] The earth gives food, shelter, and medicine to humankind and, for this reason, all things of the earth belong to human beings and nature. "The land belongs to life, life belongs to the land, and the land belongs to itself." In order to maintain himself, the Indian must maintain his relationship with nature. "Mother Earth" is the friend of the Indian, and the land belongs to the Indian.[6]

According to Indian belief, as explained by a medicine man, Rolling Thunder, the human body is divided into two halves: these halves are seen as plus and minus (yet another version of the concept that every whole is made of two opposite halves). There are also—in every whole—two energy poles: positive and negative. The energy of the body can be controlled by spiritual means. It is further believed that every being has a purpose and an identity. Every being has the power to control his own self, and from this force and the belief in its potency the spiritual power of a person is kindled.[7]

Many Native Americans with traditional orientations believe there is a reason for every sickness or pain. They believe that it is a price that is being paid, either for something that happened in the past or for something that will happen in the future. In spite of this conviction, a sick person must still be cared for. Everything is seen as being the result of something else, and this cause-and-effect relationship creates an eternal chain. Native Americans do not subscribe to the germ theory of modern medicine. Illness is something that must *be*. Even the person who is experiencing the illness may not realize the reason for its occurrence,[8] but it may, in fact, be the best possible price to pay for the past or future event(s).

The Hopi Indians associate illness with evil spirits. The evil spirit responsible for the illness is identified by the medicine man, and the remedy for the malady resides in the treatment of the evil spirit.[9]

According to legend, the Navaho people originally emerged from the depths of the earth—fully formed as human beings. Before the beginning of time, they existed with holy people, supernatural beings with supernatural powers, in a series of 12 underworlds. The creation of all elements took place in these underworlds, and there all things were made to interact in constant harmony. A number of ceremonies and rituals were created at this time for "maintaining, renewing, and mending this state of harmony."[10]

When the Navaho people emerged from the underworlds, one female was missing. She was subsequently found by a search party in the same hole from which they had initially emerged. She told the people that she had chosen to remain there and wait for their return. She became known as death, sickness, and witchcraft. Because her hair was unraveled and her body was covered with dry red ochre, the Navahos today continue to unravel the hair of their dead and to cover their bodies with red ochre. Members of the Navaho nation believe that "witchcraft exists and that certain humans, known as witches, are able to interact with the evil spirits and that these people can bring sickness and other unhappiness to the people who annoy them."[11]

Traditionally, illness, disharmony, and sadness are seen by the Navahos as the result of one or more combinations of the following actions: "(1) displeasing the holy people; (2) annoying the elements; (3) disturbing animal and plant life; (4) neglecting the celestial bodies; (5) misuse of a sacred Indian ceremony; or (6) tampering with witches and witchcraft."[12] If disharmony exists, disease can occur. The Navahos distinguish between two types of disease: (1) contagious diseases such as measles, smallpox, diphtheria, syphilis, and gonorrhea, and (2) more generalized illnesses such as "body fever" and "body ache." The notion of illness being caused by a microbe or other physiologic agent is alien to the Navahos. The cause of disease, of injury to a person or to his property, or of continued misfortune of any kind must be traced back to an action that should not have been performed. Examples of such infractions are breaking a taboo or contacting a ghost or witch. To the Navahos the treatment of an illness, therefore, must be concerned with the external causative factor(s) and not with the illness or injury itself.[13]

TRADITIONAL METHODS OF HEALING

Traditional Healers
The traditional healer of the Native American is the medicine man, and the Indians, by and large, have maintained their faith in him over the ages. He is a person wise in the ways of the land and of nature. He knows well the interrelationships of human beings, the earth, and the universe. He knows the ways of the plants and animals, the sun, the moon, and the stars. The medicine man takes his time to determine first the cause of the illness and then the proper treatment. In order to determine the cause and treatment of an illness, he performs special ceremonies that may take up to several days.

As a specific example, Boyd describes the medicine man Rolling Thunder, the spiritual leader, philosopher, and acknowledged spokesman of the Cherokee and Shoshone tribes, as being able to determine the cause of illness when the ill person does not himself know it. The "diagnostic" phase of the treatment may often take as long as three days. There are numerous causes of physical illness and a great number of reasons—good or bad—for having become ill. These causes are of a spiritual nature. When a modern physician sees a sick person, he recognizes and diagnoses only the physical illness. The medicine man, on the other hand, looks for the spiritual cause of the problem. To the Native American, "every physical thing in nature has a spiritual nature because the whole is viewed as being essentially spiritual in nature." The agents of nature, herbs, are seen as spiritual helpers and the characteristics of plants must be known and understood.[14] Rolling Thunder states that "we are born with a purpose in life and we have to fulfill that purpose."[15] The purpose of the medicine man is to cure; and his power is not dying out.

The medicine man of the Hopi Indians uses meditation in determining the cause of an illness, and sometimes he may even use a crystal ball as his focal point for meditation. At other times the Hopi medicine man chews on the root of jimsonweed. This powerful herb sends him into a trance as he meditates. The Hopis claim that this herb gives the medicine man a vision of the evil that caused a sickness. Once the medicine man concludes his meditation, he is able to prescribe the proper herbal treatment. For example, one illness, fever, is cured by a plant that smells like lightning; the Hopi phrase for fever is "lightning sickness."[16]

The Navaho Indians consider disease to result from breaking a taboo or the attack of a witch. The exact cause is diagnosed by divination, as is the ritual of treatment. There are three types of divination: motion in the hand (the most common form and often practiced by women); stargazing; and listening. The function of the diagnostician is first to determine the cause of the illness and than to recommend the treatment—that is, the type of chant that will be effective and the medicine man who can best do it. A medicine man may be called upon to treat obvious symptoms, whereas the diagnostician is called upon to ascertain the cause of the illness. (A person is considered wise if the diagnostician is called first.) Often, the same medicine man can practice both divination (diagnosis) and the singing (treatment). When any form of divination is used in making the diagnosis, the diagnostician meets with the family and discusses the patient's condition and determines the fee.

The practice of motion in the hand includes the following rituals. Pollen or sand are sprinkled around the sick person, during which time the diagnostician sits with closed eyes and with his face turned from the patient. His hand begins to move during the song. While the hand is moving, the diagnostician thinks of various diseases and various causes. When the arm begins to move in a certain way, the diagnostician knows that he has discovered the right disease and its cause. He is then able to prescribe the proper treatment.[17] The ceremony of motion in the hand may also incorporate the use of dry paintings. (These paintings are a well-known form of art.) Four colors are used— white, blue, yellow, and black—and each color has a symbolic meaning. Chanting is performed as the painting is produced, and the shape of the painting determines the cause and treatment of the illness. The chants may continue for an extended period of time,[18] depending on the family's ability to pay and the capabilities of the singer. The process of motion in the hand can be neither inherited nor learned: it comes to a person suddenly, as a gift. It is said that if an individual is able to diagnose his own illness, he is able to practice motion in the hand.[19]

Unlike motion in the hand, stargazing can and must be learned. Sand paintings are often, but not always, made during stargazing. If they are not made it is either because the sick person cannot afford to have one done or because there is not enough time to make one. The stargazer prays the star prayer to the star spirit, asking it to show him the cause of the illness. During stargazing, singing begins and the star throws a ray of light that determines the cause of the patient's illness. If the ray of light is white or yellow the patient will recover; if it is red, the illness is serious. If a white light falls on the patient's home, the person will recover; if the home is dark, the patient will die.[20]

Listening, the third type of divination, is somewhat similar to stargazing, except that something is heard rather than seen. In this instance, the cause of the illness is determined by the sound that is heard. If someone is heard to be crying, the patient will die.[21]

The traditional Navahos continue to use the medicine man, whom they call the singer, when an illness occurs. They use his service because, in many instances, the treatment that they receive from him is better than the treatment they receive from the health-care establishment. Treatments used by the singer include massage and heat treatment, the sweatbath, and use of the yucca root—approaches similar to those common in physiotherapy.[22]

The main effects of the singer are psychological. During the chant, the patient feels cared for in a deeply personal way as the center of the singer's attention, and that the patient's problem is the reason for the singer's presence. When the singer tells the patient recovery will occur and the reason for the illness, the patient has faith in what is heard. The singer is regarded as a distinguished authority and as a person of eminence with the gift of learning from the holy people. He is considered to be more than a mere mortal. The ceremony—surrounded by such high levels of prestige, mysticism, and power—takes the sick person into its circle; ultimately becoming one with the holy people by participating in the sing that is held in the patient's behalf. The patient once again comes into harmony with the universe and subsequently becomes free of all ills and evil.[23]

The religion of the Navahos is one of *good hope* when they are sick or suffer other misfortunes. Their system of beliefs and practices helps them through the crises of life and death. The stories that are told during religious ceremonies give the people a glimpse of a world that has gone by, which promotes a feeling of security because they see that they are links in the unbroken chain of countless generations.[24]

Many Navahos believe in witchcraft, and when it is considered to be the cause of an illness special ceremonies are employed to rid the individual of the evil caused by the witches. There are numerous methods employed to manipulate the supernatural. Although many of these activities may meet with strong social disapproval, Navahos recognize the usefulness of blaming witches for illness and misfortune. Tales abound concerning witchcraft and how the witches work. Not all Navahos believe in witchcraft, but for those who do it provides a mechanism for laying blame for the overwhelming hardships and anxieties of life.

Such events as going into a trance can be ascribed to the work of witches. The way to cure a "witched" person is through the use of complicated prayer ceremonies that are attended by friends and relatives, who lend help and express sympathy. The victim of a witch is in no way responsible for being sick and is therefore free of any punitive action by the community if the illness causes the victim to behave in strange ways.[25] On the other hand, if an incurably "witched" person is affected so that alterations in the person's established role severely disrupt the community, the victim may be abandoned.

Traditional Remedies

In the past, American Indians practiced an act of purification in order to maintain their harmony with nature and to cleanse the body and spirit. This was done by total immersion in water in addition to the use of sweat lodges, herb medicines, and special rituals. Today the practice is confined to total immersion of the body. Purification is seen as the first step in the control of consciousness, a ritual that awakens the body and the senses and prepares a person for meditation. It is viewed by the participants as a new beginning.[26]

The basis of therapy lies in nature: hence the use of herbal remedies. There are specific rituals to be followed when herbs are gathered. Each plant is picked to be dried for later use. No plant is picked unless it is the proper one, and only enough plants are picked to meet the needs of the gatherers. Timing is crucial and the procedures are meticulously followed. So deep is their belief in the harmony of human beings and nature that the herb gatherers exercise great care not to disturb any of the other plants and animals in the environment.[27]

One plant of interest is the common dandelion. This plant, which contains a milky juice in its stem, is said to increase the flow of milk from the breasts of nursing mothers. Another plant, the thistle, is said to contain a substance that will relieve the prickling sensation in the throats of people who live in the desert. The medicine used to hasten the birth of a baby is called a "weasel medicine" because the weasel is clever at digging through and out of difficult territory.[28]

The following is a list of common ailments and herbal treatments used by the Hopi Indians.[29]

1. Cuts and wounds are treated with globe mallow. The root of this plant is chewed to help mend broken bones.
2. To keep air from cuts, piñon gum is applied to the wound. It is also used in an amulet to protect a person from witchcraft.

3. Cliff rose is used to wash wounds.
4. Boils are brought to a head with the use of sand sagebrush.
5. Spider bites are treated with sunflower. The person bathes in water in which the flowers have been soaked.
6. Snakebites are treated with the bladder pod. The bitter root of this plant is chewed and then placed on the bite.
7. Lichens are used to treat the gums. They are ground to a powder and then rubbed on the affected areas.
8. Fleabane is used to treat headaches. The entire herb is either bound to the head or drunk as a tea.
9. Digestive disorders are treated with blue gillia. The leaves are boiled in water and drunk to relieve indigestion.
10. The stem of the yucca plant is used as a laxative. The purple flower of the thistle is used to expel worms.
11. Blanket flower is the diuretic used to provide relief from painful urination.
12. A tea is made from painted cup and drunk to relieve the pain of menstruation. Winter fat provides a tea from the leaves and roots and is drunk if the uterus fails to contract properly during labor.

CURRENT HEALTH-CARE PROBLEMS

Today, Native Americans are faced with a number of health-related problems. Many of the old ways of diagnosing and treating illness have not survived the migration and changing ways of life of the people. Because these skills have often been lost and because modern health-care facilities are not always available, the people are frequently in limbo when it comes to obtaining adequate health care. At least one-third of the Native-American population exists in a state of abject poverty. With this destitution come poor living conditions and its attendant problems, as well as diseases of the poor—including malnutrition, tuberculosis, and high maternal and infant death rates. Poverty and isolated living serve as further barriers that keep Native Americans from using limited health-care facilities even when they are available. Many of the illnesses that are familiar among white patients may manifest themselves differently in Indian patients. For example, an Indian may have a high blood sugar level but be asymptomatic for diabetes mellitus; yet the death rate for diabetes is high among pregnant Indian women.[30]

Native Americans have the highest infant mortality rate in the United States. Their birth rate is almost twice the rate of the general population. The *neonatal* death rate has been substantially reduced; however, the *postneonatal* rate is 2.3 times that for infants of all other races. This high rate is accounted for by the marked incidence of diarrhea in young babies and the harsh environment in which they must live.

Morbidity and Mortality

For the period 1979 to 1981, the life expectancy at birth for American Indians and Alaska natives was 71.1 years. This figure is an increase of 6 years from the expectancy figure of 1969 to 1971. This increased figure, however, still lags behind the life expectancy figures for all other races.[31]

The leading causes of death in the Native-American community are:

1. Accidents
2. Heart diseases
3. Cirrhosis of the liver
4. Suicide
5. Homicide[32]

The causes of morbidity are:

1. Accidental injuries
2. Cirrhosis of the liver
3. Alcoholism
4. Attempted suicide
5. Attempted homicide
6. Malnutrition
7. Pancreatitis
8. Gastrointestinal bleeding
9. Fetal alcohol deformaties
10. Mental and emotional disorders
11. Organic brain syndromes
12. Alcoholic heart disease[33]

Alcohol Abuse

All of the above problems, both in terms of mortality and morbidity, are directly related to alcohol abuse. Alcohol abuse is the most widespread and severe problem in the Native-American community. It is extremely costly to the people and underlies physical, mental, social, and economic problems. The problem is growing worse. Hawk Littlejohn, the medicine man of the Cherokee Nation, Eastern band, attributes this problem, from a traditional point of view, to the fact that Native Americans have lost the opportunity to make choices. They can no longer choose how they live their lives, how they practice their medicine, and how they practice their religion. He believes that once people return to a sense of identification within themselves, they will begin to rid themselves of this problem of alcoholism. Indeed, the problem is immense.[34]

Domestic Violence

Another problem that is related to alcohol abuse is that of domestic violence and the battering of women. A battered woman is "one who is physically assaulted by her husband, boyfriend, or some significant other." The assault may range from a push to severe, even permanent, injury, to sexual abuse, to child abuse, and to neglect. Once the pattern of abuse is established, subsequent episodes of abuse tend to get worse. This abuse is not traditional in Native-American life, but has evolved. True Indian love is based on a tradition of mutual respect and the belief that men and women are part of an ordered universe that should live in peace. In the traditional Native-American home, children were raised to respect their parents and they were not corporally punished. Violence toward women was not practiced. However, in modern times, the sanctions and protections have decreased and the women are far more vulnerable. Many women are reluctant to admit that they are victims of abuse because they believe that they will be blamed for the assault. Hence, the beatings continue. There are a number of services available to women who are victims, such as safe houses and support groups. It is believed that the long-range solution to this problem lies in teaching children to love: to nurture children and give them self-esteem; to teach boys to love and respect women; and to give girls a sense of worth. Battering of women is not part of traditional life.[35]

Domestic violence has a profound impact on the community and on the family. A pattern of abuse is easily established. It begins with tension: the female attempts to keep peace but the male cannot contain himself, a fight erupts, and then the crisis arrives. The couple may make up only to fight again. Attempts to help must be initiated or the circle will enlarge. The problem is extremely complex. Some of the services available to a household experiencing domestic violence include:

1. Tribal health: direct services for physical and mental health
2. Law enforcement: police protection may be necessary
3. Legal assistance: assistance for immediate shelter and emergency food and transportation.[36]

In addition to alcohol-related problems, recent studies indicate that the incidences of both lung cancer in males and breast cancer in females are increasing.[37]

Urban Problems

More than 50 percent of Native Americans live in urban areas. In Seattle there are 15,000 Indians. This is not a particularly dense population, but there are high rates of diphtheria; tuberculosis; otitis media, with subsequent hearing defects; alcohol abuse; inadequate immunization; iron-deficiency anemia; childhood developmental lags; mental-health problems, including depression, anxiety, and coping difficulties; and caries and other dental problems. As in all disorganized family units there are family problems related to marital difficulties and financial strain, which are usually brought about by unemployment and the lack of education or knowledge of special skills. The tension is often further compounded by alcoholism.[38]

In Boston, there are between 3,500 and 4,000 Indians. They experience the same problems as Native Americans in other cities. Yet there is an additional problem. Few non-Indian residents are even aware that there is a Native-American community in the city or that it is in desperate need of adequate health and social services.[39]

HEALTH-CARE PROVIDER SERVICES

Some historical differences in health care relate to geographical locations. Indians living in the eastern part of this country and in most urban areas are *not* covered by the services of the Indian Health Service. Native Americans living on reservations in the western portion of this country are eligible for such services. In 1923 tribal government—under the control of the Bureau of Indian Affairs—was begun by the Navahos. Treaties were established by the Navahos with the United States government, but in the areas of health and education these treaties were not honored by the United States. Health services on the reservations were inadequate; consequently the people were sent to outside institutions for the treatment of illnesses such as tuberculosis and mental-health problems. As recently as 1930 the vast Navaho lands had only seven hospitals with 25 beds each. Not until 1955 were Indians finally offered concentrated services with "modern" physicians. Only since 1965 have more comprehensive services been available to the Navahos.[40]

Indian Health Service
The Indian Health Service provides inpatient facilities and outpatient clinics. There are well-baby clinics, prenatal clinics, and diabetes clinics, in addition to public-health nursing services. Community health representatives who are tribal members serve in the community to identify health problems, to encourage people to use existing medical facilities, and to take people to the clinic when the need arises.

The Indian Health Service also makes provision for health education. Paraprofessionals and professionals in the community work to educate the people, both formally and informally, in modern health practices. A section of the Indian Health Service is concerned with alcohol abuse and mental-health problems. These mental-health workers act as liaison between the Indians and halfway houses, counselors, drug-prevention programs, and other agencies set up specifically to deal with the emotional problems of anxiety and depression. The Indian Health Service also maintains an otitis media program in view of the statistically established high incidence of this disorder among Native Americans. Young children are screened in an effort to begin early treatment so that deafness can be prevented.[41]

The ineligibility of Native Americans living on the East Coast to secure such services* has caused numerous difficulties for the needy. The providers of health care generally seem to think that Indians should receive health services from the Indian Health Service and try to send them there. However, as there simply is no Indian Health Service on the East Coast, there Native Americans tend to be shifted around among the regional health-care resources that are available.

Many providers of health care and social services are not aware that many of the Indians on the East Coast have dual citizenship as a result of the Jay Treaty of 1794, which allows for international citizenship between the United States and Canada. This raises questions whether Indians can freely cross the border between the United States and Canada, and whether those who live in the United States are eligible for welfare or medicaid if they need it.[42]

Cultural and Communication Problems

A factor that inhibits the Indian use of white-dominated health services is a deep, cultural problem: Indians suffer dis-ease when they come into contact with the white health-care provider.† Native Americans feel uneasy because for too many years they have been the victim of haphazard care and disrespectful treatment. And all too often there is conflict between what the Native Americans perceive their illness to be and what the physician may diagnose. Native Americans, like most people, do not enjoy long waits in clinics; the separation from their families; the unfamiliar, regimental environment of the hospital; or the unfamiliar behavior of the nurses and physicians, who often display demeaning and demanding attitudes. The response to this treatment varies. Sometimes it is silence; other times it is leaving and not returning. Many Native Americans request that, if the ailment is not an emergency, they be allowed to see the medicine man first and then receive treatment from the physician. Often when a sick person is afraid of receiving the care of a physician, the medicine man encourages him to go to the hospital.[44]

Health-care providers must be aware of several factors when they communicate with the Native American. One of them is recognition of the importance of nonverbal communication. Often the Native American will be observing the provider and saying very little; the patient may expect the provider to deduce the problem through in-

---

*The situation stems from the Indian Renewal Act of 1840 and the Dawes Act of 1887, legislation that disbanded tribes east of the Mississippi and established reservations west of the Mississippi.

†Dr. Red Horse explains the phenomenon of "Indian paranoia" that emerges in a predictable behavior: "It is *not* a sickness but an 'interactive reality' that Native Americans suffer whenever visits to non-Indian clinics are imminent. *Fear* is a variable and often when the fear is too great, help is not sought. For example, if a Native American child has a toothache, the parents may not take the child to the dentist because they fear the dentist's demeaning attitude."[43]

stinct rather than by the extensive use of questions during history taking. In part, this derives from the belief that direct quoting is intrusive upon individual privacy. When examining a Native American with an obvious cough, the provider might be well advised to use a declarative statement—"You have a cough that keeps you awake at night"—and then allow time for the client to respond to the statement.

It is Indian practice to converse in a very low tone of voice. It is expected that the listener will pay attention and listen carefully in order to hear what is being said. It is considered impolite to say, "Huh?" "I beg your pardon," or to give any indication that the communication was not heard. Therefore, an effort should be made to speak with clients in a quiet setting where they will be heard more easily.

Note taking is also taboo. Indian history has been passed through generations by means of verbal story telling. Native Americans are sensitive about note taking while they are speaking. When one is taking a history or interviewing, it may be preferable to use memory skills rather than to record notes. This more conversational approach may encourage greater openness between the client and the provider.

Another factor is the differing perceptions of time between the Native-American client and the provider. Life on the reservation is not governed by the clock but by the dictates of need. When an Indian moves from the reservation to an urban area, he often feels stress from this cultural conflict concerning time. This is often encountered in delivery of health care when some Native Americans may be late for specific appointments. One solution would be the use of walk-in clinics.[45]

The Indian Health Care budget was recommended for funding for the fiscal year 1985. The services that will continue to be provided include the Indian Health Service, Contract Care, Community Health Representative Program, Emergency Medical Services, and Urban Health. There are also scholarship funds available for 416 continuing students enrolled in health-care related programs and 50 extern programs.

REFERENCES

1. Alan Jon Fortney, "Has White Man's Lease Expired?" *Boston Sunday Globe*, 23 January 1977; Dee Brown, *Bury My Heart at Wounded Knee* (New York: Holt, 1970); Vine Deloria, Jr., *Custer Died for Your Sins* (New York: Avon Books 1969) and *Behind the Trail of Broken Treaties* (New York: Delacorte, 1974).
2. Martha H. Primeaux, "American Indian Health Care Practices: A Cross-Cultural Perspective," *Nursing Clinics of North America* 12, no. 1 (March 1977): 57.

3. Ibid., p. 60.
4. Doug Boyd, *Rolling Thunder* (New York: Random House, 1974), p. 96.
5. Ibid., p. 51.
6. Ibid., p. 96.
7. Ibid., p. 199.
8. Ibid., p. 123.
9. Sybil Leek, *Herbs: Medicine and Mysticism* (Chicago: Henry Regnery, 1975), p. 16.
10. Harry Bilagody, "An American Indian Looks at Health Care," in *The Ninth Annual Training Institute for Psychiatrist-Teachers of Practicing Physicians*, ed. Raymond Feldman and Dorothy Buch (Boulder: WICHE, NO. 3A30, 1969), p. 21.
11. Ibid., p. 22.
12. Ibid., p. 21.
13. Clyde Kluckhohn and Dorothea Leighton, *The Navaho*, rev. ed. (Garden City, N.Y.: Doubleday, 1962), pp. 192-93.
14. Boyd, *Rolling Thunder*, p. 124.
15. Ibid., p. 263.
16. Leek, *Herbs*, p. 16.
17. Leland C. Wyman, "Navaho Diagnosticians," in *Medical Care*, ed. W. Richard Scott and Edmund H. Volkhart (New York: Wiley, 1966), pp. 8-14.
18. Kluckhohn and Leighton, *The Navaho*, pp. 209-18.
19. Leland Wyman, "Navaho Diagnosticians," p. 14.
20. Ibid., p. 15.
21. Ibid., p. 16.
22. Kluckhohn and Leighton, *The Navaho*, p. 230.
23. Ibid., p. 232.
24. Ibid., p. 233.
25. Ibid., p. 244.
26. Boyd, *Rolling Thunder*, pp. 97-100.
27. Ibid., pp. 101-36.
28. Leek, *Herbs*, p. 17.
29. Ibid., pp. 17-26.
30. Ernestine Huffman White, "Call of the Minority Patients," *Nursing Clinics of North America* 12, no. 1 (March 1977).
31. National Indian Health Board. *NIHB Reporter* 3, no. 12 (July 1984): 4.
32. Hawk Littlejohn, Interview. Boston State College, Boston, Mass. June 1979.
33. Ibid.
34. Ibid.
35. American Indian Women of Minnesota, Inc., through a grant sponsored by the Department of Corrections, Minnesota State Task Force on Battered Women, Minnesota Council of Churches and the American Lutheran Church. "Battered Women—Definition," n.d., and "The Dakota View of Domestic Violence" in *The Circle Newspaper of the Boston Indian Council*, February/March, 1984, pp. 8-10.
36. Diane Marshall, *Family Violence*, sponsored by ACTION Grant 137-0145/1, the Mental Health Association of North Dakota and the Abused Women's Resource Closet n.d., pp. 9-11.
37. National Indian Health Board, *Reporter*, p. 8.

38. "What Are the Problems of Urban Native Americans?" (flyer distributed by the Seattle Indian Health Board, Seattle, Wash., 1974).
39. John Ginnish "The Health Needs of the Boston Indian" (Lecture given at Boston College School of Nursing, 9 April 1975.
40. Bilagody, "Health Care" pp. 22–23.
41. Ginnish, "Health Needs."
42. Ibid.
43. John Red Horse, "Urban Native-American Health Care" (Minneapolis-St. Paul: unpublished paper, 1976), p. 3.
44. Bilagody "Health Care," p. 22; Ginnish, "Health Needs."
45. Ibid., pp. 1–2.

BIBLIOGRAPHY

Boyd, Doug. *Rolling Thunder.* New York: Random House, 1974.
    An outstanding description of the work of a medicine man and his philosophy is presented.
Brown, Dee. *Bury My Heart at Wounded Knee.* New York: Holt, 1970.
    This book outlines the history of the treaties and battles between the European-American and the Native American.
Deloria, Vine, Jr. *Custer Died for Your Sins: An Indian Manifesto.* New York: Avon Books, 1969.
    A description of current philosophies and problems of today's Native Americans is presented by Deloria.
Farnsworth, Dan L. and Rome, Howard P., ed. *Psychiatric Annals* 4 (November 1974).
    This special volume of this publication contains several excellent articles regarding the issues and problems of Indian mental health.
Kluckhohn, Clyde. *Navaho Witchcraft.* Boston: Beacon Press, 1944.
    Former and current Navaho beliefs regarding witchcraft, its treatment, and its prevention are described.
Kluckhohn, Clyde, and Leighton, Dorothea. *The Navaho.* Rev. ed. Garden City, N.Y.: Doubleday, 1962.
    This book is a comprehensive anthropologic study of the Navaho. It contains much information regarding health and illness and the prevention and treatment of disease.
Stone, Eric. *Medicine among the American Indians.* New York: Hafner, 1962.
    Multiple treatments for various ailments as well as a history of these treatments are presented.

FURTHER SUGGESTED READINGS

BOOKS

Bonfante, Leo. *Biographies and Legends of the New England Indians.* Wakefield, Mass.: Pride Publ., 1974.
Brand, Johanna. *The Life and Death of Anna Mae Aquash.* Toronto: James Lorimer & Co., 1978.

Brown, Dee. *Creek Mary's Blood.* New York: Holt, Rinehart, and Winston, 1980.

Cahn, Edgar S., and Hearne, David W., eds. *Our Brother's Keeper: The Indian in White America.* New York: New American Library, 1970.

Deloria, Vine, Jr. *Behind the Trail of Broken Treaties.* New York: Delacourt Press, 1974.

Kekahbah, Janice, and Wood, Rosemary, eds. *Life Cycle of the American Indian Family.* Norman, Okla.: AIANA Publishing Co., 1980.

Leighton, Alexander, and Leighton, Dorothea. *The Navaho Door,* Cambridge: Harvard University Press, 1945.

Matthiessen, Peter. *In the Spirit of Crazy Horse.* New York: Viking Press, 1980.

Oaks, Maud: King, Jeff; and Campbell, Joseph. *Where the Two Came to Their Father: A Navaho War Ceremonial.* Princeton: Princeton University Press, 1943.

Reichard, Gladys A. *Navaho Religion: A Study of Symbolism.* New York: Pantheon Books, 1950.

——. *Prayer: The Compulsive Word.* Monograph of the American Ethnological Society. Seattle: University of Washington Press, 1944.

Storm, Hyemeyohots. *Seven Arrows.* New York: Ballantine Books, 1972.

Unger, Steven, ed. *The Destruction of American Indian Families.* New York: Association on American Indian Affairs, 1977.

Vogel, Virgil. *American Indian Medicine.* Norman, Okla.: University of Oklahoma Press, 1970.

ARTICLES

Allen, James R. "The Indian Adolescent: Psycho-Social Tasks of the Plains Indian of Western Oklahoma." *American Journal of Ortho-psychiatry* 43 (April 1973): 368–75.

Harry Bilagody. "An American Indian Looks at Health Care." In *The Ninth Annual Training Institute for Psychiatrist-Teachers of Practicing Physicians,* ed. Raymond Feldman and Dorothy Buch (Boulder: WICHE, NO. 3A30, 1969), p. 21.

Bose, D. P., and Welsh, J. D. "Lactose Malabsorbtion in Oklahoma Indians." *American Journal of Clinical Nutrition* 26 (December 1973): 1320–22.

Brod, Thomas M. "Alcoholism as a Mental Health Problem of Native Americans." *Arch Gen Psychiatry* 32 (November 1975): 1385–90.

Brosseau, James D., et al. "Diabetes among the Three Affiliated Tribes: Correlation with Degree of Indian Inheritance." *American Journal of Public Health* 69, no. 12 (December 1979): 1277–78.

Cohen, Elizabeth. "After Wounded Knee: The Feeding of the American Indian." *Food Management,* April 1974, pp. 28–80.

Coulehan, John L. "Navaho Indian Medicine: A Dimension in Healing." *Pharos* 39 (July 1976): 93–96.

Cress, J. N., and O'Donnell, J. P. "The Self-esteem Inventory and the Oglala Sioux: A Validation Study." *Journal of Social Psychology* 97 (October 1975): 135–36.

Crowell, Susanne. "Life on the Largest Reservation: Poverty and Progress in the Navajo Nation." *Civil Rights Digest* 6 (Fall 1973): 3–9.

Farris, Lorene Sanders. "Approaches to Caring for the American Indian Maternity Patient." *American Journal of Maternal Child Nursing* 1, no. 2 (March/April 1976): 80–87.

Fortney, Alan Jon. "Has White Man's Lease Expired?" *Boston Sunday Globe*, 23 January 1977.

Fuchs, M., and Bashur, R. "Use of Traditional Indian Medicine among Urban Native Americans." *Medical Care* 13 (November 1975): 915–27.

Graves, Theodore D. "The Personal Adjustment of Navajo Indian Migrants to Denver, Colorado." *American Anthropologist* 72 (1970): 38–51.

Hardy, Mary Kniep, and Burckhardt, Margaret A. "Nursing the Navaho." *American Journal of Nursing* 77 (January 1977): 95–96.

Johnson, Carmel-Acosta. "A Case of a Psychotic Navaho Indian Male." In *Social Interaction and Patient Care*, edited by James K. Skipper, Jr., and Robert C. Leonard, pp. 184–95. Philadelphia: Lippincott, 1965.

Kniep-Hardy, Mary, and Burkhardt, Margaret A. "Nursing the Navajo." *American Journal of Nursing*, January 1977, pp. 95–96.

Kunitz, S. J. "Navaho and Hopi Fertility 1971–1972." *Human Biology* 46 (September 1974): 435–51.

Loughlin, Bernice W. "Pregnancy in the Navajo Culture." *Nursing Outlook*, March 1965, pp. 55–58.

McCauley, M. A. "Indian Nurse Considers Cultural Traits." *American Journal of Nursing*, May 1975, pp. 5, 15.

Maynard, E. "Negative Ethnic Image among Oglala Sioux High School Students." *Pine Ridge Research Bulletin* 6 (December 1968): 18–25.

Nagel, Gerald S. "American Indian Life: Unemployment, Ill Health, and Skid Rows." *Current*, January 1975, pp. 34–42.

Omelas, Ramona. "The Beat of a Different Drum." *Diabetes Forecast*, July/August 1977, pp. 25–27.

Peretti, Peter O. "Enforced Acculturation and Indian-White Relations." *Indian Historian* 6 (Winter 1973): 38–52.

Primeaux, Martha. "American Indian Health Care Practices: A Cross-Cultural Perspective." *Nursing Clinics of North America* 12 (March 1977): 55–65.

———, "Caring for the American Indian Patient." *American Journal of Nursing* 77 (January 1977): 91–94.

Robinson, Shirley. "Self-Help Programs for Indians and Native Alaskans." *Alcohol Health and Research World*, Summer 1974, pp. 11–15.

Rosenblum, Estelle H. "Conversation with a Navajo Nurse." *American Journal of Nursing*, August 1980, pp. 1459–61.

Saland, J.; McNamara, H.; and Cohen, M. I. "Navaho Jaundice: A Variant of Neonatal Hyperbilirubinemia Associated with Breast Feeding." *Journal of Pediatrics* 85 (August 1974): 271–75.

Samet, Jonathan M. et al. "Respiratory Disease Mortality in New Mexico's American Indians and Hispanics." *American Journal of Public Health* 70, no. 5 (May 1980): 492–97.

Satz, Karen J. "Integrating Navajo Tradition into Maternal-Child Nursing." *Image* 15, no. 3 (October 1982): 89–91.

Wauneka, Annie D. "Helping a People to Understand." *American Journal of Nursing* 62, no. 7 (July 1962): 88–90.

Webster, Noel. "WARN Against Battering on the Reservations." *Guardian*, 4 April 1984, p. 4.

Westermeyer, Joseph. "The Drunken Indian: Myths and Realities." *Psychiatric Annals* 4, no. 9 (November 1974): 29–35.

Whittaker, James O. "Alcohol and the Standing Rock Sioux Tribe II: Psychodynamic and Cultural Factors in Drinking." *Journal of Studies on Alcohol,* 1963, pp. 80–90.

CHAPTER 11

Health and Illness in the White Ethnic Communities

Members of the white ethnic communities have their origins in Europe. They have immigrated to this country ever since the very first settlers came to the shores of New England. The white population is comprised of diverse and multiple origins. The recent literature in the area of ethnicity and health has focused on people of color, and little has been written about the white ethnic communities. In this chapter an overview of the differences, by ethnicity, will be presented. Earlier chapters have focused on religious differences with respect to health and healing. The focus on this chapter will be on ethnic differences. Given that we are talking about well over 80 percent of the American population, the enormity of the task of attempting to describe each difference is readily apparent. Instead, I intend to highlight some of the basic beliefs of selected groups; for now, the groups with whom I have had the greatest exposure. I have not only been able to do library research but also firsthand research by interviewing and observing people in their daily experiences with the health-care delivery system, both as inpatients and as community residents receiving home care.

BACKGROUND

The major groups migrating to this country between 1820 and 1975 include people from: Germany—14.8 percent; Italy—11.1 percent; Great Britain—10.3 percent; Ireland—10 percent; Austro-Hungary—9.2 percent; Canada—8.6 percent; and Russia—7.1 percent, of the total number of immigrants to arrive in this country.[1] The most populous "foreign stock"—that is, people who are foreign-born Americans or native-born Americans with at least one foreign-born parent—include Italian, German, Canadian, British, and Poles.[2]

The 1980 census asked a general question relating to ancestry (ethnicity) for the first time in a decennial census. The question was based on self-identification and was open-ended. Ancestry refers to a person's nationality group, lineage, or the country in which the person or the person's parents or ancestors were born before they came to the United States. The responses to the question were a reflection of the ethnic group(s) with which the person identified and they were able to indicate their ethnic group regardless of how many generations they were removed from it.[3]

The 1980 census collected information on both single- and multiple-ancestry groups. A large number of people (about 83 percent) reported single ancestry, but many also reported double and triple ancestry. The results of the 1980 census with respect to ancestry were as follows:

English	50 million
German	49 million
Irish	40 million
Afro-American	21 million
French	13 million
Italian	12 million
Scottish	10 million
Polish	8 million
Mexican	8 million
American Indian	7 million
Dutch	6 million[4]

Tables 11-1 and 11-2 show the percent of distribution of European ancestry groups by region and the largest five states for European ancestry groups. Both tables were compiled from the 1980 census data.

The following discussion will focus on several white ethnic groups and attempt to describe some of the history of their migration to America, the areas where they now live, the common beliefs regarding health and illness, some kernels of information regarding family and social life, and problems that members from a given group may have in interacting with health-care providers. The intention is not to create a vehicle for stereotyping, but to whet the reader's appetite: to realize the vast differences among whites and to search out more information about the people the reader may be caring for from them, themselves.

TABLE 11-1. PERCENT DISTRIBUTION OF EUROPEAN (EXCLUDING SPANIARD) ANCESTRY GROUPS WITH 1,000,000 OR MORE PERSONS BY REGION: 1980

Ancestry group	Number (1,000)	Percent distribution				
		Total	Northeast	North Central	South	West
English	49,598	100	16	23	40	21
German	49,224	100	19	41	22	18
Irish	40,166	100	24	26	32	18
French[a]	12,892	100	26	27	27	19
Italian	12,184	100	57	16	13	14
Scottish	10,049	100	19	23	35	24
Polish	8,228	100	41	38	11	10
Dutch	6,304	100	18	35	26	20
Swedish	4,345	100	15	43	12	31
Norwegian	3,454	100	7	55	7	31
Russian n.e.c.[b]	2,781	100	48	17	16	19
Czech	1,892	100	18	49	18	15
Hungarian	1,777	100	39	33	13	14
Welsh	1,665	100	25	27	22	27
Danish	1,518	100	9	38	10	43
Portuguese	1,024	100	50	3	6	41

NOTE: Includes persons who reported single and multiple ancestry group(s). Persons who reported a multiple ancestry group may be included in more than one category.
[a]Excludes French Basque.
[b]Includes persons who reported as Russian, Great Russian, Georgian, and other related European or Asian groups.

TABLE 11-2. LARGEST FIVE STATES FOR EUROPEAN (EXCLUDING SPANIARD) ANCESTRY GROUPS WITH 1,000,000 OR MORE PERSONS: 1980

Ancestry group	Rank of States				
	First	Second	Third	Fourth	Fifth
English	Calif.	Tex.	Ohio	N.Y.	Fla.
German	Calif.	Pa.	Ohio	Ill.	N.Y.
Irish	Calif.	N.Y.	Pa.	Tex.	Ohio
French[a]	Calif.	La.	Mich.	Mass.	N.Y.
Italian	N.Y.	N.J.	Pa.	Calif.	Mass.
Scottish	Calif.	Tex.	Pa.	Fla.	N.Y.
Polish	N.Y.	Ill.	Pa.	Mich.	N.J.
Dutch	Calif.	Mich.	Pa.	N.Y.	Ohio
Swedish	Calif.	Minn.	Ill.	Wash.	Mich.
Norwegian	Minn.	Wis.	Calif.	Wash.	N.D.
Russian n.e.c.[b]	N.Y.	Calif.	Pa.	N.J.	Fla.
Czech	Ill.	Tex.	Calif.	Wis.	N.Y.
Hungarian	N.Y.	Ohio	Pa.	N.J.	Calif.
Welsh	Pa.	Calif.	Ohio	N.Y.	Fla.
Danish	Calif.	Utah	Minn.	Iowa	Wis.
Portuguese	Calif.	Mass.	R.I.	Hawaii	N.J.

NOTE: Includes persons who reported single and multiple ancestry group(s). Persons who reported a multiple ancestry group may be included in more than one category.
[a]Excludes French Basque.
[b]Includes persons who reported as Russian, Great Russian, Georgian, and other related European or Asian groups.
Source: U.S., Department of Commerce, Bureau of the Census. 1980 Census of Population—Ancestry of the Population by State: 1980—Supplementary Report. (Washington, D.C.: Government Printing Office, 1983), p. 2.

ITALIAN-AMERICANS

The Italian-American community is comprised of immigrants who came here from mainland Italy, from Sicily and Sardinia, and other Mediterranean islands that are part of Italy. The number of Americans claiming Italian ancestry is 12 million; the states with the highest concentration of Italians are New York, New Jersey, Pennsylvania, California, and Massachusetts; and the cities with the largest Italian populations are New York, Philadelphia, Chicago, Boston, and Newark.[5]

Italian-Americans indeed have a proud heritage in the United States, for America was "founded" by an Italian—Christopher Columbus; named for an Italian—Amerigo Vespucci—and explored by several Italian explorers, including Verrazano, Cabot, and Tonti.[6]

History of Migration

Between 1820 and 1976, over 5 million people from Italy immigrated to the United States. The peak years were from 1901 to 1920 and only a small number of people are coming today. The Italians came to this country to escape poverty and to search for a better life in a country where they expected to reap rewards for their hard labor. The early years were not easy, but people chose to remain in this country and not return to Italy. The Italians tended to live in neighborhood enclaves and these neighborhoods, such as the North End in Boston and Little Italy in New York, still exist as Italian neighborhoods. Although the younger generation may have moved out, they still return home to maintain family, community, and ethnic ties.[7]

The family has served as the main tie that has kept the people together, for it provides the person with the strength to cope with the surrounding world and produces a sense of continuity in all situations. The family is the primary focus of the Italian's concern and the Italian takes pride in the family and the home. The Italians are resilient, yet fatalistic, and they take advantage of the present. As mentioned, the home is a source of great pride, and it is a symbol of the family, not a status symbol, per se. The church is also an important focus for the life of the Italian.[8] Many of the festivals and observances continue to exist today and in the summer the North End of Boston is alive each weekend with the celebration of a given saint (Fig. 11-1).

The father is the head of the Italian household and the mother is said to be the heart of the household.

Italian-Americans have tended to attain low levels of education in the United States, but their incomes are comparable to or higher than those of other groups.[9]

The Italian population falls into four generational groups: (1) the elderly, living in Italian enclaves; (2) a second generation living both within the neighborhoods and in the suburbs; (3) a younger, well-educated group living mainly in the suburbs; and (4) new immigrants.[10]

70th GRAND RELIGIOUS FEAST

IN HONOR OF THE PROTECTRESS

SAINT AGRIPPINA
DI MINEO

THE THREE-DAY FEAST IS IN HONOR AND PRAISE OF SAINT AGRIPPINA, THE PROTECTRESS AND PATRON SAINT OF THE IMMIGRANTS FROM THE SMALL TOWN OF MINEO IN SICILY AND THEIR DESCENDANTS.

EACH YEAR FOR THE PAST 69 YEARS THIS GROUP OF DEVOTED 'PAESANI', NOW SCATTERED THROUGHOUT THE STATE, COME TOGETHER IN THE NORTH END SECTION TO PROCLAIM ANEW THEIR FAITH, AS WAS THE CUSTOM IN THEIR LAND OF ORIGIN. EACH YEAR EVERYONE IS INVITED TO PARTICIPATE AND WITNESS THE HONOR AND GLORY THAT IS BESTOWED TO THIS MARTYRED SAINT.

Advisory Consultant · Peter Tardo
Maestro di Banda · Gaetano Giaraffo
Capo di Banda · Stanley Pugliese

SANT'AGRIPPINA DI MINEO

A beautiful blonde maiden Saint'Agrippina was a princess by birth. This beautiful virgin martyr who was unmercifully scorged and tortured to death by the Emperor Valerion (256 AD). After her death, her relics were taken from Rome to Mineo by Saints Agatha Bassa and Paula.

The Greeks honor her in a lesser degree and claim to have relics of her. Also, in the city of Constantinople, they claim to have her body.

Saint Agrippina is the Patron Saint of thunderstorms, leprosy and evil spirits.

ST. AGRIPPINA PRAY FOR
OUR DECEASED MEMBERS

A Tug of War will take place when the procession is over. The Saint is being carried by 20 men, namely Sicilians against the Romans.

Figure 11-1. Announcement of a North End (Boston) Festival. (From the author's collection.)

Health and Illness

Italians tend to present their symptoms to their fullest point and to expect immediate treatment for ailments. In traditional belief terms, they may view the cause of illness to be one of the following: (1) winds and currents that bear diseases; (2) contagion or contamination; (3) heredity; (4) supernatural or human causes; and (5) psychosomatic interactions.

Moving air, in the form of drafts, causes irritation and then a cold that can lead to pneumonia. A belief an elderly person may express in terms of cancer surgery is that it is not a good idea to have surgery because surgery exposes the inner body to the air and if the cancer is "exposed to the air the person is going to die quicker." Just as drafts are considered to be a cause of illness, fresh air is considered to be vital for the maintenance of health. Homes and the workplace must be well ventilated, to prevent illness from occurring.

One sees the belief in contamination manifested in the reluctance of people to share food and objects with people who are considered unclean and they will often not enter the homes of those who are ill. There is also a strong sense of modesty and shame among women, resulting in an avoidance of discussions relating to sex and menstruation.

Blood is regarded by some, especially the elderly, to be a "plastic entity" that responds to fluids and food and is responsible for many variable conditions. Various adjectives, such as "high" and "low" and "good" and "bad," are used to describe blood. Some of the "old superstitions" include the beliefs that:

1. Congenital abnormalities can be attributed to the unsatisfied desire for food during pregnancy.
2. If a woman is not given food that she smells, the fetus will move inside and a miscarriage will result.
3. If a pregnant woman bends or turns or moves in a certain way, the fetus may not develop normally.
4. A woman must not reach during pregnancy because reaching can harm the fetus.

Italians may also attribute the cause of illness to the evil eye or to curses. There is a difference between these two causes in that less serious illnesses such as headaches may be caused by *malocchio,* while more severe illness, which can often be fatal, may be attributed to more powerful curses—*castiga.* Curses are sent either by God or by evil people. An example of a curse is the punishment from God for sins and bad behavior.[11]

It is also recognized by Italians that illness can be caused by the suppression of emotions, as well as stress from fear, grief, and anxiety. If one is unable to find an emotional outlet, one well may "burst." It is not considered healthy to bottle up emotions.[12]

Often the care of the ill is managed in the home, with all members of the family sharing in the responsibilities. The use of home remedies is ostensibly decreasing, although several students have reported the continued use of rituals for the removal of the evil eye and the practice of leeching. One practice described for the removal of the evil eye was to take an egg and olive oil and to drip them into a pan of water, make the sign of the cross, and recite prayers. If the oil spreads over the water, the cause of the problem is the evil eye, and the illness should get better. Mineral waters are also used and tonics are used to cleanse the blood. There is also a strong religious influence among Italians who believe that faith in God and the saints will see them through the illness. One woman that I worked with had breast cancer. She had had her surgery several years ago and did not have a recurrence. She attributed her recovery to the fact that she attended mass every single morning and that she had total faith in Saint Peregrine, whose medal she wore pinned to her bra by the site of the mastectomy. In regard to terminal illness and death, people tend to take a fatalistic stance and believe that it is God's will. Death is often not discussed between the dying person and the family members. I recall caring for an elderly Italian man at home and, in working with the family, it was not possible to have the man and his wife discuss the situation. Although each knew that he was dying and would talk with the nurse, to each other he "was going to recover," and everything possible was done to that end.

The families observe numerous religious traditions surrounding death, and funeral masses and anniversary masses are observed. It is the custom for the widow to wear black, although this is not as common with the younger generations.

Health-related Problems
Two diseases commonly seen among Italians are of genetic origin; one is favism, a severe hemolytic anemia produced by the eating of fava beans and the deficiency of an X-linked enzyme. The second problem is the Thalassemia syndromes, including Cooley's anemia and alpha thalassemia.[13]

Language problems frequently occur when the elderly or new immigrants are seeking care. Often, due to modesty, people are reluctant to answer the questions asked through interpreters and the gathering of pertinent data is most difficult.

Problems related to time also occur. Physicians tend to diagnose emotional problems more often for Italian patients than other ethnic groups because of the Italian pattern of reporting more symptoms and reporting them more dramatically.[14]

In general, Italian-Americans are motivated to seek explanations with respect to their health status and the care they are to receive. If instructions and explanations are well given, they tend to cooperate with health-care providers. It is often necessary to actually spell out directions in the greatest detail and then to provide written instructions to insure compliance with necessary regimens.

GERMAN-AMERICANS

(The following material, relating to both the German-American and Polish-American communities was obtained from research conducted in southeastern Texas in May 1982. It is by no means indicative of the health and illness beliefs of the entire German-American and Polish-American communities. It is included here to demonstrate the type of data that can be gleaned using an "emic"* approach of col-

---

*Emic: description of behavior dependent on the person's categorization of the action. Etic: description of behavior based on categories created by the investigator and employed to compare phenomena cross-culturally. These are two forms of anthropological research described by Pelto and Pelto in *Anthropological Research: The Structure of Inquiry,* 2nd ed. Cambridge: Cambridge University Press, 1978.

lecting data. It cannot be generalized, but it allows the reader to grasp the diversity of beliefs that surround us!)

Since 1830 almost 7 million Germans have immigrated to the United States. There are presently 49 million Americans who claim German ancestry. The Germans represented a cross section of German society and came from all social strata and walks of life. Some came to escape poverty, others came for religious or political reasons, and others came to take advantage of the opportunity to open up the new lands. Many were recruited to come here, as were the Germans who settled in the German enclaves in Texas. The immigrants represented all religions, including primarily Lutherans, Catholics, and Jews. There were the rich and the poor, the educated and the ignorant, all coming here. The immigrants were of all ages. Present-day descendants are farmers, educators, artists, and so forth. The Germans brought to the United States the cultural diversity and folkways that they observed in Germany. The festivals of Corpus Christi, Kinderfeste (children's feast), and Sangerfeste (singing festival) all originated in Germany.[15]

The states with the greatest number of people with German ancestry are California, Pennsylvania, Ohio, Illinois, and New York. The cities with the greatest numbers are New York, Chicago, Philadelphia, Milwaukee, and Detroit.[16]

The Germans began to migrate to the United States in the seventeenth century and have contributed 15 percent of the total immigration population. They are the least visible ethnic group in the United States and often people are surprised to discover there is such a large Germanic influence in this country. In other places, the German communities maintain strong identification with their German heritage: for example, the city of Fredericksberg, Texas, maintains an ambience of German culture and identity. People born there who are fourth generation and more, continue to learn German as their first spoken language.[17]

The German ethnic community is the second largest foreign-stock group in the state of Texas and is exceeded only by the Mexican community. Germans have been immigrating to Texas since 1840 and continue to arrive. They are predominantly Catholic, Lutheran, and Methodist. Many of these people have maintained their German identity. The major German communities in Texas are Victoria, Cuero, Gonzales, New Braunfels, and Fredericksberg.

Texas, during the European freedom revolutions of 1830 and 1848, was quite popular especially in Germany, and was seen as a "wild and fabulous land." However, for the tradition-bound German families, the abandonment of the homeland was difficult. They were enticed, however, by the hopes of economic and social improvement and political idealism. An additional reason for the mass migration was the overpopulation of Germany, and the immigrants' desire to escape an imminent European catastrophe. By the 1840s several thousand Northern Germans had come to Texas, and another large migration occurred in 1890. This second cluster of people came because there was a severe crop failure in Russian-occupied Germany and the Russian language had become a required subject in German schools. Other German migrations occurred from 1903 to 1905.

The Germans found pleasure in the small things of everyday life. They were tied together by the German language for it bound them to the past, entertained them with games, riddles, folk songs and literature, and folk wisdom. The greatest amusement was singing and dancing. Religion for the Lutherans, Catholics, and Methodists was a part of everyday life. The year was measured by the church calendar; observance of church ritual paced the milestones of the life cycle. The Germans believed that each individual was a "part of the fabric of humanity," that "history was a continued process," and "everything had a purpose as mankind strove to something better."[18]

The Germans had a penchant for forming societies and clubs and the longest lasting of these clubs are the singing societies. The first was organized in 1850 and it exists now. The Germans brought with them their customs and traditions, their cures, curses, and recipes, and their tools and ways of building.[19]

Health and Illness

Among the Germans, health may be described as a state of well-being—physically and emotionally; the ability to do your duty; more than not being ill, positive energy to do things—enjoy life; and the ability to do and think and act the way you would like to—to go and congregate, to enjoy life. Illness may be described as the absence of well-being, pain; malfunction of body organs; not being able to do what you want to do; a blessing from God to suffer; and a disorder of body, imbalance.

Causes of Illness

Most people believe in the germ theory and in the stress-related theories. However, other causes of illness are identified, such as drafts, environmental changes, and belief in the evil eye and punishment from God.

The methods of maintaining health include the requirement of dressing properly for the season, proper nutrition, and the wearing of shawls to protect oneself from drafts. Also, the taking of cod-liver oil, exercise, and hard work. Methods for preventing illness include wearing an asafetida bag around the neck in the winter to prevent colds, wearing scapulars, religious practices, sleeping with the windows open, and cleanliness.

The use of home remedies to treat illness continues to be practiced. Table 11–3 gives examples of commonly used home remedies.

Current Health Problems

There do not appear to be any unusual health problems particular to German-Americans.[20]

TABLE 11–3. ILLNESS SYMPTOMS AND REMEDIES AMONG GERMAN-AMERICANS

Gastrointestinal Problems

Symptom	Remedy
Constipation	Castor oil Black draught
Diarrhea or vomiting	Don't eat for 24 hours Chicken soup
Stomachache	Peppermint tea Tea and toast Berries - elderberry

Respiratory Problems

Symptom	Remedy
Cold	Wet compress around throat - cover with wool Lemon juice and whiskey Apply chopped onions in a sack to the soles of the feet *Olbas* oil (made in Germany)
Cough	Goose fat - rub on chest Honey and milk *Tausend Gülden Kraut* (thousand golden herb) - rum
Earache	Put warm oil in ear Warm towels Bitter geranium leaves
Sore throat	Put camphor on a wet rag - wind around the throat Gargle with salt water Onion compress Chicken soup Linaments

Physical Injuries

Symptom	Remedy
Bumps	Hard knife (cold metal), place on bump
Cuts	Iodine - clean well
Puncture wound (nail)	Soak in kerosene
Wounds	Clean well with water - apply iodine

Miscellaneous Problems

Symptom	Remedy
Aches and pains	Kytle's linament *Olbas* oil Volcanic oil Salves and linaments

(continued)

TABLE 11-3—Continued

Miscellaneous Problems–Continued

Symptom	Remedy
Arthritis	Warm water soaks
	Honey, vinegar, and water soaks
Boils	"Capital water" - sulfur water - drink this (this is available at the Texas Capital)
Clean body after winter	Kur (similar to hot springs) drink
Fever	Cold compress on head - fluids
Headache	Iced cloth on head
Menstrual cramps	Cardui
Rheumatism	Aloe Vera - rub on sore area
	Cod-liver oil - massage
Ringworm	Apply fig juice
Sty	Camomile-tea compress
	One half of a hard-boiled egg - apply warm white on eye
Toothache	Cloves
	Salbec tea
	Olbas oil
Warts	Apply fig juice and fig leaf milk

Source: Rachel E. Spector, "A Description of the Impact of Medicare on Health-Illness Beliefs and Practices of White Ethnic Senior Citizens in Central Texas." Ph.D. diss. University of Texas at Austin School of Nursing, 1983; Ann Arbor, Mich.: University Microfilms International, 1983.

POLISH-AMERICANS

The first people immigrating to this country from Poland came with Germans in 1608 to Jamestown, Virgina, to help develop the timber industry. Since that time, Poland, too, has given America one of its largest ethnic groups, with well over 8 million people claiming Polish ancestry. Many of the people arriving before 1890 came for economic reasons. Those coming here since that time came for both economic and political reasons and also for religious freedom. The present situation in Poland is a source of concern for the many people who have family ties to their homeland today. Polish heros include Casimir Pulaski and Thaddeus Kosciuszko who were heros in the American Revolution. The major influx of Poles to the United States began in 1870 and ended in 1913. The people who arrived were mainly peasants seeking food and release from the political oppression of three foreign governments in Poland. The immigrants who came both before and after this mass of immigrants were better educated and not as poor. In the United States, the Polish immigrants lived in poor conditions either because they had no choice or because that was the way they were able to meet their own priorities. They were seen by other Americans to live as animals and were often mocked and called stupid. Quite often, the Polish people spoke and understood several European languages but had difficulty learning English, and they were scorned. The Polish people shared the problem as a community and banded together in tight enclaves called "Polonia." They attempted to be as self-sufficient as possible. They worked at preserving their native culture and voluntary Polish ghettos grew up in close proximity to the parish church.[21]

An example of the Polish experience in the United States is that of the Polish immigrants in Texas. The first Poles came to Texas in the second half of the nineteenth century and most of them settled in Victoria, San Antonio, Houston, and Bandera. The first Polish colonies in America were located in Texas, the oldest being Panna Maria (Virgin Mary) in Karnes County, 50 miles southeast of San Antonio. Unlike other Poles who wanted to return to Poland, the colonists who arrived in Texas after 1850 came to settle permanently and had no intention of returning to their homeland. These people came to Texas for economic, political, and religious reasons; severe poverty was the major reason for leaving Poland.

The first collective Polish immigration to America was in 1854 when 100 families came to Texas. They landed in Galveston where a few in the party remained. The rest traveled in a procession northwestward, bringing with them a few belongings such as featherbeds, crude farm implements, and a cross from their parish church. Their dream of living in the fertile lands of Texas was to raise crops, speak their own language, educate their children, and worship God as they pleased. This dream did not materialize and members of the band grew discouraged. Some of the immigrants remained in Victoria and others went to San Antonio.

The people who went to San Antonio continued to travel and on Christmas Eve, 1854, they stopped at the junction of the San Antonio and Cibolo rivers. Here, under a live oak tree, they celebrated mass and founded Panna Maria. In 1855, 1856, and 1857 others followed this small group in moving to this part of Texas.

These settlers were exposed to many dangers from nature, such as heat, drought, snakes, and insects. The Polish settlers were not accepted by the other settlers in the area because their language, customs, and culture were different. But the immigrants survived and many moved to settle other areas near Panna Maria. Today, the people of Panna Maria continue to live simple lives close to nature and God and speak mainly Polish.

Much of the history of the Polish people in Texas is written around the foundings and the locations of the various church parishes. For example, in 1873 the Parish of the Nativity of the Blessed Virgin Mary was begun in Cestohowa. Within this church above the main altar is a large picture of the Virgin Mary of Czestohowa. This picture was taken to the church from Panna Maria. It is a copy of the famous Madonna of Czestohowa, Poland, a city 65 miles east of where the immigrants to Texas originated. The Black Madonna is a beloved, miraculous image and a source of faith to the Polish people. The shrine of Our Lady in Czestohowa, Poland, is one of the largest shrines in the world. Since the fourteenth century that picture had been the object of veneration and devotion of Polish Catholics. It is claimed to have been painted by Saint Luke the Evangelist; its origin is traced to the fifth or sixth century A.D.; and it is the oldest picture of the Virgin in the world. The scars on the face date from 1430 when bandits struck it with a sword. The history, traditions, and miracles of Czestohowa are the heritage of the Polish people.[22] One woman that I interviewed said that she had been ill with a fatal disease. The entire time that she lay close to death she prayed to the Virgin. When she finally did recover, she made a pilgrimage back to her homeland in Poland and visited the shrine to give thanks to the Virgin. The woman was positive that this was the source of her recovery.

The states with the greatest numbers of Polish people are New York, Illinois, Pennsylvania, New Jersey, and Michigan; the cities with the largest Polish communities are New York, Chicago, Detroit, Philadelphia, and Buffalo.[23]

Health and Illness
The definitions of health among the Polish people I interviewed included: feeling O.K.—as a whole—body, spirit, everything a person can't separate; happy, until war, don't need doctor, don't need medicine; active, able to work, feel good, do what I want to do; and good spirit, good to everybody, never cross. The definitions for illness may include: something wrong with body, mind, or spirit, one wrong affects them all; not capable of working, see the doctor often; not right, something ailing you; not active; feeling bad; and opposite of health, not doing what I want to do. The methods for maintaining health include the following: Happy home, kind and loving, healthy food, pure, walk, exercise, proper clothing, sweaters, well-balanced diet, try not to worry, faith in God, activity, dress warm, go to bed early, and work hard. The methods for preventing illness include: cleanliness, the wearing of scapulars, avoiding drafts, following the proper diet, not gossiping, keeping away from people with colds, and wearing medals because "God is with you all the time to protect you and take care of you." Other ideas about illness include the beliefs that illnesses are caused by poor diets and that the evil eye may well exist as a causative factor (but not really sure). This belief was attributed to the older generations and is not regarded as prevalent among younger people.

The home remedies listed in Table 11–4 were described and were in common use.

Health-Care Problems
There are no outstanding problems between the Polish community and the health-care deliverers. Language may be a barrier if members of the older generation do not speak English and the taking of health

TABLE 11-4. ILLNESS SYMPTOMS AND REMEDIES AMONG POLISH-AMERICANS

Gastrointestinal Problems

Symptom	Remedy
Colic	Tea - peppermint or camomile Sugar, water, vinegar, and soda, makes soda water Bess-plant tea Homemade sauerkraut
Constipation	Epsom salts - teaspoon in water - cleans out stomach Cascara Castor oil Senna-leaf tea
Cramps	Camomile tea
Diarrhea	Paregoric Cinnamon tea Dried blueberries Chew coffee beans
Gas	Drink soda water
Indigestion	Aloes vulgaris - juniper and elder-berries Peppermint and spearmint teas Blackberries

Respiratory Problems

Symptom	Remedy
Cold	Castor oil - mentholatum Flaxseed or mustard poultice - on chest Dried raspberries and tea with wine Mustard plaster Oatmeal poultice - hot bricks to feet Cupping Camphor salve Oxidine Rub goose fat on chest
Cough	Honey and hot water; bed rest Hot lemonade with whiskey; honey Few drops of turpentine and sugar "Gugel Mugel" - warm milk with butter, whiskey, and honey Honey and warm milk Milk with butter and garlic Mustard plaster Linden tea Onion poultice

(continued)

TABLE 11-4—Continued

Respiratory Problems–Continued

Symptom	Remedy
Croup	Few drops of kerosene and sugar
Sore throat	Honey
	Warm water, salt - gargle
	Goose grease around throat covered with a dry rag
	Paint throat with kerosene
	Goose fat in milk

Physical Injury

Symptom	Remedy
Burns	Aloe Vera
Cuts	Vinegar, water, flour paste
	Clean with urine
	Carbolic salve
Puncture wounds (nail)	Turpentine and linament
	Put salt pork on wound and soak in hot water
	Hunt's lightning oil
Frostbite	Put snow on frozen place
Scratches, sores	Linament
	Moss
	Spider webs
Sprains	Linaments - Sloan's Volcanic

Miscellaneous Problems

Symptom	Remedy
Earache	Hot water bottle to ear
	Camphor on cotton - place in ear
Fever	Camomile tea
Flu	Novak oil - rub on head
	Knorr's Green Drops
Headache	Vinegar on a cloth applied to head
	Steam kettle - cover head and inhale
High blood pressure	Cooked garlic
	Garlic oil
Lice	Cover head with kerosene
Toothache	Hot salt compress
Neuralgia	Bed rest
Pyorrhea	Drink yarrow
Rheumatism	Lemon juice - rub on sore places
Trouble urinating	Juice of pumpkin seeds made into a tea
	Swamp root medicine

Source: Rachel E. Spector, "A Description of the Impact of Medicare on Health-Illness Beliefs and Practices of White Ethnic Senior Citizens in Central Texas." Ph.D. diss. University of Texas at Austin School of Nursing, 1983; Ann Arbor, Mich.: University Microfilms International, 1983.

histories is complicated when the providers cannot communicate directly with the informant. Again, the problems of using an interpreter may develop when there is difficulty finding someone who is conversant in Polish, whom the informant will trust to reveal personal matters to, and who will translate accurately.[24]

In Poland, there is a shortage of medical supplies and there is the use of faith healers and the belief in miracle workers. On the main street of Warsaw all sorts of folk-medicine and miracle-worker paraphernalia are on sale: divining rods, cotton sacks filled with herbs to be worn over an ailing heart or liver, coils of copper wire to be placed under food to rid it of poisons, and pendulums.[25]

In this chapter I have attempted to open the door to the enormous diversity regarding health and illness beliefs that exists in the white communities. I have only opened the door and peeked inside. There is a richness of knowledge to be gained. It is for you to acquire it as you care for all patients. Ask them what they believe about health and illness and what their practices and remedies may be. The students that I am working with find this to be a most enlightening experience.

REFERENCES

1. Stephanie Bernardo, *The Ethnic Almanac* (New York: Doubleday, 1981), p. 24.
2. Ibid., p. 474.
3. U.S., Department of Commerce, Bureau of the Census. *1980 Census of Population—Ancestry of the Population by State: 1980* (Washington, D.C.: Government Printing Office, 1983), p. 6.
4. Ibid., p. 2.
5. Bernardo, *Ethnic Almanac*, p. 29.
6. Ibid., p. 26.
7. Humbert S. Nelli. "Italians," in *Harvard Encyclopedia of American Ethnic Groups,* ed. Stephan Thernstrom (Cambridge: Harvard University Press, 1980), pp. 545–60.
8. Marie Rotunno and Monica McGoldrick, "Italian Families," in *Ethnicity and Family Therapy* ed. Monica McGoldrick, John K. Pearce, and Joseph Giordano (New York: Guilford Press, 1982), p. 341.
9. Ibid., p. 344.
10. Antoinette T. Ragucci, "Italian Americans" in *Ethnicity and Medical Care,* ed. Alan Harwood (Cambridge: Harvard University Press, 1981), p. 216.
11. Ibid., pp. 223–32.
12. Ibid., p. 232.
13. Ibid., p. 222.
14. Rotunno and McGoldrick, "Italian Families," p. 350.
15. Kathleen Neils Conzen, "Germans" in *Harvard Encyclopedia of American Ethnic Groups,* ed. Stephan Thernstrom (Cambridge: Harvard University Press, 1980), pp. 405–25.
16. Bernardo, *Ethnic Almanac* p. 35.

17. Rachel E. Spector, "A Description of the Impact of Medicare on Health-Illness Beliefs and Practices of White Ethnic Senior Citizens in Central Texas." Ph.D. diss. University of Texas at Austin School of Nursing, 1983; Ann Arbor, Mich.: University Microfilms International, 1983.
18. G. E. Lich, *The German Texans* (San Antonio: University of Texas Institute of Texan Cultures, 1982), pp. 33–72.
19. Ibid. p. 81.
20. Spector, *Impact of Medicare,* pp. 120–33.
21. Victoria Green, "Poles," in *Harvard Encyclopedia of American Ethnic Groups,* ed. Stephan Thernstrom (Cambridge: Harvard University Press, 1980), pp. 787–803.
22. E. J. Dworaczyk, *The First Polish Colonies of America in Texas* (San Antonio: Naylor Co., 1979) and B. Grzelonski, *Poles in the United States: 1776–1865* (Warsaw: Interpeirs, 1976).
23. Bernardo, *Ethnic Almanac,* p. 48.
24. Spector, *Impact of Medicine,* pp. 120–33.
25. "Letter from Poland—Of Faith Healers and Miracle Workers," *Boston Globe,* 21 August 1983.

BIBLIOGRAPHY

Bernardo, Stephanie. *The Ethnic Almanac.* New York: Doubleday, 1981.
    Bernardo describes the customs, culture, and traditions of numerous ethnic groups in America. She also provides pertinent information regarding the numbers of people in various ethnic groups, the states where they live, and interesting facts about the contributions members have made to American life.
Hand, Wayland D., ed. *American Folk Medicine: A Symposium.* Berkeley: University of California Press, 1976.
    A description of the practice of folk medicine in the United States, this symposium covers such topics as folk medicine among the Amish, the powwow in Pennsylvania, and folk medicine among French Canadians.
Harney, Robert F. and Harold Troper. *Immigrants.* Toronto: Van Nostrand Reinhold, 1975.
    This well-illustrated text provides a history of the ethnic groups who immigrated to Canada.
Harwood, Alan, ed. *Ethnicity and Medical Care.* Cambridge: Harvard University Press, 1981.
    This book covers the health and illness beliefs and practices among the Italian-Americans in addition to the beliefs of various ethnic groups of color.
McGoldrick, Monica; John K. Pearce; and Joseph Giordano, eds. *Ethnicity and Family Therapy.* New York: Guilford Press, 1982.
    In this excellent text, the experiences of several family therapists working with families of diverse backgrounds are described. Among the ethnic groups included are the Greeks, Irish, Germans, Iranians, and Polish. It is one of the few sources that contains background information to any great extent on white ethnic groups.
McLemore, S. Dale. *Racial and Ethnic Relations in America.* Boston: Allyn and Bacon, 1980.
    McLemore describes theories of Americanization and the experiences of various groups in socializing to the American culture.

Thernstrom, Stephan, ed. *Harvard Encyclopedia of American Ethnic Groups.*
   Cambridge: Harvard University Press, 1980.
   This outstanding text provides information about all aspects of immigration and the immigrants in terms of their social and cultural backgrounds. It is a valuable library resource for every nursing school.

FURTHER SUGGESTED READINGS

BOOKS

Anderson, J. Q. *Texas Folk Medicine.* Austin: Encino Press, 1970.

Bauwens, Eleanor F. *The Anthropology of Health.* St. Louis: C. V. Mosby,
   1979.

Benjamin, G. G. *The Germans in Texas.* (originally published in 1910) Austin:
   Jenkins Publishing Co., 1974.

Boney, Wilfrid. *The French Canadians Today.* London: J. M. Dent and Sons,
   1939.

Bracq, Jean C. *The Evolution of French Canada.* New York: MacMillan Co.,
   1924.

Candill, Harry M. *Night Comes to the Cumberlands.* Boston: Little, Brown
   and Co., 1962.

Crispino, Joseph A. *Assimilation of Ethnic Groups: The Italian Case.* Newark:
   New Jersey Center for Migration, 1980.

Gambino, R. *Blood of My Blood: The Dilemma of Italian-Americans.* Garden
   City, N.Y.: Doubleday, 1974.

Greeley, Andrew M. *The Irish Americans.* New York: Harper and Row, 1981.

Hufford, David J. *American Healing Systems: An Introduction and
   Exploration. Conference Booklet.* Philadelphia: University of Pennsylvania,
   1984.

Miner, Horace. *St. Denis: A French Canadian Parish.* Chicago: University of
   Chicago Press, 1939.

Shepard, Richard F. and Levi, Vickie G. *Live and Be Well.* New York:
   Ballantine Books, 1982.

Wade, Mason. *The French-Canadian Outlook.* New York: Viking Press, 1946.
———. *The French Canadians, 1876-1945.* New York: MacMillan Co., 1955.

CHAPTER 12

The Use of *Parteras* in the Rio Grande Valley, Texas

A Case Study

January 2, 1925

Malone Duggan, M.D.
State Health Officer
Capital Station
Austin, Texas

Dear Sir:

. . . The conclusions, based on a study (of the midwife situation in Texas) and information gained by contact and correspondence during the past sixteen months, are:

This final chapter is an example of two health care systems—modern and traditional—existing side by side. It is an edited and abridged edition of a paper originally published as Working Paper Number 23, The Lyndon B. Johnson School of Public Affairs, The University of Texas at Austin, 1983. It represents one outcome of the U.S.-Mexico Border Maternal and Child Health Care Project. The overall project was directed by Drs. David C. Warner, Chandler Stolp, and Bernard Portnoy. The project was conducted under a contract with the American Academy of Pediatrics and funded by a grant from the Robert Wood Johnson Foundation, the Hogg Foundation, the Lyndon B. Johnson Foundation, and the Henry J. Kaiser Family Foundation. The research was conducted in 1981 and 1982.

1. That the midwives have practiced without restraint and have practically ignored state laws.

2. That the midwives have no training, not even in the simplest rudiments of surgical cleanliness.

3. That many of the midwives are not capable of being trained.

4. That many deaths and much disability both of mothers and babies, are directly traceable to the lack of proper care.

5. That despite the above enumerated conclusions, the midwife is still a necessity in some communities. . . .

> Respectfully submitted,
> H. Garst, M.D.
> Director
> Bureau of Child Hygiene

INTRODUCTION

The preceding letter—written 60 years ago—may well illustrate an aspect of the current paradoxical view the medical and public health professions take toward the practicing lay midwife, especially the *partera.**

Midwifery, one of the oldest female professions, is the art and practice of attending women during childbirth, and the practice has been recognized throughout the history of humankind. Midwife means "with women" and until the seventeenth century, midwives were women. Women have always been healers—passing on skills and knowledge from one to another.[1]

Female healers were called "wise women" by the populace— witches or charlatans by the authorities.[4] As the male physician ascended to power over the centuries, women were more and more excluded from the healing profession, first by the suppression of "witches" in medieval Europe and later by the rise of male medical professionals. In the United States, male physicians began to include the delivery of babies in their practice during the eighteenth century. The number of hospital deliveries has rapidly increased over the years;

The following definitions are presented to clarify terms:
Lay midwife, a person who practices lay midwifery.
Lay midwifery, assisting childbirth for compensation.[2]
Partera, a Mexican-American or Mexican lay midwife, is a member of the indigenous health-care system of the Mexican-American and Mexican communities.[3] Because the majority of lay midwives residing in the Texas border counties are Mexican-American, or Mexican, the term *partera* will be used here. The only occasion for using the term midwife is in a discussion of state birth certificates because there is no way of isolating the *parteras* from the midwife category. It is assumed that in the counties along the United States-Mexico border, the midwives are predominantly *parteras.*

the numbers of midwife deliveries have in turn decreased. It is only recently that a change has been seen in this trend and the demand for female-attended births is increasing.[5]

In Mexico, too, there is a long history of the use of midwives—*parteras*. The practice of midwifery predates Cortes. The goddess Tlozoteotl was the goddess of childbirth, and the midwives were known as "Tlamatqui-Tuti." They, too, cared for the pregnant woman, attended the delivery, and cared for the newborn.[6]

OVERVIEW OF THE BORDERLANDS

"The United States-Mexico border presents a unique situation of human interdependence in a bi-national, multi-social-cultural and economic world."[7] The border extends for 2,000 miles—from Brownsville, Texas, and Matamoros, Mexico, in the east to San Diego, California, and Tijuana, Mexico, in the west. The border is one of the most rapidly developing areas in the United States. In Mexico, the population is growing even more rapidly than in the United States; there are 4 million people living along the Mexican side of the border, most in extreme poverty. Many of the people cross the border legally on a daily basis for work—many more cross the border illegally and disperse throughout the United States.[8]

I became most familiar with the lower Rio Grande Valley, and will focus on this part of the border. The South Texas border area is one of contrasts: economically, from the very rich to the very poor, the migrant and rural farm workers. Many of the poor live in *colonias,* where the water is not potable and there is inadequate food and shelter. Diseases, such as hepatitis, are endemic.[9] Culturally, the United States side of the border is bicultural—nearly 80 percent of the population is either bilingual or speaks only Spanish, and Mexican customs are observed. The major industry in the Valley is agriculture—oranges, grapefruit, and vegetables. The other important industry is tourism. Several small factories are beginning to be developed along the border.

The water supply in the valley is of a poor quality. It is contaminated with insecticides and other agricultural runoffs.[10] In addition, there are times when the water is in critically short supply; large amounts of water are lost to irrigation up-river. The local population nearly doubles each fall when the migrant workers return to their base camps.[11]

The major health problems in the valley's children are lack of immunization, anemia, lack of parental health education, and the lack of money to pay for health care.[12]

Mr. E. Garcia, the Clinic Manager of the McAllen Family Health Center in McAllen, Texas, and Mr. R. Garza, Clinic Director of *Su Clinica Familiar* in Harlingen, Texas believe the lack of money has led to an increased use of *parteras* (lay midwives) and *curanderas* (folk healers) to treat childhood illnesses. One can easily purchase both herbal and prescription medications over the counter in Mexico. Many Mexican women come to the United States side, especially Brownsville, for the delivery of their babies by *parteras*. The children are United States citizens by birth, and eligible for numerous benefits. Several problems have developed from this practice, such as the sale of illegal birth certificates and an unusually low neonatal mortality rate in Brownsville. If a baby dies in Mexico, its death is not recorded in the United States. There were two maternal deaths in Hidalgo county in 1981: both women were delivered by *parteras*. One woman died from a hemorrhage due to a retained placenta, the other from eclampsia. Also, in Hidalgo County, a mother who was not immunized against tetanus delivered a baby who developed tetanus of the umbilical cord. The baby survived.[13]

In the spring of 1981 there was a large measles epidemic in the valley. Several hundred children contracted measles, one died. Many of the children who developed measles were between the ages of 6 to 15 months. The practice of delaying measles immunization until 18 months was changed and babies are now immunized at 5 to 6 months. A door-to-door immunization program was initiated and 98 percent of the children were immunized against the measles. It has been estimated that 92 percent of the resident children are immunized against all childhood communicable diseases.[14]

PARTERAS

The Background of *Parteras*

Definition. The *partera*, midwife, is viewed as a healer by many members of the Mexican-American/Mexican communities. She is described as "an individual who is recognized in her community as having the ability to heal."[15] The *partera* is almost always a female, and is described as outgoing, warm, gentle, caring, and cooperative.

Function and Role. A *partera's* duties include: (1) giving advice to the pregnant woman; (2) giving physical aid, such as treating any illness the woman may experience during pregnancy; (3) guiding the woman through her pregnancy in terms of nutrition or activities she can and cannot do; and (4) being in attendance during labor and delivery.[16]

Profile. The following description of *parteras* has been developed from the Philpott dissertation[17] based on data collected in 1977 from *partera* interviews (Table 12-1). The *parteras* practiced in the Rio Grande Valley of Texas, six in Cameron County, 25 in Hidalgo County, and 1 in Willacy County. Thirty-one of the *parteras* had Spanish surnames, 21 (65.6 percent) were United States citizens and 11 (34.4 per-

**TABLE 12-1. PROFILE SUMMARY: 32 PARTERAS
IN THE LOWER RIO GRANDE VALLEY, TEXAS**

Characteristic	Number	Percentage	Range	Mean
Spanish surname	31	97.0		
U.S. citizen	21	65.6		
Mexican citizen residing in U.S.	11	34.4		
Spanish—Primary language	31	97.0		
Number of children			1–21	5.1
Age			38–50	60.5
Years residing in U.S.			3–78	35.4
Living conditions				
Beautiful	5	16.0		
Very nice	10	31.0		
Nice	5	16.0		
Not very nice	10	31.0		
Apartment	1	3.0		
Missing	1	3.0		
Years in school			0–17	
No education	11	34.3		
1–6 years	10	31.3		
7–12 years	7	21.9		
More than 12 years	4	12.5		
Years in practice				30
Age beginning practice				
Before 20	3	9.3		
20–30	15	46.9		
30–40	8	25.0		
40+	6	18.8		
Cost of delivery			$185–300	
Place where delivered				
Mother's home only	10	31.0		
Patera's home only	8	25.0		
Choice of location	14	44.0		
Emergency actions				
Refer to hospital	21	65.6		
Call M.D. first	11	34.3		
Record keeping	24	75.0		
Experienced stillbirths	14	44.0		
Practice within a religious context	11	34.3		
Herbalists	11	34.3		
Use home remedies	18	56.0		

cent) were Mexican citizens residing in the United States. Spanish was
the primary language for 31 of the women; while 1, an Anglo, stated
English was her primary language. All had been married, 19 still were;
all had given birth to children, the mean being 5.1 and the range 1 to
21. The mean age of the *parteras* was 60.5 years, with a range of 38
to 80 years. The mean number of years that the *parteras* had been

residing in the United States was 35.4, with a range of 3 to 78. Most of the *parteras* were themselves attended by *parteras* when they delivered their babies.

The homes the *parteras* lived in were rated with the word "nice," which meant a clean, comfortable, relatively modern edifice. Of the homes visited, 5 were described as beautiful, 10 very nice, 5 as nice, 10 not nice, and 1 was an apartment.

Education. The educational background of the *parteras* was diverse. The numbers of years spent in school ranged from 0 to 17; 7 were found to be illiterate, 11 had no education, 10 had from 1 to 6 years of school, 7 had from 7 to 12 years, 4 women had 12 or more years. One woman was a registered nurse and one had attended 2 years of medical school in Mexico.

In terms of "training"—they all had many years of experience. Many of them began their practice as young women: three before the age of 20; 15 between the ages of 20 and 30 years; eight between 30 and 40 years old; and the remainder when they were over 40. The average number of years in practice was thirty. The empirical midwife has no "formal" training; rather, she learns her craft from a family member or under the tutelage of an older midwife. One of the *parteras* reported that she was out on a delivery with another midwife. The other woman left her alone with the woman in labor while she ran an errand. While the "teacher" was gone, the woman delivered. The younger woman assisted in the birth and began her practice at that time.

Many of the *parteras* were from families where there had been three to four generations of *parteras*. "My mother, grandmother, aunt—all were midwives." Another claimed that as a child she knew that she would be a midwife. One woman reported that she had observed several deliveries and that she "just went out and delivered babies." Several of the midwives did have formal nursing or practical nursing education. As mentioned, one was a nurse, another attended medical school for two years.

The Functioning of *Parteras*

Use. Patients are most often referred to the *parteras* by their friends or relatives. "A *partera* with a good reputation is always busy." Several *parteras* claimed that they received referrals from the health department they were registered with, one advertised in the local newspaper, another in the telephone book, and several had signs on their homes.

Costs. The costs of a *partera* delivery have risen from an average of $175 in 1977. They now range between $185 to $300. The *parteras* purchase their own supplies, such as cotton and maternity pads; birth certificates are filed by them.

The *parteras,* in general, believe that the women come to them because they are poor and cannot afford a hospital delivery. However, there are other reasons. For example, some *parteras* believed that the mothers have more confidence in them than in the doctors because they speak Spanish, understand modesty, and work within the mother's cultural and religious context.

Facilities. Many of the *parteras* have birthing rooms in their own homes; in fact, eight of the *parteras* will only deliver in their homes. Ten of the *parteras* will deliver only in the mother's home, and the remainder will deliver where the mother wants. Most of the *parteras* do have a contact with a doctor whom they can call if they have a problem. In case of an emergency, 21 (65.6 percent) of the *parteras* send the mother to the hospital; 11 (34 percent) call a doctor first. Several reported that they felt "the doctors do not want to help. I guess they think that we are going to take their job away." All of the *parteras* that had been interviewed for the Philpott study were registered with the county (Cameron, Hidalgo, or Willacy) health departments.

Practice. The *parteras* avoid delivering women with high blood pressure; anemia; a history of diabetes; multiple babies; and transverse presentations. Several *parteras* also prefer to send women with breech presentations to the hospital. If an unfamiliar woman in labor appears at their door "in the middle of the night" who is very poor with no place to go to deliver, most claim they will "take her in."

Seventy-five precent (24) of the *parteras* keep records of their deliveries. Included in these records are such data as the name of the mother, date, time of admission, stage of labor, time in labor, contractions, time of delivery, presenting part, time of delivery and condition of placenta, and the physical condition of the mother and baby.

Several of the midwives reported that they did deliver stillborn babies. Eighteen reported, however, that they had never had a stillborn. A study by Sanchez in 1971 reported that many midwives in South Texas had delivered defective children. The midwives that he interviewed differentiated between physically defective children and mentally defective children. He reported that the *parteras* were "aware of the problems of defective children, and some felt that much more effort was needed in this area to eliminate the causes of defective children and to help those already born." Sanchez also reported that a majority of the *parteras* he interviewed had beliefs (folk) about the causes of birth defects that included "eclipses," or "punishment from God." Others expressed concern about blood problems and syphillis.

Prenatal Care. The amount of prenatal care that the *parteras* deliver ranges from "a lot to a little." In general, the mothers seek assistance during their third or fourth month of pregnancy. When the *partera's* assistance is sought, the mother is sent either to the health department or to a doctor for blood work. The *partera* is able to follow the mother's case and gives her advice and massages and may charge $1 to $3 for this prenatal care. Sanchez found that one important service that the midwife performed was the repositioning of the fetus in the womb through massaging.[18]

There are several forms of advice that a *partera* may give the pregnant woman. For example, she may advise the woman who is experiencing pica (the craving for and ingestion of nonfood substances such as clay and laundry starch) to purchase solid milk of magnesia in Mexico. The milk of magnesia tastes like clay, thereby satisfying the pica, and is not considered harmful. The mother with food cravings is advised to satisfy them. The mothers are also instructed not to lift heavy objects, to take laxatives to prevent constipation, to exercise often by walking frequently, and not to cross their legs, or bathe in hot water. The reason for the last two admonitions is the belief that crossing the legs and taking hot baths can cause the baby to assume the breech position.

If the *partera* knows the exact date of the mother's last period, she is able to tell exactly when she is going to deliver. She calculates eight lunar months and 27 days from the onset of the last period.

Labor and Delivery Care. With the onset of labor, the mother contacts the *partera*. She either goes to the home of the *partera*, or the *partera* comes to her home. The mother is examined vaginally to determine how far along in labor she is and the position of the baby. She is instructed to shower and to empty her bowels, with an enema, if necessary. She is encouraged to walk and move around until the delivery is impending. Some of the *parteras* elect to shave the pubic hair, others trim it, and others simply clean the area with a disinfectant.

The mother is helped to relax and is kept walking. Once she is ready to deliver, she is put to bed. Most of the mothers are delivered lying down in bed. However, if the mother chooses to do so, she is delivered in a squatting or sitting position.

Several home remedies are used during labor. *Comino* (cumin seed) tea or *canela* (cinnamon) tea may be used to stimulate labor. Occasionally, pitocin is given to speed labor and ergotrate is given to prevent hemorrhage after delivery. These medications are purchased in Mexico. However, dispensing them in Texas is illegal, and most of the *parteras* claimed NOT to use them. Olive oil is used to lubricate the abdomen during massage and it is later massaged on the perineum to prevent tearing. It is believed that the gentle touch of the *partera* in massaging the abdomen and later the perineum helps the mother to relax during her labor.

Many of the *parteras* will deliver a woman who has had a previous cesarean section. Twelve of the *parteras* work alone and require no assistance during the delivery; six require assistance occasionally. Many state that they depend on "the Virgin or Saint Raymond, the patron saint of *parteras*" for help.

Equipment. The equipment that the *partera* uses consists of: gloves (the majority use gloves while delivering the baby), umbilical cord ties, scissors, eye drops (they instill silver nitrate eye drops that are procured at the health department), a scale, alcohol, gauze and cotton, a bulb syringe (to suction mucus from the newborn's mouth), hemostats (to clamp the cord), and plastic bags, to place the placenta in. The *partera* washes her hands and dons gloves for the delivery.

Care of the Baby and Mother. The baby is stimulated if needed and the mucus is removed from the mouth and nose as needed, with the use of a bulb syringe. The cord is clamped, tied with cord ties, and cut with scissors that have been boiled and soaked in alcohol. The stump is then treated with Mercurochrome, alcohol, or a combination of the two. The baby is weighed and some time after the delivery it is bathed. Most of the *parteras* bind both the mother and the baby. The baby may be fed oregano or cumin tea right after birth or later on to help it spit up the mucus. Other *parteras* give the baby sugar water, weak *comino* tea, or boiled water. Eye drops are instilled in the baby's eyes, in compliance with state laws (silver nitrate is most frequently used).

The *partera* stays at the mother's home for several hours after the delivery and then returns to check her and the baby the next day. If the mother delivers at the home of the *partera*, she generally stays 12 to 14 hours.

Disposal of the Placenta. There are several ways of disposing of the placenta: it may just be placed in a plastic bag and thrown in the trash, or it may be buried in the yard. Some placentas are buried with a religious or folk ceremony.

There are several folk reasons given for the burial of the placenta. The reason given for not burning it was that it was like "burning a person." The placenta must be buried so that the animals will not eat it. If it is eaten by a dog, the mother will not be able to bear any more children. If it is thrown in the trash, the mother's womb may become "cold." Another reason given for the burial of the placenta is that to do so prevents the mother from having pain. If the baby is a girl, the placenta is buried near the home so the daughter will not go far away. If it is a boy, it is thrown far away.

Folk Beliefs. Several of the *parteras* who were interviewed discussed the following folk beliefs:

The pregnant woman is "hot" and she must avoid "hot" foods. There was also mention, primarily in Sanchez's study, of such folk beliefs as *mal de ojo* (evil eye), *susto* (shock or fright), eclipse (the viewing of the moon at the wrong time of the month, thus causing birth defects), *empacho* (food not passing through the stomach), *latido* (chronic lack of appetite causing emaciation), and *bilis* (nervous tension and fatigue caused by extreme anger). Eleven of the *parteras* claimed that they practiced within a religious context, 11 claimed to be herbalists, and 18 used home remedies.

Cross-Check: *Partera* Visit

In order to verify the findings of Philpott and to obtain answers to questions she did not deal with, a visit was made to a *partera* in Weslaco, Texas. The following is a description of that visit and the *partera*'s answers to the questions that were discussed. This woman had been described by the public health nurse as a *partera* who "loves her work, does the job well, and is one to whom people come back because she is able to establish excellent rapport with her clients."

The visit was made to this *partera* shortly after 1:00 P.M. on a sunny December afternoon. We turned off the superhighway onto a small unpaved road and drove up to a yellow house that was surrounded by a neatly trimmed lawn, with flowers and statues. There was a small sign on the front of the house that had a stork painted on it, the word "partera," and a telephone number.

We were greeted at the door by a four-year-old boy who invited us in and said that his grandmother would help us in a moment. When the *partera* came, we explained the purpose of the visit, and we were invited to come in and sit down. The home was well furnished and decorated for Christmas, which was in two weeks. The woman was warm, friendly, and receptive. She spoke no English but was willing to talk slowly and was able to understand "Boston"-accented Spanish.

She was 51 years old, had studied some nursing in Mexico, had previously practiced for 10 years in Victoria, Texas, 3 years in Reynosa, Mexico, and had been practicing in Weslaco for four years. She had established a good relationship with the nurses in the county and also with the doctors.

The women who come to her are from Rio Grande, McAllen, San Juan, Weslaco, and Donna, Texas. Some also come from Mexico. She is very popular and delivers from 5 to 9 babies a month. She charges $185 a delivery. She sends her patients to the public health department for prenatal care. The ages of the women that she sees are 15 to 42. Most come to her during their fourth or fifth month of pregnancy. She will not accept as a patient a woman who is anemic, has high blood pressure, has a history of diabetes or other medical problems, or indicates a malpresentation. She feels that a major problem is that of the baby's presentation. If the baby is in a transverse presentation, she will not deliver it and sends the mother to a doctor. She is cautious with breech presentations and has delivered twins.

She then took us to her "birthing room" in the back of the house. The home had appeared small from the outside. However, it went straight back for quite a distance and we passed several rooms, including a dining room, several bedrooms, and a kitchen on the way to the "birthing room." The home was extremely clean and well furnished and comfortable. The walls were adorned with family and religious pictures.

The "birthing room" consisted of two single beds, an examining table, an instrument table with a scale on it and the following equipment: hemostats and scissors (soaking in basins filled with alcohol), cotton, gauze, gloves, and eye medications. There are also a sphygmomanometer and stethoscope. In the back corner of the room there was a washing machine and dryer and a large carton of maternity pads. There was a statue of the Virgin with a candle in front of her on the washing machine and there were religious pictures on the walls. The room was clean and both beds were neatly made up. There was a separate entrance into the room from outside. There was also one small window covered with a colorful curtain.

The *partera* explained that she keeps the mothers active until they are ready to deliver. When the woman comes to her house, she examines her to determine how far along she is in labor. If this is her first baby and she has not started to dilate and everything appears normal, the *partera* sends her home with instructions to return when the "labor" comes more often or if "her water breaks." If the mother is in more active labor, or if this is more than her first child, she keeps her at her home. But she keeps her active and maybe walking in the neighborhood until her labor is quite active. When the delivery appears imminent; that is, when the head begins to crown, she puts the mother to bed. If the baby's head is in a posterior position she rests the mother's hips on rolled towels or a bed pan to elevate her hips and lower back. She massages the mother's abdomen and perineum with oil. The abdomen is massaged to relax the mother and the perineum is massaged to prevent tearing. She cleanses the perineum with soap, water, and then Mercurochrome. If needed, she shaves the mother. She may also give the mother an enema earlier in labor if it is needed. Before the baby is delivered, she washes her hands and puts on gloves. She does not wear a mask or special clothes, but does wear an apron. She works alone, but prays to the Virgin for assistance.

Once the baby is delivered, she suctions it with the bulb syringe to remove excess mucus. She clamps the cord with the hemostats, cuts it with the scissors, and ties it with the cord ties. She instills silver nitrate in the baby's eyes. She wraps the baby and places it with the mother and waits for the placenta. She related that if she has difficulty delivering the placenta, she has the mother blow into a coke bottle and the placenta then "pops out." The placenta is disposed of in accordance with the patient's wishes.

She encourages the father of the baby to remain with the mother, or else she has some other relative stay with the mother. She wants them to see what she does and to be aware of the "good job" that she does. She keeps the mother in her home for eight hours after the delivery.

She also assumes the responsibility for registering the baby's birth at the county courthouse.

MIDWIFE DELIVERIES IN THE TEXAS-MEXICO BORDER AREA

Statistical Background

Midwives, or *parteras*, deliver a significant percentage of babies along the Texas-Mexico border. Cameron County has both the greatest number of registered *parteras* and the greatest number of *partera* deliveries. In 1976 there were 39 lay midwives in Cameron County; 30 in Brownsville; and 31 in Hidalgo County. This population tends to remain constant. However, in 1977 the city of Brownsville passed a strict city ordinance to control the midwives. An examination was given and passage was required to practice within the city limits. Several of the midwives were unable to pass the new requirements and moved outside the city limits.[19]

As can be seen in Table 12-2, 97 percent of the rural deliveries in 1974 were performed by midwives. From 1975 to 1977, the number of rural midwife deliveries declined from 10.5 (1975) to 3 (1976) to 5 (1977) percent. In 1978, after the city of Brownsville passed the Lay Midwife Ordinance, the number of rural area midwife deliveries rose to 43 percent. In 1980, 48 percent of the rural Cameron County babies were delivered by midwives.

In Brownsville, from 67 to 80 percent of the live births were delivered by midwives from 1974 to 1977. In 1978, after passage and enforcement of the Lay Midwife Ordinance, the number dropped to 43.5 percent. By 1980, it rose to 49 percent. These figures illustrate the changes that can occur with changes in policy.

Not only do the midwives in rural Cameron County and Browns-

TABLE 12-2. TOTAL MIDWIFE-DELIVERED BIRTHS, BY OCCURRENCE, RURAL CAMERON COUNTY AND BROWNSVILLE, TEXAS, 1974–1980

	Rural Cameron County			Brownsville		
Year	Total Births	Midwife Delivered	Percent- age	Total Births	Midwife* Delivered	Percent- age
1974	76	74	97.0	4921	3309	67.0
1975	702	74	10.5	4145	3162	76.0
1976	994	30	3.0	3716	2965	80.0
1977	920	47	5.0	2665	1893	71.0
1978	1469	627	43.0	1592	693	43.5
1979	1970	982	49.8	1696	745	44.0
1980	2101	1011	48.0	1681	824	49.0

*In the creation of this table, the category "other" was added to the midwife category since a small number of births were in this particular category.
Source: *Texas Department of Health, Bureau of Vital Statistics, Austin, Texas, 1974–1980.*

ville deliver a significant percentage of babies overall; they also deliver a high percentage of the babies born to teenage mothers as shown in Table 12-3. For example, in Brownsville there was a total of 718 births to teenage mothers in 1974; 470, or 65 percent, of these deliveries were performed by midwives. In that same year, there were 13 teenagers delivered in the rural area; 100 percent of these deliveries were by midwives.

In 1977, 76 percent of the babies born to teenage mothers in Brownsville were delivered by midwives; in 1978, after passage of the ordinance, 46 percent were delivered by midwives. However, in these same years (1977, 1978) there were 9 percent midwife deliveries of teenage mothers in the rural areas in 1977 and in 1978 there were 46 percent.

In 1980, midwives delivered 50 percent of the babies born to teenage mothers in rural Cameron County and 53 percent of the babies born to teenage mothers in Brownsville.

Tables 12-4 and 12-5 demonstrate the numbers and percentages of midwife deliveries in selected Texas border counties, from east to west, by occurrence and by place of mother's residence. Overall, the percentages of midwife deliveries decline as one travels east to west. For example, the percent of midwife deliveries by occurrence in 1980 was 30.8 percent in Cameron County, while the percentage in El Paso was 10.2 percent. In terms of residence, 18.6 percent of the Cameron County residents were delivered by midwives in 1980 and 7.6 percent of those in El Paso.

A striking difference appears in the rate of midwife deliveries by occurrence compared with midwife deliveries by residence (see Tables 12-6 and 12-7). In 1980, for example, 3,263 midwife deliveries occurred in the four Rio Grande Valley counties as compared to 1,866 midwife-delivered residents of the area. One explanation of this is an in-migration to the midwives for delivery, both from other counties and from Mexico. A substantially high number of women from Mexico do deliver in Texas. It appears from these data that a high number of these "missing" births may be attributed to women from Mexico.

Since 1982, when the peso was devalued, the numbers of *partera* deliveries by occurrence have remained nearly constant in both Cameron and Hidalgo counties. In Cameron County the percentage difference between occurrence and residency is 10 percent.

Midwifery: Issues and Problems
The following are examples of issues and problems that have been raised about the practice of lay midwifery.

Birth Practices. The Philpott study reported that:

1. Midwives often administered medications without consulting a physician.

TABLE 12-3. CROSSCLASSIFICATION OF LIVE BIRTHS, BY OCCURRENCE, TO TEENAGE MOTHERS BY CAMERON COUNTY PLACE OF BIRTH, YEAR OF DELIVERY, AND BIRTH ATTENDANT, 1974–1980

Year	Location	Maternal Age	M.D.	Percentage	C.N.M.	Percentage	Midwife	Percentage	Total
1974 (Total Births: 731)	Rural Cameron County	12–15	0		0		1	100	1
		16–19	0		0		12	100	12
		Total	0	0	0	0	13	100	13
	Brownsville	12–15	18	51	0		17	49	35
		16–19	230	34	0		453	66	683
		Total	248	35	0		470	65	718
1975 (Total Births: 752)	Rural Cameron County	12–15	2	100	0		0	0	2
		16–19	97	92	0		9	8	106
		Total	99	92	0		9	8	108
	Brownsville	12–15	11	32	0		23	68	34
		16–19	154	25	0		456	75	610
		Total	165	26	0		479	74	644
1976 (Total Births: 712)	Rural Cameron County	12–15	9	100	0		0	0	9
		16–19	128	95	0		7	5	135
		Total	137	95	0		7	5	144
	Brownsville	12–15	11	30	0		26	70	37
		16–19	120	23	0		411	77	531
		Total	131	23	0		437	77	568
1977 (Total Births: 521)	Rural Cameron County	12–15	5	83	0		1	16	6
		16–19	101	91	0		10	9	111
		Total	106	91	0		11	9	117
	Brownsville	12–15	8	26	0		23	74	31
		16–19	90	24	0		283	76	373
		Total	98	24	0		306	76	404

(continued)

TABLE 12-3–Continued

Year	Location	Maternal Age	M.D.	Percentage	C.N.M.	Percentage	Midwife	Percentage	Total
1978 (Total Births: 395)	Rural Cameron County	12–15	6	66	0		3	33	9
		16–19	79	53	0		70	47	149
	Total		85	54	0		73	46	158
	Brownsville	12–15	9	64	0		5	36	14
		16–19	105	47	0		118	53	223
	Total		114	48	0		123	52	237
1979 (Total Births: 477)	Rural Cameron County	12–15	2	29	0		5	71	7
		16–19	89	45	0		111	55	200
	Total		91	44	0		116	56	207
	Brownsville	12–15	10	53	2	11	7	36	19
		16–19	96	38	39	16	116	46	251
	Total		106	39	41	15	123	46	270
1980 (Total Births: 497)	Rural Cameron County	12–15	2	33	0		4	67	6
		16–19	118	50	0		117	50	235
	Total		120	50	0		121	50	241
	Brownsville	12–15	9	47	0		10	53	19
		16–19	111	47	0		126	53	237
	Total		120	47	0		136	53	256

*In the creation of this table, the category "other" was added to the midwife category since a small number of births were in this particular category.
Source: Texas Department of Health, Bureau of Vital Statistics, Austin, Texas, 1974–1980.

TABLE 12-4. PERCENTAGE OF MIDWIFE DELIVERIES IN SELECTED TEXAS BORDER COUNTIES FROM EAST TO WEST IN 1979 AND 1980, BY PLACE OF OCCURRENCE

County	Total Number of Births		Total Number of Midwife Deliveries		Percentage of Midwife Deliveries	
	1979	*1980*	*1979*	*1980*	*1979*	*1980*
Cameron	6387	6927	2035	2131	31.9	30.8
Willacy	236	259	34	57	14.4	22.0
Hidalgo	7881	8538	1042	1075	13.2	12.6
Zapata	1	0	1	0	100.0	0.0
Webb	3536	3621	876	661	24.7	18.3
El Paso	11629	11785	1276	1202	11.0	10.2
Total	29760	31130	5264	5126	17.7	16.5

Source: Texas Department of Health, Bureau of Vital Statistics, 1979–1980.

2. Substandard sanitary conditions existed in midwives' clinics or homes.
3. Many of the midwives did not use silver nitrate in the baby's eyes, in violation of the law.
4. Many of the midwives did not know or practice sterile technique.
5. Folk medications and folk remedies were often used in the midwife's care of the mother and baby.[20]

Maternal Mortality. In 1980 there was a maternal death reported in Hidalgo County. The mother, a 24-year-old gravida 1, was a Mexican national. She was delivered by a *partera* in Mission, Texas. The cause of death was found to be related to:

1. Severe shortness of breath on exertion during pregnancy causing limitation of activities.

TABLE 12-5. PERCENTAGE OF LAY MIDWIFE DELIVERIES IN SELECTED TEXAS BORDER COUNTIES FROM EAST TO WEST IN 1979 AND 1980, BY PLACE OF MOTHER'S RESIDENCE

County	Total Number of Births		Total Number of Midwife Deliveries		Percentage of Midwife Deliveries	
	1979	*1980*	*1979*	*1980*	*1979*	*1980*
Cameron	5094	5489	997	1019	19.6	18.6
Willacy	430	449	34	59	7.9	13.0
Hidalgo	6982	7614	780	788	11.0	10.3
Zapata	129	154	3	11	2.0	7.7
Webb	2445	2643	207	195	8.4	7.3
El Paso	9809	9915	865	756	8.8	7.6
Total	24889	26264	2886	2828	11.6	10.8

Source: Texas Department of Health, Bureau of Vital Statistics, 1979–1980.

TABLE 12-6. PERCENTAGE OF MIDWIFE DELIVERIES IN THE RIO GRANDE VALLEY, TEXAS, COUNTIES 1979–1983 BY OCCURRENCE

County	Total Number of Births					Total Number of Midwife Deliveries					Percentage of Midwife Deliveries				
	1979	1980	1981	1982	1983	1979	1980	1981	1982	1983	1979	1980	1981	1982	1983
Cameron	6387	6927	7082	6616	6232	2035	2131	2350	1798	1807	32	31	33	27	29
Willacy	236	259	256	231	237	34	57	25	19	9	14	22	10	8	4
Hidalgo	7881	8538	8642	8327	7907	1042	1075	1135	1055	1188	13	13	13	15	15
Zapata	1	0	0	0	2	0	1	0	0	0	100	—	—	—	—

Source: Texas Department of Health, Bureau of Vital Statistics, Austin, Texas, 1979–1983.

TABLE 12-7. PERCENTAGE OF THE MIDWIFE DELIVERIES IN THE RIO GRANDE VALLEY, TEXAS, COUNTIES 1979–1983 BY PLACE OF MOTHER'S RESIDENCE

County	Total Number of Births					Total Number of Midwife Deliveries					Percentage of Midwife Deliveries				
	1979	1980	1981	1982	1983	1979	1980	1981	1982	1983	1979	1980	1981	1982	1983
Cameron	5094	5489	5511	5466	5278	997	1019	1065	905	1004	20	19	19	17	19
Willacy	430	449	420	437	395	34	59	32	24	28	8	13	8	5	7
Hidalgo	6982	7614	7648	7646	7477	780	788	866	847	985	11	10	11	11	13
Zapata	129	154	148	172	157	3	11	6	2	3	2	8	4	1	2

Source: Texas Department of Health, Bureau of Vital Statistics, Austin, Texas, 1979–1983.

2. Severe abdominal pain two hours after delivery.
3. A hemoglobin of 8 grams on admission to the hospital.[21]

In 1981 there was another maternal death in Hidalgo county—this one was that of a 48-year-old gravida 4, para 3, woman. She, too, was a Mexican national. With her last pregnancy she had been advised to "have no more children." The family was very poor and she had had no prenatal care. The mother arrived at the *partera*'s home at the "last moment" with no records of blood tests and prenatal care. The *partera* attempted to refuse to take care of her, but was unable to refuse her because of the advanced stage of labor. The woman was pushing, and it was too late to send her elsewhere. The baby was delivered and the cord was greenish-yellow. The placenta did not deliver; after 20 to 30 minutes the woman began to bleed. The *partera* attempted to stop the bleeding and to get an ambulance to come to take the woman to the hospital. There were a number of delays and two hours passed before the lady got to the hospital. She was dead on arrival. The death was most likely due to a postpartum hemorrhage.[22]

Infant Morbidity.   An infant developed tetanus of the cord in 1981. This baby was delivered by a *partera* who had been delivering babies since the early 1950s. This particular *partera* had been defensive about visits by the public health nurses, and she was reluctant to allow them into her home. She was illiterate and had a vision impairment.

According to the mother, the *partera* had cut the baby's cord with scissors that she removed from her instrument bag; and tied the cord with string that she cut from a ball of string. In other words, neither the scissors nor the cord ties were sterile. The baby was treated and recovered with some residual neurological damage. The mother, who did not know if she had received tetanus immunization, was immunized.[23]

Crossover Births.   Crossover births, that is, births to women from Mexico who cross over the border to deliver, represent a large share of the number of *partera* deliveries. These births have caused numerous problems in the communities along the border. Many of the mothers do not receive adequate or any prenatal care. There are problems with welfare and food stamps and immigration practices and policies. In some areas along the border there are a large number of *crossover* births, for example, Cameron County, Texas. In other areas the numbers are smaller, either because there are no *parteras* to deliver the mothers or because the United States hospitals are able to return the women to Mexico.

As of August 1984, the immigration policy of the United States toward crossover births stated that:

1. All people born in the United States are citizens of the United States.

2. A child born in the United States can attend public school at the United States place of residence.
3. When a person born in the United States reaches the age of 21 the person can petition for permanent resident status for the parents. Permanent residents are granted permanent resident status, also known as "green cards" or "A numbers." (Prior to 1977, parents of children born in the United States could apply for permanent resident status after the child was born.) As of January 1982, permanent residents no longer have to register yearly.[24]

Associated Problems.   Additional, tangential issues surround *partera* deliveries. For example:

1. The extreme poverty of large numbers of people residing along the border who are migrant workers or unemployed.
2. The lack of medicaid cards or other types of health insurance.
3. The refusal of some doctors to care for Medicaid patients; for example, it was reported that not one doctor in Edinburg, Texas, will accept medicaid mothers.
4. The practice of hospitals of not accepting patients without pre-payment. Several hospitals were cited for turning away patients, and in several places the practice of sending women in labor back to Mexico to deliver still exists.
5. The alleged issuance of false birth certificates by some *parteras* for babies born in Mexico.
6. The asserted performance of abortions by some *parteras.*
7. The lack of back-up and follow-up care. It was often difficult to trace crossover mothers and to follow up on PKUs and other well-baby care practices and on the issues of neonatal mortality.[25]

Although problems have existed for many years in *partera* deliveries, serious medical problems that have been reported are few in number, considering the high numbers of *partera* deliveries.

Research and Policy Recommendations
To improve the quality of maternal and child health care the following recommendations are offered.

Conduct a Community Survey.   In addition to the training of TBAs (Traditional Birth Attendants), the United Nations has developed a program for surveying community people, including mothers, as to their needs for maternal and child health care. Such a survey should be made along the United States-Mexico border, primarily in the Texas area, because of the prevalence of traditional midwives. Most people state that poverty is the chief reason why women elect to be delivered by *parteras,* but this may not be the only reason. Only a survey of the mothers who choose either to go to the doctor or to a *partera* will shed light on this situation.

An example of a community survey is the study "Use of a Maternity Center as a Birthing Alternative in the El Paso-Juarez Area," by Eastman and Loustaunau. The study was undertaken from October 1980 through January 1981. The researchers discovered that women who used the maternity center in El Paso "strongly endorsed it as their first choice of location for birthing and overwhelmingly supported the use of female midwives." This preference for a female birth attendant fits in with the Mexican-American and Mexican culture. The researchers also found that the main reason for using this center was NOT cost—the women did not want a hospital birth. A third finding was that 66 percent of those using the center were Mexican nationals while the number of Anglo women using the center was 8 percent. The reason offered for the high use of this clinic by Mexican nationals was the guarantee of United States citizenship for their children. Lastly, the researchers found that a large percentage of women using this clinic had no family doctor or gynecologist.[26]

Each society has its own customs, beliefs, values, and practices regarding childbirth and the care of mothers and children. These vary from society to society. Prior to making policy and laws, one must be aware of and sensitive to, the practices within the society they are focusing on. In an area that includes a heterogeneous society, such as the United States-Mexico border, one must be cognizant—prior to legislation—of the role the *partera* is playing in the community that she serves. It is important for the policy makers to:

1. Identify aspects of traditional practice that need to be changed
2. Determine the extent to which the *parteras* would be willing to receive training
3. Determine the incentives that may be needed to obtain their cooperation
4. Be aware of the rituals and techniques and procedures used in the management of labor and delivery—that is, the scope of the *parteras'* practice
5. Determine the level to which the *parteras* wish to be trained
6. Determine how the people in the community feel about *parteras*
7. Be sensitive to existing language barriers. The training programs must be in a language that the *parteras* understand, both the connotations and denotations of words. If the *partera* is illiterate, other forms of learning beside the written word must be devised. This also holds true for testing. The *parteras* ought to be tested in the language that they understand, be it spoken or written.

Use the Spanish Language. Those who deliver health services to Mexican and Mexican-American mothers must speak and understand

Spanish. Health education materials—films, books, pamphlets, and posters—must be available in Spanish.

Establish Collaboration. Close collaboration between the public health nurses and the *parteras* is vital. An example of this collaboration is found in Hidalgo County where public health nurses recognize that the *parteras* will not change their ways. The nurses are able to work with them, however, by insisting that they WILL do certain things, such as register the births within the correct time and instill eye drops in the baby's eyes. The nurses in the Hidalgo County Health Department have been able to upgrade the care that the indigent prenatal patients receive by ensuring that every woman has prenatal blood work done, regardless when she seeks the service; that each woman has a prenatal physical examination done by a nurse midwife; and that health education play a predominant role in their maternal-child health program. It has been observed that women are seeking the services of the health department maternity nurses earlier in their pregnancy.

A goal of health policy must be to improve maternal-child health care by developing cooperative and collaborative relationships between the various parties (physicians, nurses, certified nurse midwives and lay midwives) who deliver maternal-child health care.

CONCLUSION

This chapter has focused primarily on the *parteras* who practice midwifery in Texas along the United States-Mexico border. It has described their background and practice, the issues and problems related to their practice, present regulation, and research and policy recommendations.

The practice of midwifery is ancient—the role of women in the birthing process continues to be popular in this geographic region. Observation of the practice of *parteras*, interviews with the leading characters, the midwives and health-care providers, and literature reviews, have led to the conclusion that given safeguards (adequate prenatal care and prenatal screening, and adequate medical backup, such as access to the hospital if an emergency develops) the practice of the *partera* can be safe and effective. It provides women with a *choice*—the choice to be delivered by someone who (1) speaks their language; (2) shares a similar culture or religious world view; and (3) is willing to deliver them in the privacy of their home or in a birthing center. Alternatively, the woman has the choice of delivering in the hospital and being delivered by a physician or certified nurse midwife. In these circumstances the pregnant women is not constrained by only one choice: that of the hospital way of childbirth.

Yes, there have been problems with midwife deliveries, and several of these problems have been discussed. Iatrogenic problems also continue to occur in hospital labor and delivery rooms, so those who do criticize midwife births ought to be familiar with these problems, too. Childbirth in itself involves risks and often problems are inherent in the nature of the event. For the normal woman, however, who is delivering a child in an uncomplicated delivery (about 97 percent of all births) many of the interventions espoused by the medical professionals may not be necessary.

It is important for public policy discussion, decision making and legislation, as well as for the major deliverers of health care to understand the intricacies of midwifery. The goal of health care has been to provide safe and adequate services to all recipients. Only with the mutual collaboration and respect of health-care providers and midwives can the prenatal and perinatal care of the indigent and others desiring traditional birthing services be sustained and upgraded.

The situation described by Dr. Garst in 1925 may also exist today. He recognized then that the "midwife is still a necessity in some communities." These words are also true today. Avenues of collaboration and mutual respect must be explored and followed.

The practice of the *partera* in the Rio Grande Valley is the life of the past, the present, and of the future: "a way of life *de ayer, hoy y mañana.*"[27]

REFERENCES

1. Thomas R. Forbes, *The Midwife and the Witch* (New Haven: Yale University Press, 1966) and J. B. Donegan, *Women and Men Midwives: Medicine, Morality, and Misogyny in Early Amercia* (Westport, Conn.: Greenwood Press, 1978).
2. Robert T. Trotter, II, and Juan A. Chavira, "*Curanderismo:* An Emic Theoretical Perspective of Mexican-American Folk Medicine," *Medical Anthropology,* Fall 1980, pp. 423–87.
3. Hector Uribe. Texas S. B. #1093, 1981.
4. Barbara Ehrenreich and D. English, *Witches, Midwives, and Nurses: A History of Women Healers,* 2nd. ed. (Old Westbury, N.Y.: Feminist Press, 1973).
5. J. B. Litoff, *American Midwives 1860 to the Present* (Westport, Conn.: Greenwood Press, 1978).
6. I. Kelly, *Folk Practice in North Mexico Birth Customs, Folk Medicine, and Spiritualism in the Laguna Zone* (Austin: University of Texas Press, 1965).
7. Anthony N. Zavaleta, ed., "Mexican American Health Status: Selected Topics from the Borderlands," *Borderlands Journal—Special Issue* 4, no. 1 (Fall 1980): 1.
8. Robert S. Landmann, ed., *The Problem of the Undocumented Worker* (Alburquerque: Latin American Institute, University of New Mexico, 1981).
9. E. Garcia, Clinic Manager, McAllen Family Health Center, McAllen, Tex., personal interview, 19 November 1981.
10. R. Garza, Clinic Director, *Su Clinica Familiar,* Harlingen, Tex., personal interview, 18 November 1981.

11. B. N. Shenkin, *Health Care for Migrant Workers: Policies and Politics* (Cambridge: Ballinger Publishing Co., 1974).
12. Sister Mary N. Vincelli, Director of Nursing, Hidalgo County Health Department, Edinburg, Tex., personal interview, 19 November 1981.
13. Ibid.
14. Garcia and Garza interviews.
15. Trotter and Chavira, "Curanderismo."
16. Margaret A. Kay, "The Mexican American," in *Culture, Child Bearing, Health Professionals*, ed. Ann Clark (Philadelphia: F. A. Davis, 1978).
17. Laura L. Philpott, "A Descriptive Study of Birth Practices and Midwifery in the Lower Rio Grande Valley of Texas" (Ph.D. diss., University of Texas Health Science Center at Houston, School of Public Health, 1979).
18. A. R. Sanchez, "An Exploratory Study of Mexican American Midwives' Attitudes, Practices, and Beliefs Regarding Children Born with Congenital Defects." Master's thesis, University of Texas at Austin, 1971.
19. Bertrand Chavez, Director, Brownsville Health Department, Brownsville, Tex., personal interview, 19 November 1981.
20. Philpott, "Descriptive Study."
21. Vincelli, interview.
22. Ibid.
23. Ibid.
24. Leonel J. Castillo, Former Commissioner of Immigration and Naturalization, personal interviews, Austin, Texas and Houston, Texas, 18 November 1981 and 30 June 1984.
25. Eve Powell-Griner and D. Streck. "A Closer Examination of Neonatal Mortality Rates Among the Texas Spanish Surname Population," *American Journal of Public Health* 8, no. 43 (March 1983).
26. K. Eastman and M. Loustaunau, "Use of a Maternity Center as a Birthing Alternative in the El Paso-Juarez Area" (n.p., n.d.).
27. Julian Castillo, Director, Division of Health Related Professions, personal letter, 6 April 1982.

ANNOTATED BIBLIOGRAPHY

Alvarez, Humberto Romero. *Health without Boundaries*, Mexico: United States-Mexico Border Public Health Association, 1975.

In this extensive report, Alvarez describes the unique, thirty-year-old public health center that serves the United States-Mexico border area. The author stresses the point that "health problems do not recognize boundaries between two countries." Numerous factors—biologic, social, cultural, economic, and geographic—that contribute to health problems are described in depth. Alvarez also compares morbidity and mortality rates for the two countries over the past thirty years. He describes health areas where change is desperately needed, such as in the area of maternal child care in Mexico. He also describes several joint projects where cooperation has led to better health conditions, such as a sanitation project in Baja, California, and Tijuana. This report provides the reader with a broad, general awareness of the scope of health problems on the United States-Mexico border.

Clark, Margaret. *Health in the Mexican-American Culture.* 2nd ed. Berkeley: University of California Press, 1970.

In this book, Clark describes the traditional health and illness beliefs and practices of Mexican-Americans in California. The book is based on a study that was designed to secure sociocultural information helpful to health workers. Clark describes such phenomena as family life, attitudes and beliefs relating to health and illness, and specifically to pregnancy and childbirth. For example, she describes the specific practices of *la cuarentena* (forty days after delivery) and the diet during and after pregnancy in great detail. In addition, she describes the traditional beliefs and practices relating to infant care, such as feeding practices, the fondling of babies, and the methods of protecting the babies from *mal d'ojo,* "evil eye." The descriptive and anecdotal information in this book is valuable for health-care providers who work in the Mexican-American community. This book is well written and documented and is considered a "classic" in the early work done in medical sociology and anthropology.

Kessner, David M. *Infant Death: An Analysis by Maternal Risk and Health Care.* Washington, D.C.: Institute of Medicine, 1973.

Kessner's theme throughout this book is that one cannot discuss health care without first realizing that those who are receiving the health care must have their basic needs—food and water, clothing, and shelter—met first. He vividly describes the social risks—maternal age, birth order of children, maternal education, and the given legitimacy status of each child—that affect infant morbidity and mortality. Kessner also describes the medical risks—the time of the first prenatal visit, the time spent in receiving medical care both in pregnancy and labor, and the early detection of complications—and their relationship to maternal morbidity and mortality rates and the effect on infant morbidity and mortality. He illustrates this presentation with numerous case studies that point out the need for comprehensive maternity care. The contents of this book not only provide an in-depth understanding of the medical risks related to infant mortality, but also an analysis of the social conditions that relate to the phenomena. In addition, this book facilitates the reader's understanding of the role that the poverty present along the United States-Mexico border is playing in the higher-than-expected infant mortality rates.

Landmann, Robert S., ed. *The Problem of the Undocumented Worker.* Albuquerque: Latin American Institute, University of New Mexico, 1981.

This series of thirteen articles deals with one of the most sensitive and pressing issues facing today's immigration policy makers—the monumental problems of undocumented workers and their families. The anthology represents a spectrum of scholarly opinion on the illegal migration of Mexicans to the United States and it explores this issue from several dimensions, such as:

1. Why do people come to the United States illegally?
2. What is the impact on labor?
3. What are the human rights of the migrants?

In general, the present literature relating to this topic is fragmented and not in consensus. There is confusion about the extent of the social, political, economic, and health consequences of the undocumented workers and their families. The United States-Mexico border is the focal point of this problem—hence, the importance of this document (or other related literature) for the acquisition of knowledge in this area. This particular document provides the reader with an in-depth analysis. In order for one to begin to understand the complexities of the maternal/child-health issues on the border, one must be knowledgeable about the issues discussed in this anthology.

Louv, Richard. *Southwind: The Mexican Migration.* San Diego: San Diego Union, 1980.

In this book, Louv attempts to describe the life of the undocumented alien. Louv discusses issues such as the history of migration, the people who are coming to the United States from Mexico, the numbers of illegals, the underground railroad, and other aspects of this complex problem. He paints a vivid picture, in personal terms, of the life that is enmeshed in poverty and exploitation. The book is designed to provide answers to the questions of human rights and economic and political problems. It is a much more "personal" account than the Landmann anthology and presents another facet of this complex problem. It, too, helps to enhance one's understanding of the United States-Mexico border area and the maternal/child-health problems that exist there.

Shenkin, Budd N. *Health Care for Migrant Workers: Policies and Politics.* Cambridge, Mass.: Ballinger Publishing Co., 1974.

In this book, Shenkin describes the migrant workers in the United States. A migrant is a person who moves far away from the place called home to work in the fields. Included in Shenkin's description of the migrants are who they are, where they originate, and where they journey to—that is, the three major streams. In addition to a sociologic description, he provides a comprehensive description of the health of the migrant workers and their families. He states that "valid health statistics of migrants and of the rural poor are hard to find, but that despite these limited figures a strong case can be made to demonstrate that the health status is generally *wretched.* Poor people are sicker than non-poor people in the United States. The sicker groups get less medical care." Shenkin describes, in depth, several health programs that have been created to provide health services to the migrants. Yet, despite these attempts, their health status remains poor. There are several reasons, such as mobility, the fact that services do not extend far enough, and health education and motivation are deficient, that explain this on-going problem. Several solutions are proposed: alleviation of poverty, alleviation of discrimination, and increasing the capacity of the rural medical care delivery system. In summary, this book is highly informative as to the overall health conditions of a large number of residents in the border area.

Silver, George A. *Child Health: America's Future Generation.* Germantown, Md.: Aspen System's Corp., 1978.

Silver states that "the future of social policy is embodied in child health." He focuses on the belief that children's health is more a matter of protection and prevention than adult health is. The author argues that the United States child-health services are not operating at their peak and he describes several reasons for this failure. Silver documents that 40 percent of children from poverty areas (urban and rural) are not immunized. He further demonstrates that these children receive inadequate prevention and curative services. "The value of children is reflected in the care they receive." In summary, this book presents a comprehensive description of the care that children ought to receive and examples where this care does not exist.

Tidemann, Marjorie. "Maternal/Child Health: Background Paper for a Border Health Research Agenda Development Conference." (Paper presented Sept. 20, 1981, at the Border Health Focused Research Agenda Development Conference, Westwood Look Resort, Tucson, Arizona, 20–22 September 1981.)

In this paper, Tidemann reviews the status of maternal and child health-care problems on both sides of the United States-Mexico border. The first issue that the author describes is that of infant mortality rates. These rates ranged from 32.8 to 52.1/1,000 births in Northern Mexico in 1974; and from 5.1 to 40.3/1,000 births in the United States border counties. Secondly, she describes the childbearing practices of women in the border area. Traditionally, women bear children early, and families of 12 to 16 children are not uncommon. Thirdly, children of the poor in this area are "extremely" vulnerable to infectious diseases because of poor nutrition. Tidemann also introduces the plight of migrant workers, undocumented aliens, environmental problems, and cultural problems. She concludes her presentation by describing the nature of the problems on the border as "historic." She believes that an approach to their resolution must be "creative and acknowledge the interrelationships among the multiple groups of problems."

Trotter, Robert T., II, and Chavira, Juan A. "*Curanderismo:* An Emic Theoretical Perspective of Mexican-American Folk Medicine," *Medical Anthropology,* Fall 1980, pp. 423–87.

In this outstanding, highly informative article, Trotter and Chavira describe the actual practice of *curanderismo,* Mexican-American folk medicine, as a systematic body of healing theories. There are three levels at which *curanderismo* is practiced, each demanding a higher degree of learning. This article is unique in that it describes in great detail how the *curandero* actually carries out the rituals. The underlying meanings of rituals are also explained. The informants were several *curanderos* in South Texas. The information was collected through participant-observation methods over a span of four years. (The *curanderos* were informed as to the purpose of the research and gave their consent to be observed.) The authors describe the relationship of the *curandero* to the patient and the family, the methods the *curandero* uses in the prevention, detection, and healing of illness, and the underlying unity of the preception of illness. The use of *curanderos* and other traditional healers such as *parteras* (midwives) is widespread along the United States-Mexico border. Their advice and services are sought throughout the life cycle of family members, including pregnancy and the child-rearing years.

Warner, David. *The Health of Mexican-Americans in South Texas.* Austin: LBJ School of Public Affairs, University of Texas at Austin, 1979.

In this report on the physical and mental health of Mexican-Americans, Warner describes the following situations in great depth:

1. Socioeconomic and health conditions
2. Morbidity and mortality rates
3. Living conditions in urban and rural areas of South Texas

4. Nutritional, mental health services, and migrant health services
5. Folk medicine

This report is a well-executed study of the area.

Zavaleta, A. N., ed. "Mexican-American Health Status: Selected Topics from the Borderlands." *Borderlands Journal—Special Issue,* 4. no. 1 (Fall 1980).

  The material contained in this journal is similar to other material presented thus far, but for this quote: Zavaleta states "The United States-Mexico border presents a unique situation of human interdependence in a bi-national, multi-social-cultural-and economic world."

BIBLIOGRAPHY

Aiken, R. *Mexican Folk Tales from the Borderland.* Dallas: Southern Methodist University Press, 1980.

Alexander, J. "Statement on the Use of Midwives in Texas." Prepared for the Texas Department of Health, January 1978.

Alvarez, H. R. *Health without Boundaries: United States-Mexico Border Public Health Association.* Mexico: 1975.

Bradley, C. J. "Characteristics of Women and Infants Attended by Lay Midwives in Texas, 1971: A Case Comparison Study." Master's thesis, University of Texas Health Science Center at Houston, School of Public Health, 1980.

Campos, E. *Medicina Popular—Supersticione, Credios, E Meizinhas.* 2nd. ed. Rio de Janeiro: Livraria—Editora da Casa, 1955.

Chavira, L. *Curanderismo—An Optional Health-Care System.* Edinburg, Tex.: Pan American University, 1975.

Eastman, K., and Loustaunau, M. "Use of a Maternity Center as a Birthing Alternative in the El Paso-Juarez Area." n.p., n.d.

Ehrenreich, B. and English, D. *Witches, Midwives, and Nurses: A History of Women Healers,* 2nd ed. Old Westbury, N.Y.: Feminist Press, 1973.

Forbes, Thomas R. *The Midwife and the Witch.* New Haven: Yale University Press, 1966.

Fuller, S. "The Role of the Nurse Midwife and the Lay Midwife in the Rio Grande Valley." Health Policy Paper, LBJ, School of Public Affairs: n.p., May 1979.

Kay, M. A. "Health and Illness in a Mexican American Barrio." In *Ethnic Medicine in the Southwest,* edited by E. H. Spicer. Tucson: University of Arizona Press, 1977.

———, "The Mexican American." In *Culture, Childbearing, Health Professionals,* edited by A. Clark. Philadelphia: F. A. Davis Co., 1978.

Kelly, I. *Folk Practice in North Mexico Birth Customs, Folk Medicine, and Spiritualism in the Laguna Zone.* Austin: University of Texas Press, 1965.

Kessner, D. M. *Infant Death: An Analysis by Maternal Risk and Health Care.* Washington, D.C.: Institute of Medicine, 1973.

Myles, M. D. *Textbook for Midwives.* London: Churchill Livingstone, 1975.

Philpott, L. L. "A Descriptive Study of Birth Practices and Midwifery in the Lower Rio Grande Valley of Texas. Ph. D. dissertation, University of Texas Health Science Center at Houston School of Public Health, 1979.

Powell-Griner, E., and Streck, D. "A Closer Examination of Neonatal Mortality Rates among the Texas Spanish Surname Population," *American Journal of Public Health,* 8, no. 43 (March 17, 1982).

Sanchez, A. R. "An Exploratory Study of Mexican American Midwives' Attitudes, Practices, and Beliefs Regarding Children Born with Congenital Defects." Master's thesis, University of Texas at Austin, 1971.

Shutter, M. E. "Disease and Curing in a Yaqui Community." In *Ethnic Medicine in the Southwest,* edited by E. H. Spicer. Tucson: University of Arizona Press, 1977.

Epilogue

Why must health-care deliverers study ethnicity, culture, and cultural sensitivity? Why must they know the difference between "hot" and "cold" and yin and yang? Why must they be concerned with the consumer's failure to practice what professionals believe to be good preventive medicine, or with the consumer's failure to comply with a given treatment regimen, or with the consumer's failure to seek medical care during the initial phase of an illness?

There is little disagreement that health-care services in this country are unevenly distributed and that the poor and the ethnic people of color get the short end of the stick in terms of the care they receive (or do not receive). Yet it is often maintained that, when such care *is* provided, these same people fail to use it or use it inappropriately. Why is this seeming paradox so?

The major focus of this book has been on the provider's and the consumer's differing perceptions of health and illness. These differences may account for the health-care provider's misconception that services are used inappropriately and that people do not care about their health. What to the casual observer appears to be "misuse" may represent our failure to meet the needs and expectations of the consumer. This possibility may well be difficult for health-care providers to face, but careful analysis of the available information seems to indicate that this may—at least in part—be the case. How, then, can health-care providers change their method of operation and provide both safe and effective care for ethnic people of color and, at the same time, for the population at large? The answer to this question is not an easy one. However, there are a number of measures that can and must be taken to ameliorate the current situation.

Although curricula in professional education are quite full, ethnic studies must be taken by all people who wish to deliver health care. It is no longer sufficient to teach a student in the health professions to "accept the patient for who he is." The question arises: Who is he? Introductory sociology and psychology courses fail to provide this information; it is learned best by meeting with the people themselves and letting them describe who they are from their own perspective. I have suggested two approaches to the problem. One is to have ethnic people of color who work as patient advocates or as nurses and physicians come to the class setting and explain how people of their ethnic group view health and illness, and describe the kinds of health care they practice. Another approach is to send students out into communities where they will have the opportunity to meet with people in their own settings. It is not necessary to memorize all the available lists of herbs, hot-cold imbalances, folk diseases, and so forth. The objective is to become more sensitive to the crucial fact that there are multiple factors underlying given patient behaviors. One, of course, is that the patient may well *perceive* and *understand* health and illness from quite a different perspective than that of the health-care provider. Each person comes from a unique culture and a unique socialization process.

The health-care provider must be sensitive to his own perceptions of health and illness, and the practices he employs. Even though the perceptions of most health professionals are based on a middle-class and medical-model viewpoint, providers must realize that there are other ways of regarding health and illness. The first three chapters of this book are devoted to consciousness-raising about self-treatment. It is always an eye-opening experience to publicly scrutinize ourselves in this respect. Quite often we are amazed to see how far we stray from the system's prescribed methods of keeping healthy. The journals confirm that we, too, delay in seeking health care and fail to comply with treatment regimens. Often our ability to comply rests on quite pragmatic issues such as "What is it doing for me?" and "Can I afford to miss work and stay in bed for two days?" As we gain insight into our own health-illness attitudes and behaviors, we tend to be much more sympathetic to and empathetic with the person who fails to come to the clinic or who hates to wait for the physician or who delays in seeking health care.

The health-care provider should be aware of the complex issues that surround the delivery of health care from the patient's viewpoint. Calling the medical society for the name of a physician (because a "family member has a health problem") and visiting and comparing the services that are rendered in an urban and a suburban emergency room are exercises that can enable us to better appreciate some of the difficulties that the poor, the ethnic minorities, and the population at large all too often experience when they attempt to obtain health care. Members of the health-care team have a number of advantages in gaining access to the health-care system. For example, they can choose a physician whom they know because they work with him or because someone they work with has recommended him. But health-care providers must never forget that most people do not have these advantages. It is indeed an unsettling, anxiety-provoking, and frustrating experience to be forced to select a physician from a list. It is an even more frustrating experience to be a patient in an unfamiliar location—for example, an urban emergency room, where, quite literally, anything goes.

Another barrier to adequate health care is the financial burden imposed by treatments and tests. There are other issues as well. For example, a Chinese patient—who traditionally does not believe that his body replaces blood that is taken for testing purposes—should have as little blood work as necessary, and the reasons for the tests should be carefully explained. A Hispanic woman who believes that taking a pap smear is an intrusive procedure that will bring shame to her should have the procedure performed by a female physician or nurse. When this is not possible, she should have a female chaperone with her for the entire time that the male physician or nurse is in the room.

More ethnic people of color must be represented in the health-care professions.   There are multiple issues related to the problem of underrepresentation. Many of the programs designed to increase the number of ethnic people of color in the health-care team have failed. The continued use of the quota system in medical schools is an example of this failure. Difficulties surrounding successful entrance into and completion of professional education programs are complex and numerous, having their roots in impoverished community structures and early educational deprivation. While society is in some ways dealing with such issues—for example, initiating improvements in early education—we are faced with an *immediate* need to bring more ethnic people of color into health-care services.

One method would be the more extensive use of patient advocates and "outreach" workers from the given ethnic community who may be recognized there as healers. These people can provide an overwhelmingly positive service to both the provider and the consumer in that they will serve as the bridge in bringing health-care services to the people. The patient advocate can speak to the client in language that the client understands and in a manner that is acceptable. Advocates are also able to coordinate medical, nursing, social, and even educational services to meet the patient's needs as he perceives them. In settings where advocates are employed, many problems are resolved to the convenience of both the health-care member and, more importantly, the client!

The nettlesome issue of language bursts forth with regularity. There is always a problem when a non-English-speaking person tries to seek help from the English-speaking majority. The more common languages, French, Italian, and Spanish, should ideally be spoken by at least some of the professional people that staff hospitals, clinics, neighborhood health-care centers, and home health agencies. The use of an interpreter is always difficult because the interpreter generally "interprets" what he translates as he translates. To bring this thought home, the reader should recall the childhood game of "gossip": a message was passed around the room from person to person, and by the time it got back to the sender its content was usually substantially changed. This game is not unlike trying to communicate through an interpreter, and the situation is even more frustrating when—as can often be the case in urban emergency rooms—the interpreter is a 6-year-old child. It is, obviously, far more satisfying and productive if the patient, nurse, and physician can all speak the same language.

Health services must be made far more accessible and available to ethnic people of color. I believe that one of the most important events in this modern era of health-care delivery is the advent of neighborhood health centers. They are successful essentially because people who work in them know the people of the neighborhood. In addition, the people of the community can contribute to the decision making involved in governing and running the agency so that services are tailored to meet the needs of the clients. Concerned members of the health-care team have a moral obligation to support the increased use of health-care centers and *not* their decreased use, as currently tends to occur because of cutbacks in response to allegations (frequently politically motivated) of too-high costs or the misuse of funds. These neighborhood health-care centers provide greatly needed personal services in addition to relief from the widespread depersonalization that occurs in larger institutions. When health-care providers who are genuinely concerned face this reality, perhaps they will be more willing to fight for the survival of these centers and strongly urge their increase rather than acquiesce in their demise. In rural areas, the problem is even greater, and far more comprehensive health planning is needed to meet patient needs.

I should like to reiterate that this book was written with the hope that by sharing the material I have been trying to teach, some small changes will be made in the thinking of all health-care providers who read it. There is nothing new in these pages; perhaps it is simply a recombination of material with which the reader is familiar. But I hope it serves its purpose: the sharing of beliefs and attitudes, and the stimulation of lots of consciousness-raising concerning issues of vital concern to health-care providers who must confront the needs of clients with diverse cultural backgrounds.

BIBLIOGRAPHY

Branch, Marie Foster, and Paxton, Phyllis Perry. *Providing Safe Nursing Care for Ethnic People of Color.* New York: Appleton-Century-Crofts, 1976.
    This outstanding book has a threefold purpose: (1) to describe how deficient knowledge about cultural health beliefs impedes health care; (2) to

describe a set of approaches to nursing care directed toward the enhancement of *wellness* for ethnic people of color; and (3) to provide models for nursing education.

Brink, Pamela J., ed. *Transcultural Nursing: A Book of Readings*. Englewood Cliffs, N.J.: Prentice-Hall, 1976.

Transcultural nursing is a blend of anthropology and nursing. The many readings in this book demonstrate this blend in a number of situations.

Epstein, Charlotte. *Effective Interaction in Contemporary Nursing*. Englewood Cliffs, N.J.: Prentice-Hall, 1974.

Epstein explores what nurses should know about communications; how to deal with stereotypes, such as the "ideal" patient and nurse; the nurse in the community; and the nurse and social change.

Leininger, Madeline. *Nursing and Anthropology: Two Worlds to Blend*. New York: Wiley, 1970.

In this work we find an overview of transcultural nursing concepts in several settings.

Storlie, Frances. *Nursing and the Social Conscience*. New York: Appleton-Century-Crofts, 1970.

This book helps the reader to look forward and to examine the purpose of nursing and the profession. It offers no answers to the problems of society, but it raises significant questions.

FURTHER SUGGESTED READINGS

BOOKS

American Nurses' Association. *A Strategy for Change*. Papers presented at the conference held 9–10 June 1979, Commission on Human Rights, Alburquerque, N. Mex.

Brownlee, Ann Templeton. *Community, Culture and Care: A Cross Cultural Guide for Healthworkers*. St. Louis: C. V. Mosby, 1979.

Bullough, Vern L. and Bullough, Bonnie. *Health Care for Other Americans*. New York: Appleton-Century-Crofts, 1982.

Feagin, Joe R. and Feagin, Clairece B. *Discrimination American Style*. Englewood Cliffs, N.J.: Prentice-Hall, 1978.

Katz, Judy H. *White Awareness*. Norman, Okla.: University of Oklahoma Press, 1978.

Mushkin, S. V. *Consumer Incentives for Health Care*. New York: Prodist, 1974.

ARTICLES

Branch, Marie. "Faculty Development to Meet Minority Group Needs: Recruitment, Retention, and Curriculum Change, 1971–1974." Western Interstate Commission for Higher Education, no. 2060.

Buckley, John. "Faculty Commitment to Retention and Recruitment of Black Students." *Nursing Outlook,* January 1980, pp. 46–50.

Claerbaut, David. "The Black Nursing Student at the Liberal Arts College: A Study in Alienation." *Nursing Forum*, 15, no. 2 (February 1976): 211–18.

Cofer, Audre. "Autobiography of a Black Nurse." *American Journal of Nursing,* October 1974, pp. 1836–38.

Group, T. M. "If a Nurse Is to Help in Ghettos." *American Journal of Nursing* 69 (December 1969): 2635–36.

Harvey, Lillian H. "Educational Problems of Minority Group Nurses." *Nursing Outlook* 18, no. 9 (September 1970): 48–50.

Hess, Gertrude, and Stroud, Florence. "Racial Tensions: Barriers in Delivery of Nursing Care." *Journal of Nursing Administration,* May-June 1972, pp. 46–49.

La Fargue, Jane. "Role of Prejudice in Rejection of Health Care." *Nursing Research* 21 (January-February 1972): 53–58.

Malhiot, Grete and Ninan, Mary. "A Seminar for Minority Students." *Nursing Outlook,* July 1979, pp. 473–75.

Milio, Nancy. "Values, Social Class, and Community Health Services." *Nursing Research* 16 (Winter 1967): 26–31.

Miller, Michael H. "On Blacks Entering Nursing." *Nursing Forum* 11, no. 3 (March 1972): 248–63.

Paxton, Phyllis, and Robinson, Stella P. "Continuing Education Needs of Nurses Serving Minorities and the Poor." *Journal of Continuing Education in Nursing* 5 (March-April 1974): 12–17.

Piero, Phyllis. "Black White Crises." *American Journal of Nursing,* February 1974, pp. 280–81.

Richeck, H. G. "A Note on Prejudice in Prospective Professional Helpers." *Nursing Research* 19 (March-April 1970): 172–75.

Sellers, Rudolph V. "The Black Health Worker and the Black Health Consumer—New Roles for Both." *American Journal of Public Health* 60, no. 11 (November 1970): 2154–70.

Smith, Gloria R. "From Invisibility to Blackness: The Story of the Black Nurses' Association." *Nursing Outlook* 23, no. 4 (April 1975): 225–29.

Suggested Course Outline

NU301. CULTURAL DIVERSITY IN HEALTH AND ILLNESS*

The purpose of this course is to bring the student into a direct relationship with the ethnic person—both of color and white, black, Chinese, Hispanic, Native American—and the American health-care delivery system. The course content will include discussion of the following topics:

- The perception of health and illness among health-care providers and consumers.
- The cultural and institutional factors that affect the consumers' access to and use of health-care resources.
- Health-care providers' ways of coping with illness and related problems.
- The manner in which ethnic people, both of color and white, and their problems have been depicted in the literature (e.g., the works of Lewis, Kiev, Clark) and their implications for nursing practice.

Goal
The goal of this course is to broaden the student's perception and understanding of health and illness and the variety of meanings of these terms for members of ethnic groups of color and white ethnic groups.

Objectives
Upon completion of this course the student will be able to:

---

*From the Boston College School of Nursing, Chestnut Hill, Massachusetts 02167.

1. Understand more fully the perception and meaning of health and illness for the student and for the ethnic consumer both of color and white.
2. Enter into dialogue with people who have experienced problems in dealing with the American health-care system.
3. Understand the conflicts between the consumer and the American health-care system and its impact on nursing practice and action.
4. Develop ideas as to what nursing practice can do to intervene in this conflict and diminish it.

Texts

The following texts will be read in total and are suggested for purchase:

Bullough, Bonnie, and Bullough, Vern L. *Health Care for other Americans.* New York: Appleton-Century-Crofts, 1982.

Ehrenreich, Barbara, and Ehrenreich, John. *The American Health Empire: Power, Profits, and Politics.* New York: Random House, Vintage Books, 1971.

Spector, Rachel E. *Cultural Diversity in Health and Illness.* 2nd ed. New York: Appleton-Century-Crofts, 1985.

Assignments and Evaluation

1. Weekly readings, class attendance, preparedness, and participation	15%
2. Health interviews	5%
3. Health diaries	10%
4. Reaction papers	20%

The purpose of these papers is to express the student's reactions to the assigned readings up to date of the paper, as well as to the classroom discussion.

5. Term paper (maximum 8 to 10 pages)	25%

This paper must deal with the problems and issues presented in class and the student's interpretation of how professional nurses must cope with them in practice. All papers must be submitted in proper Turabian format, typed and double-spaced.

6. Term project	25%

Class presentation, with a small group, on perspectives of health and illness in one of the four communities studied; class presentation must include the following data:

1. History of ethnic group in the United States
2. Traditional perceptions of health and illness

3. Traditional healing methods
4. Current health-care problems

Sources must include a bibliography, interviews with people within the given community, and observations.

COURSE OUTLINE

Week I   **Course Introduction: Discussion of General Concepts of Health**
Assignments for Class II:
1. Interview an older member of your family to determine (a) what practices were used to prevent illness and maintain health; (b) what was done to treat illness.
2. Begin a daily diary of your health status for one month. (Both assignments must be handed in.)

Week II   **Discussion: Concepts of Illness and Practices for Maintaining Health and Preventing Illness**
Readings:†
*Bullough and Bullough, pp. 1–18
*Ehrenreich and Ehrenreich, Introduction
Dubos, *Mirage of Health*
Dubos, *Man Adapting*

Week III   **The Delivery of Health Care in the United States**
Readings:
*Silver, *A Spy in the House of Medicine*
*Ehrenreich and Ehrenreich—complete this book
*Kennedy, *In Critical Condition*

Week IV   **Culture: Its Effect on the Perception of Health and Illness**
Readings:
*Bullough and Bullough—complete this book
*Zola, "Culture and Symptoms: An Analysis of Patients Presenting Complaints"
*Brink, *Transcultural Nursing,* pp. 93–126

Week V   **Poverty and Its Impact on Health Care**
Readings:
*Trattner, *From Poor Law to Welfare State*
Freire, *Pedagogy of the Oppressed*
Feagin, *Subordinating the Poor*
Piven, *Regulating the Poor*

---

†For complete bibliographic data on the listed readings, see the following Bibliography. The asterisks indicate required reading.

Week VI   **Faith and Healing**
               Readings:
                   Kelsey, *Healing and Christianity*
                   Leek, *Herbs: Medicine and Mysticism*
                   MacNutt, *Healing*
                   Film: "We Believe in Nino Fidencio"

Week VII   **Health and Illness in the Hispanic Communities**
               Readings:
                   *Thomas, *Down These Mean Streets* or *Savior, Savior, Hold My Hand*
                   *Lewis, *La Vida*
                   Clark, *Health in the Mexican-American Culture: A Community Study*
                   *Branch, *Providing Safe Nursing Care for Ethnic People of Color*, Chap. 3

Week VIII   **Health and Illness in the Native American Community**
               Readings:
                   *Deloria, *Custer Died for Your Sins*
                   Kluckhohn, *The Navaho*
                   *Branch, Chap. 4
                   Brown, *Bury My Heart at Wounded Knee*

Week IX   **Health and Illness in the Chinese Community**
               Readings:
                   *Brink, *Transcultural Nursing,* pp. 240–47
                   *Branch, Chap. 5

Week X   **Health and Illness in the Black Community**
               Readings:
                   Haley, *Roots*
                   *Grier, *Black Rage*
                   Wright, *Black Boy* or *Native Son*
                   *Branch, Chap. 6
                   Gutman, *The Black Family in Slavery and Freedom*
                   Angelou, *I Know Why the Caged Bird Sings*

Week XI   **Health and Illness in the White Community**
               Readings:
                   Background information about specific groups of instructor's or student's selection.

Week XII   **Institutional Barriers and Advocacy**
               Readings:
                   *Branch, Part I

Week XIII   **Implications for Nursing and Health-Care Delivery**
               Readings:

*Storlie, *Nursing and the Social Conscience*
*Brink, *Transcultural Nursing,* last section, pp. 215–75.
*Branch, Parts III and IV

Week XIV   **Evaluation and Interethnic Dinner**

Bibliography

Achebe, Chinua. *Things Fall Apart.* Greenwich, Conn.: Fawcett Crest, 1959.
Aiken, Linda G. *Health Policy and Nursing Practice.* New York: McGraw-Hill, 1981.
Aiken, R. *Mexican Folk Tales from the Borderland.* Dallas: Southern Methodist University Press, 1980.
Allport, Gordon W. *The Nature of Prejudice* (abridged). Garden City, N.Y.: Doubleday and Co., 1958.
Alvarez, H. R. *Health without Boundaries,* Mexico: United States-Mexico Border Public Health Association, 1975.
American Nurses' Association. *A Strategy for Change.* Papers presented at the conference of the Commission on Human Rights, Alburquerque, N.M., 9–10 June 1979.
Anderson, J. Q. *Texas Folk Medicine.* Austin: Encino Press, 1970.
Andrade, Sally Jones. *Chicano Mental Health: The Case of Cristal.* Austin: Hogg Foundation for Mental Health, 1978.
Angelou, Maya. *I Know Why The Caged Bird Sings.* New York: Random House, 1970.
Apple, Dorion, ed., *Sociological Studies of Health and Sickness: A Source Book for the Health Professions.* New York: McGraw-Hill, Blakiston Division, 1960.
Arnold, Mark G., and Rosenbaum, Greg. *The Crime of Poverty.* Skokie, Ill.: National Textbook Co., 1973.
Ashely, Joann. *Hospitals, Paternalism, and the Role of the Nurse.* New York: Teachers College Press, 1976.
Ausubel, Nathan. *The Book of Jewish Knowledge.* New York: Crown Publishers, 1964.
Bakan, David. *Disease, Pain and Sacrifice: Toward a Psychology of Suffering.* Chicago: University of Chicago Press, 1968.
Bauwens, Eleanor F. *The Anthropology of Health.* St. Louis: C. V. Mosby, 1979.
Becker, Marshall H. *The Health Belief Model and Personal Health Behavior.* Thorofare, N.J.: 1974.
Benjamin, G. G. *The Germans in Texas.* 1910. Reprint. Austin: Jenkins Publishing Co., 1974.
Berman, Edgar. *The Solid Gold Stethoscope.* New York: MacMillan Co., 1976.
Bermann, Eric. *Scapegoat.* Ann Arbor: University of Michigan Press, 1973.

Bernardo, Stephanie. *The Ethnic Almanac.* Garden City, N.Y.: Doubleday and Co., 1981.

Bishop, G. *Faith Healing: God or Fraud?* Los Angeles: Shervourne Press, 1967.

Boney, Wilfrid. *The French Canadians Today.* London: J. M. Dent and Sons, 1939.

Bracq, Jean C. *The Evolution of French Canada.* New York: MacMillan Co., 1924.

Bradley, C. J. "Characteristics of Women and Infants Attended by Lay Midwives in Texas, 1971: A Case Comparison Study." Master's thesis, University of Texas Health Science Center at Houston, School of Public Health, 1980.

Branch, Marie Foster, and Paxton, Phyllis Perry. *Providing Safe Nursing Care for Ethnic People of Color.* New York: Appleton-Century-Crofts, 1976.

Brink, Pamela J., ed. *Transcultural Nursing: A Book of Readings.* Englewood Cliffs, N.J.: Prentice-Hall, 1976.

Brown, Dee. *Bury My Heart at Wounded Knee.* New York: Holt, Rinehart and Winston, 1970.

———. *Creek Mary's Blood.* New York: Holt, Rinehart and Winston, 1980.

Brownlee, Ann Templeton. *Community, Culture and Care: A Cross Cultural Guide for Healthworkers.* St. Louis: C. V. Mosby, 1979.

Bullough, Bonnie, and Bullough, Vern L. *Poverty, Ethnic Identity and Health Care.* New York: Appleton-Century-Crofts, 1972.

Bullough, Vern L., and Bullough, Bonnie. *Health Care for Other Americans.* New York: Appleton-Century-Crofts, 1982.

Buxton, John. *Religion and Healing in Mandari.* Oxford: Clarendon Press, 1973.

Cafferty, Pastora San Juan; Chiswick, Barry R.; Greeley, Andrew M.; and Sullivan, Teresa A. *The Dilemma of American Immigration: Beyond the Golden Door.* New Brunswick: Transaction Books, 1983.

Calhoun, Mary, *Medicine Show.* New York: Harper and Row, 1976.

Campos, E. *Medicina Popular—Supersticione Credios E Meizinhas.* 2nd ed. Rio de Janeiro: Livraria—Editora da Casa. 1955.

Candill, Harry M. *Night Comes to the Cumberlands.* Boston: Little, Brown and Co., 1962.

Chavira, L. *Curanderismo: An Optional Health-Care System.* Edinburg, Tex.: Pan American University, 1975.

Chenault, Lawrence R. *The Puerto Rican Migrant in New York City.* New York: Columbia University Press, 1938.

Clark, Ann L. *Culture and Child Rearing.* Philadelphia: F. A. Davis Co., 1981.

———. *Culture, Childbearing Health Professionals.* Philadelphia: F. A. Davis Co., 1978.

Clark, Margaret. *Health in the Mexican-American Culture: A Community Study.* Berkeley: University of California Press, 1959.

Conway, Mimi. *Rise Gonna Rise.* New York: Anchor Books, 1974.

Cramer, M. E. *Divine Science and Healing.* Denver: Colorado College of Divine Science, 1923.

Crichton, Michael. *Five Patients.* New York: Alfred A. Knopf, 1970.

Crispino, Joseph A. *Assimilation of Ethnic Groups: The Italian Case.* Newark: New Jersey Center for Migration, 1980.

Davis, Fred, ed. *The Nursing Profession: Five Sociological Essays.* New York: John Wiley and Sons, 1966.

De Castro, Josue. *The Black Book of Hunger.* Boston: Beacon Press, 1967.

Deloria, Vine, Jr. *Custer Died for Your Sins—An Indian Manifesto.* New York: Avon Books, 1969.

Densmore, Frances. *How Indians Use Wild Plants for Food, Medicine, and Crafts.* New York: Dover, 1974.

Donegan, Jane B. *Women and Men Midwives: Medicine, Morality and Misogyny in Early America.* Westport, Conn.: Greenwood Press, 1978.

Donin, Hayim Halevy. *To Be a Jew.* New York: Basic Books, 1972.

Dubos, René Jules. *Man Adapting.* New Haven: Yale University Press, 1965.

———. *Man, Medicine and Environment.* New York: Mentor, 1968.

———. *Mirage of Health.* Garden City, N.Y.: Anchor Books, Doubleday and Co., 1961.

Ehrenreich, Barbara, and Ehrenreich, John. *The American Health Empire: Power, Profits, and Politics.* New York: Random House, Vintage Books, 1970.

Ehrenreich, B., and English, D. *Witches, Midwives, and Nurses: A History of Women Healers,* 2nd. ed. Old Westbury, N.Y.: Feminist Press, 1973.

Elling, Ray H. *Socio-Cultural Influences on Health and Health Care.* New York: Springer Co., 1977.

Elworthy, R. T. *The Evil Eye: The Origins and Practices of Superstition.* N.Y.: Julian Press, 1958. (originally published by John Murray, London, 1915).

Epstein, Charlotte. *Effective Interaction in Contemporary Nursing.* Englewood Cliffs, N.J.: Prentice-Hall, 1974.

Feagin, Joe R. *Subordinating the Poor—Welfare and American Beliefs.* Englewood Cliffs, N.J.: Prentice-Hall, 1975.

Feagin, Joe R. and Feagin, Clairece B. *Discrimination American Style.* Englewood Cliffs, N.J.: Prentice-Hall, 1978.

Finney, Joseph C., ed. *Culture Change, Mental Health and Poverty.* New York: Simon and Schuster, 1969.

Fleming, Arthur S., chairman, U.S. Commission on Civil Rights. *The Tarnished Golden Door—Civil Rights Issues on Immigration.* Washington, D.C.: Government Printing Office, 1980.

Forbes, Thomas R. *The Midwife and the Witch.* New Haven: Yale University Press, 1966.

Ford, P. S. *The Healing Trinity: Prescriptions for Body, Mind, and Spirit.* New York: Harper and Row, 1971.

Foy, F. A., ed. *Catholic Almanac.* Huntington, Ind.: Our Sunday Visitor, 1980.

Freeman, Howard; Levine, Sol; and Reeder, Leo G., eds. *Handbook of Medical Sociology.* 2nd ed. Englewood Cliffs, N.J.: Prentice-Hall, 1972.

Freidson, Eliot. *Profession of Medicine.* New York: Dodd, Mead and Co., 1971.

Freire, Paulo. *Pedagogy of the Oppressed.* Translated by Myra Bugman Ramos. New York: Seabury Press, 1970.

Gambino, R. *Blood of My Blood: The Dilemma of Italian-Americans.* Garden City, N.Y.: Doubleday and Co., 1974.

Gelfond, D. E. and Kutzik, A., eds. *Ethnicity and Aging: Theory, Research and Policy.* New York: Springer, 1979.

Genovese, Eugene D. *Roll, Jordan, Roll.* New York: Vintage Books, 1972.

Giordano, Joseph, and Giordano, Grace Pineiro. *The Ethno-Cultural Factor in Mental Health.* New York: New York Institute of Pluralism and Group Identity, 1977.

Glazer, N., and Moynihan, D., eds. *Ethnicity: Theory and Experience.* Cambridge: Harvard University Press, 1975.

Gordon, David M. *Theories of Poverty and Underemployment.* Lexington, Mass.: D. C. Heath and Co., 1972.

Gordon, Ferald, *Role Theory and Illness.* New Haven, Conn.: College and University Press, 1966.

Greeley, Andrew M. *The Irish Americans.* New York: Harper and Row, 1981.
_____. *Why Can't They Be Like Us? America's White Ethnic Groups.* New York: E. P. Dutton, 1975.

Grier, William H., and Cobbs, Price M. *Black Rage.* New York: Bantam Books, 1968.

Gutman, Herbert G. *The Black Family in Slavery and Freedom, 1750-1925.* New York: Pantheon Books, 1976.

Haley, Alex. *Roots.* Garden City, N.Y.: Doubleday and Co., 1976.

Hand, Wayland D. *American Folk Medicine: A Symposium.* Berkeley: University of California Press, 1973.

Harney, Robert F. and Troper, Harold. *Immigrants: A Portrait of Urban Experience 1890-1930.* Toronto: Van Nostrand Reinhold, 1975.

Harwood, Alan, ed. *Ethnicity and Medical Care.* Cambridge: Harvard University Press, 1981.

Hecker, M. *Ethnic American, 1970-1977.* Dobbs Ferry, N.Y.: Oceana Publications, 1979.

Henderson, George, and Primeaux, Martha, eds. *Transcultural Health Care.* Menlo Park, Calif.: Addison-Wesley, 1981.

Herzlich, Claudine. *Health and Illness—A Social Psychological Analysis.* Translated by Douglas Graham. New York: Academic Press, 1973.

Hickel, Walter J. *Who Owns America?* New York: Paperback Library, 1972.

Howe, Irving. *World of Our Fathers.* New York: Harcourt Brace Jovanovich, 1976.

Hufford, David J. *American Healing Systems: An Introduction and Exploration.* Conference Booklet, Philadelphia: University of Pennsylvania, 1984.

Hughes, Langston, and Bontemps, Arna, eds. *The Book of Negro Folklore.* New York: Dodd, Mead, 1958.

Hutchens, Alma R. *Indian Herbalogy of North America.* Windsor, Ont.: Meico, 1973.

Hutton, J. Bernard. *The Healing Power.* London: Leslie Frewin, 1975.

Illich, Ivan. *Medical Nemesis: The Expropriation of Health.* London: Marion Bogars, 1975.
_____ ; Zola, Irving K.; McKnight, John; Caplan, Jonathan; and Shaiken, Harley. *Disabling Professions.* Salem, N.H.: Boyars, 1977.

Jaco, E. Gartly, ed., *Patients, Physicians, and Illness: Sourcebook in Behavioral Science and Medicine.* Glencoe, Ill.: Free Press, 1958.

Jarvis, D. C. *Folk Medicine: A Vermont Doctor's Guide to Good Health.* New York: Henry Holt and Co., 1958.

Jonas, Steven. *Health Care Delivery in the United States.* 2nd. ed. New York: Springer, 1982.

Jung, Carl G., ed. *Man and His Symbols.* Garden City, N.Y.: Doubleday and Co., 1964.

Kain, John F., ed. *Race and Poverty: The Economics of Discrimination.* Englewood Cliffs, N.J.: Prentice-Hall, 1969.

Katz, Judy H. *White Awareness.* Norman, Okla.: University of Oklahoma Press, 1978.

Kekahbah, Janice, and Wood, Rosemary, eds. *Life Cycle of the American Indian Family.* Norman, Okla.: AIANA Publishing Co., 1980.

Kelly, Isabel. *Folk Practice in North Mexico. Birth Customs, Folk Medicine and Spiritualism in the Laguna Zone.* Austin: University of Texas Press, 1965.

Kelsey, Morton T. *Healing and Christianity.* New York: Harper and Row, 1973.

Kennedy, Edward M. *In Critical Condition: The Crises in America's Health Care.* New York: Simon and Schuster, 1972.

Kennett, Frances. *Folk Medicine, Fact and Fiction.* New York: Crescent Books, 1976.

Kiev, Ari. *Curanderismo: Mexican-American Folk Psychiatry.* New York: Free Press, 1968.

———. *Magic, Faith, and Healing: Studies in Primitive Psychiatry Today.* New York: Free Press, 1964.

Klein, Judith Weinstein. *Jewish Identity and Self-Esteem: Healing Wounds through Ethnotherapy.* New York: Institute on Pluralism and Group Identity, 1980.

Kluckhohn, Clyde. *Navaho Witchcraft,* Boston: Beacon Press, 1944.

———, and Leighton, Dorothea. *The Navaho.* Rev. ed. Garden City, N.Y.: Doubleday and Co., 1962.

Knutson, Andie L. *The Individual, Society and Health Behavior.* New York: Russell Sage Foundation, 1965.

Kordel, Lelord, *Natural Folk Remedies.* New York: G. P. Putnam's Sons, 1974.

Kosa, John, and Zola, Irving Kenneth. *Poverty and Health—A Sociological Analysis* 2nd ed. Cambridge: Harvard University Press, 1976.

Kotelchuck, David, ed. *Prognosis Negative.* New York: Vintage Books, 1976.

Kotz, Nick. *Let Them Eat Promises.* Garden City, N.Y.: Doubleday and Co., 1971.

Kreiger, Dolores. *The Therapeutic Touch.* Englewood Cliffs, N.J.: Prentice-Hall, 1979.

Krippner, S., and Villaldo, A. *The Realms of Healing.* Millbrae, Calif.: Celestial Arts, 1976.

Landmann, Robert S., ed. *The Problem of the Undocumented Worker.* Albuquerque: Latin American Institute, University of New Mexico, 1981.

Leek, Sybil. *Herbs: Medicine and Mysticism.* Chicago: Henry Regnery Co., 1975.

Leff, S., and Leff, Vera. *From Witchcraft to World Health.* New York: Macmillan Co., 1957.

Leininger, Madeleine. *Nursing and Anthropology: Two Worlds to Blend.* New York: John Wiley and Sons, 1970.

———. *Transcultural Nursing: Concepts, Theories and Practices.* New York: John Wiley and Sons, 1978.

Lewis, Oscar. *The Children of Sanchez: Autobiography of a Mexican Family.* New York: Random House, 1961.

———. *A Death in the Sanchez Family.* New York: Random House, 1966.

———. *Five Families: Mexican Case Studies in the Culture of Poverty.* New York: New American Library Basic Books, 1959.

———. *La Vida: A Puerto Rican Family in the Culture of Poverty—San Juan and New York.* New York: Random House, 1966.

Lieban, Richard W. *Cebuano Sorcery.* Berkeley: University of California Press, 1967.

Litoff, J. B. *American Midwives 1860 to the Present.* Westport, Conn.: Greenwood Press, 1978.

Louv, Richard. *Southwind: The Mexican Migration.* San Diego: San Diego Union, 1980.

Lynch, L. Reddick, ed. *The Cross-Cultural Approach to Health Behavior.* Rutherford, N.J.: Fairleigh Dickenson University Press, 1969.

McGill, O. *The Mysticism and Magic of India.* South Brunswick, N.J. and New York: A. S. Baines and Co., 1977.

McGoldrick, Monica; Pearce, John K.; and Giordano, Joseph. *Ethnicity and Family Therapy.* New York: Guilford Press, 1982.

McLemore, S. Dale. *Racial and Ethnic Relations in America.* Boston: Allyn and Bacon, 1980.

MacNutt, Francis. *Healing.* Notre Dame, Ind.: Ave Maria Press, 1974.

_____. *The Power to Heal.* Notre Dame, Ind.: Ave Maria Press, 1977.

Malinowski, Bronislaw. *Magic, Science and Religion.* Garden City, N.Y.: Doubleday and Co., 1954.

Maloney, Clarence, ed. *The Evil Eye.* New York: Columbia University Press, 1976.

Mandell, Betty Reid, ed., *Welfare in America: Controlling the "Dangerous Classes."* Englewood Cliffs, N.J.: Prentice-Hall, 1975.

Mann, Felix. *Acupuncture—The Ancient Chinese Art of Healing and How It Works Scientifically.* New York: Vintage Books, 1972.

Marsella, A. B., and Pedersens, P. B., eds. *Cross Cultural Counseling and Psychotherapy.* New York: Pergamon, 1981.

Martinez, R. A., ed. *Hispanic Culture and Health Care.* St. Louis: C. V. Mosby, 1978.

Matthiessen, Peter. *In the Spirit of Crazy Horse.* New York: Viking Press, 1980.

Mechanic, David. *Medical Sociology: A Selective View.* New York: Free Press, 1968.

Metraux, Alfred. *Voodoo in Haiti.* New York: Schocken Books, 1972.

Milio, Nancy. *The Care of Health in Communities: Access for Outcasts.* New York: Macmillan Co., 1975.

Millman, Marcia. *The Unkindest Cut.* New York: William Morrow and Co., 1977.

Mindel, C. H., and Habenstein, R. W., eds. *Ethnic Families in America.* New York: Elsevier, 1976.

Miner, Horace. *St. Denis, A French Canadian Parish.* Chicago: University of Chicago Press, 1939.

Montgomery, Ruth. *Born to Heal.* New York: Coward, McCann, and Geoghegan, 1973.

Morley, Peter, and Wallis, Roy, eds. *Culture and Curing.* Pittsburgh: University of Pittsburgh Press, 1978.

Mushkin, S. V. *Consumer Incentives for Health Care.* New York: Prodist, 1974.

Newman, Katharine D. *Ethnic American Short Stories.* New York: Pocket Books, 1975.

Norman, John C., ed. *Medicine in the Ghetto.* New York: Appleton-Century-Crofts, 1969.

Novak, Michael. *The Rise of the Unmeltable Ethnics.* New York: Macmillan Co., 1972.

O'Berennan, Junius, and Smith, Nopal. *The Crystal Icon.* Austin: Galahad Press, 1981.

Opler, Marvin K., ed. *Culture and Mental Health*. New York: Macmillan Co., 1959.

Orque, Modesta Soberano; Block, Bobbie; and Monrray, Lidia S. Ahumada. *Ethnic Nursing Care: A Multi-Cultural Approach*. St. Louis: C. V. Mosby, 1983.

Osofsky, Gilbert. *Harlem: The Making of a Ghetto*. New York: Harper and Row, 1963.

Padilla, Elena. *Up From Puerto Rico*. New York: Columbia University Press, 1958.

Parsons, Talcott, and Clark, Kenneth B. *The Negro American*. Boston: Beacon Press, 1965.

Paul, Benjamin, ed. *Health, Culture, and Community: Case Studies of Public Reactions to Health Programs*. New York: Russell Sage Foundation, 1955.

Pearsall, Marion. *Medical Behavior Science: A Selected Bibliography of Cultural Anthropology, Social Psychology, and Sociology in Medicine*. Louisville: University of Kentucky Press, 1963.

Pelto, P. J. and Pelto, G. H. *Anthropological Research: The Structure of Inquiry*, 2nd. ed. Cambridge: Cambridge University Press, 1978.

Philpott, Laura L. "A Descriptive Study of Birth Practices and Midwifery in the Lower Rio Grande Valley of Texas." Ph.D. diss., University of Texas Health Science Center at Houston School of Public Health, 1979.

Piven, Frances Fox, and Cloward, Richard A. *Regulating the Poor: The Functions of Public Welfare*. New York: Vintage Books, 1971.

Rand, Christopher. *The Puerto Ricans*. New York: Oxford University Press, 1958.

Read, Margaret. *Culture, Health and Disease*. London: Javistock Publications, 1966.

Redman, Eric. *The Dance of Legislation*. New York: Simon and Schuster, 1973.

Roby, Pamela, ed. *The Poverty Establishment*. Englewood Cliffs, N.J.: Prentice-Hall, 1974.

Rogler, Lloyd H. *Migrant in the City*. New York: Basic Books, 1972.

Rude, Donald, ed. *Alienation: Minority Groups*. New York: John Wiley and Sons, 1972.

Russell, A. J. *Health in His Wings*. London: Metheun and Co., 1937.

Ryan, William. *Blaming the Victim*. New York: Vintage Books, 1971.

S., E. M. *The House of Wonder—A Romance of Psychic Healing*. London: Rider and Co., 1927.

Saunders, Lyle. *Cultural Difference and Medical Care: The Case of the Spanish-Speaking People of the Southwest*. New York: Russell Sage Foundation, 1954.

Saunders, Ritt. *Healing through the Spirit Agency*. London: Hutchinson and Co., 1927.

Senior, Clarence. *The Puerto Ricans, Strangers—Then Neighbors*. Chicago: Quadrangle Books, 1961.

Sexton, Patricia Cayo. *Spanish Harlem*. New York: Harper and Row, 1965.

Shaw, W. *Aspects of Malaysian Magic*. Kuala Lumpur, Malaysia: Naziabum Nigara, 1975.

Shenkin, B. N. *Health Care for Migrant Workers: Policies and Politics*. Cambridge, Mass.: Ballinger Publishing Co., 1974.

Shepard, Richard F., and Levi, Vickie G. *Live and Be Well*. New York: Ballantine Books, 1982.

Shih-Chen, Li. *Chinese Medicinal Herbs.* Translated by F. Porter Smith and G. A. Stuart. San Francisco: Georgetown Press, 1973.

Shostak, Arthur B.; Van Til, Jon; and Van Til, Sally Bould. *Privilege in America: An End to Inequality?* Englewood Cliffs, N.J.: Prentice-Hall, 1973.

Silver, George. *A Spy in the House of Medicine.* Germantown, Md.: Aspen Systems Corp., 1976.

Silverstein, Martin Elliot; Chang, I-Lok; and Macon, Nathaniel, trans. *Acupuncture and Moxibustion.* New York: Schocken Books, 1975.

Simmen, Edward, ed. *Pain and Promise: The Chicano Today.* New York: New American Library, 1972.

Smith, Lillian. *Killers of the Dream.* Garden City, N.Y.: Doubleday and Co., 1963.

Sowell, T. *Ethnic America.* New York: Basic Books, 1981.

Spector, Rachel E. "A Description of the Impact of Medicare on Health-Illness Beliefs and Practices of White Ethnic Senior Citizens in Central Texas." Ph.D. diss. University of Texas at Austin School of Nursing, 1983; Ann Arbor, Mich.: University Microfilms International, 1983.

Spicer, Edward, ed. *Ethnic Medicine in the Southwest.* New York: Russell Sage Foundation, 1977.

Stack, Carol B. *All Our Kin.* New York: Harper and Row, 1974.

Steinberg, Milton. *Basic Judaism,* New York: Harcourt, Brace and World, 1947.

Steiner, Stan. *La Raza: The Mexican Americans.* New York: Harper and Row, 1969.

Stone, Eric. *Medicine among the American Indians.* New York: Hafner Publishing Co., 1962.

Storlie, Frances. *Nursing and the Social Conscience.* New York: Appleton-Century-Crofts, 1970.

Storm, Hyemeyohots. *Seven Arrows.* New York: Ballantine Books, 1972.

Styron, William. *The Confessions of Nat Turner.* New York: Random House, 1966.

Tallant, Robert. *Voodoo in New Orleans.* New York: Collier Books, 1946.

Te Selle, Sallie, ed. *The Rediscovery of Ethnicity: Its Implications for Culture and Politics in America.* New York: Harper and Row, 1973.

Thernstrom, Stephen, ed. *Harvard Encyclopedia of American Ethnic Groups.* Cambridge: Harvard University Press, 1980.

Thomas, Clarke. *They Came to Pittsburgh.* Pittsburgh: *Post-Gazette,* 1983.

Thomas, Piri. *Down These Mean Streets.* New York: Signet Books, 1958.

_____. *Savior, Savior, Hold My Hand.* Garden City, N.Y.: Doubleday and Co., 1972.

Trattner, Walter I. *From Poor Law to Welfare State: A History of Social Welfare in America.* New York: Free Press, 1974.

Trotter, Robert, II, and Chavira, Juan Antonio. *Curanderismo—Mexican American Folk Healing.* Athens: University of Georgia Press, 1981.

Unger, Steven, ed. *The Destruction of American Indian Families.* New York: Association on American Indian Affairs, 1977.

U.S. Commission on Civil Rights. *Mexican Americans and the Administration of Justice in the Southwest.* Washington, D.C.: Government Printing Office, 1970.

U.S. Department of Commerce, Bureau of the Census. *Ancestry of the Population by State: 1980.* Washington, D.C.: Government Printing Office, 1980.

————. *Population Profile of the United States: 1981.* "Population Characteristics," ser. 20, no. 374, Sept., 1982.

U.S. Department of Justice. Immigration and Naturalization Service. *Immigration Literature: Abstracts of Demographic Economic and Policy Studies.* Washington, D.C.: Government Printing Office, 1979.

Valentine, Charles A. *Culture and Poverty.* Chicago: University of Chicago Press, 1968.

Wade, Mason. *The French-Canadian Outlook.* New York: Viking Press, 1946.

————. *The French-Canadians, 1876–1945.* New York: Macmillan Co., 1955.

Wallnöfer, Heinrich, and von Rottauscher, Anna. *Chinese Folk Medicine.* Translated by Marion Palmedo. New York: New American Library, 1972.

Warner, David. *The Health of Mexican Americans in South Texas.* Austin: LBJ School of Public Affairs, University of Texas at Austin, 1979.

Warren, N., ed. *Studies in Cross-Cultural Psychology.* New York: Academic Press, 1980.

Weil, Andrew. *Health and Healing.* Boston: Houghton Mifflin Co., 1983.

Weinberg, R. D. *Eligibility for Entry to the United States of America.* Dobbs Ferry, N.Y.: Oceana Publications, 1967.

Wheelwright, Edith Grey. *Medicinal Plants and Their History.* New York: Dover, 1974.

Williams, Richard Allen, ed. *Textbook of Black-Related Diseases.* New York: McGraw-Hill, 1975.

Winkler, Gershon. *Dybbuk.* New York: Judaica Press, 1981.

Wright, Richard. *Black Boy.* New York: Harper and Brothers, 1937.

————. *Native Son.* New York: Grosset and Dunlop, 1940.

Young, James H. *The Medical Messiahs.* Princeton: Princeton University Press, 1967.

Zavaleta, Anthony N., ed. "Mexican American Health Status: Selected Topics from the Borderlands." *Borderlands Journal—Special Issue* 4, no. 1 (Fall 1980).

Zborowski, Mark. *People in Pain.* San Francisco: Jossey-Bass, 1969.

Zolla, Elemire. *The Writer and the Shaman.* New York: Harcourt Brace Jovanovich, 1969.

Index

Page numbers followed by *f* indicate illustrations; page numbers followed by *t* indicate tables; page numbers followed by *n* indicate footnotes.